POCKET GOOD GUIDES MOTORWAY BREAKS

Edited by Alisdair Aird and Fiona Stapley

Managing Editor Karen Fick
Additional Research Fiona Wright

EBURY PRESS

This edition first published in Great Britain in 2005

1 3 5 7 9 10 8 6 4 2

© Random House Group Ltd 2005

Alisdair Aird and Fiona Stapley have asserted their right to be identified as authors of this work under the Copyright, Designs and Patents Act 1988.

All rights reserved. No part of this publication may be reproduced, stored in a retrieval system, or transmitted in any form or by any means, electronic, mechanical, photocopying, recording or otherwise without the prior permission of the copyright owners.

First published by
Ebury Press
Random House, 20 Vauxhall Bridge Road, London SW1V 2SA

Random House Australia (Pty) Limited
20 Alfred Street, Milsons Point, Sydney, New South Wales 2061, Australia

Random House New Zealand Limited
18 Poland Road, Glenfield, Auckland 10, New Zealand

Random House South Africa (Pty) Limited
Endulini, 5A Jubilee Road, Parktown 2193, South Africa

The Random House Group Limited Reg. No. 954009

www.randomhouse.co.uk

A CIP catalogue record for this book is available from the British Library.

ISBN 0091904854

Papers used by Ebury Press are natural, recyclable products made from wood grown in sustainable forests.

Text design and typesetting by Textype, Cambridge.

Jacket design by Main Artery

Cover image © Masterfile

Printed and bound by Norhaven Paperback A/S, Viborg

Introduction

Escape from the traffic

Minutes away from motorway junctions and other major trunk roads, hundreds of relaxing escapes make for an ideal journey break - if you're in the know.

For this new book, we have drawn on our years of experience in scouring the country to put together Britain's leading guide books, and our hot tips from thousands of readers who report regularly to us, to put together the best guide to these tucked-away treats. You'll find all sorts of places here, from cafés or pubs just right for a quick but tasty bite, through fine restaurants ideal for a more leisurely meal, to peaceful spots for a sunny-day stroll or picnic.

We've added two more useful ingredients, too. First, we've put in all sorts of interesting attractions that most people will be surprised to find so close to a motorway or trunk, and might well want to plan a journey-break outing or even a longer visit to. And secondly, we've tracked down around 300 good places to stay in, perfectly poised for a quiet and restorative night to break a long journey.

To contact the Pocket Good Guides team,
please write to

Pocket Good Guides
Freepost TN1 569
Wadhurst
E. Sussex
TN5 7BR

or check out
www.goodguides.co.uk

Contents

Introduction iii

Using the Guide vii

Motorways 1

Trunk Roads 34

Maps 209

Using the Guide

We've listed this book starting with motorways, working in numerical order through the junctions. The junction numbers are also shown on the maps.

In the second half of the book we also list the major trunk roads (those with big green road signs) in numerical order. As most trunk roads do not have junction numbers we have ordered entries along these roads working from either South to North or from East to West depending on the principal orientation of the road. Running in numerical order along the road, each entry on a trunk road is labelled in the text and on the map with a number and with the town or village name nearest to the attraction. Note that these numbers are our own numbers (and we have stuck with our own numbers even on roads like the A55 which do have junction numbers).

We have included three types of information in this book. Things to do (this could be an attractive village, a historic house or a park for a walk and represented by two walkers), places to eat (this might be a pub, restaurant or tearoom and shown by a knife and fork symbol), and places to stay (indicated by a bed) which could include anything from a farm, pub or inn or smart hotel.

Prices and other factual details

THINGS TO DO 🥾
The price we give is for an adult visitor. When we say 'cl Nov-Easter' we mean that the establishment reopens for Easter. NT after the price means that a property is owned by the National Trust, EH means that it is owned by English Heritage, HS means that it is owned by Historic Scotland

WHERE TO STAY 🛏
The price we show is the total for two people sharing a double or twin-bedded room with its own bathroom for one night in high season. It includes a full English breakfast, VAT and any automatic service charge that we know about. Dinner may be included in the price at some of the more remote places, in which case we say so. We always mention

USING THE GUIDE

a restaurant if we know there is one and we commend food if we have information supporting a positive recommendation. Many B&Bs will recommend nearby pubs for evening meals if they do not offer dinner.

WHERE TO EAT ✖
These range from smart restaurants to gastro pubs to more down-to-earth pubs where you can get a basic meal. Many of the pubs and restaurants listed are very popular and without booking you may not get a table. We say when places are closed, but it is worth checking before you turn up.

M1

1. ✕ ⋈ MOULSOE
Carrington Arms *(2.1 miles from M1 **junction 14**; A509 towards Newport Pagnell, then first right)*
£49.50; well refurbished old brick house with comfortable traditional furnishings, meat and fish displayed in refrigerated glass case with friendly staff who guide you through what is on offer (it is then sold by weight and cooked on a sophisticated indoor barbecue), separate bar menu as well, an oyster bar, well kept real ales, and a good range of wines inc champagne by the glass; disabled access *(01908) 218050*

2. ✕ ⋈ ROADE
Roade House *(2.4 miles off M1 **junction 15**; High St, off A508 S)*
£70; smart and popular restaurant-with-rooms with comfortable surroundings, courteous service, reliably enjoyable food using first-class ingredients, and reasonably priced wines; cl Sun, Mon am, Sat am, 1 wk Christmas; disabled access *(01604) 863372*

3. ✕ NETHER HEYFORD
Old Sun *(1.8 miles off M1 **junction 16**: village signed left off A45 W – Middle St)*
18th-c golden stone pub, its small linked low-beamed rooms packed with interesting bric-a-brac and curios, enjoyable home cooking (not Mon evening or Sun – and evening meals kept to dining end), well kept ales, friendly family service, big inglenook log fire, traditional games; children in eating areas, picnic-sets out on terrace with antique farm machinery *(01327) 340164*

4. ✕ CRICK
Red Lion *(1 mile off M1 **junction 18**, via A428)*
Good generous home cooking (not Sun evening) in pretty stone and thatched pub, quick friendly service, well kept ales, cosy low-ceilinged bar with big inglenook, no smoking pub; tables outside, some under cover, children (lunchtimes) and dogs welcome *(01788) 822342*

MOTORWAY BREAKS

5. ✕ ⌂ KILSBY
George *(2.5 miles off M1 **junction 18**: A428 towards Daventry, left on to A5 – look out for pub off on right at roundabout)*
£50; relaxing motorway/A5 refuge with hospitable hard-working landlady, good value wholesome bar food, well kept ales, decent wines and fine range of malt whiskies, plush banquettes, dark panelling, cheerful no smoking dining area, back games bar; children and dogs allowed, picnic-sets in back garden *(01788) 822229*

6. ✕ KEGWORTH
Cap & Stocking *(1 mile off M1 **junction 24**: follow A6 towards Loughborough; in village, turn left at chemist's down one-way Dragwall opposite High St, then left and left again, into Borough St)*
Sensibly priced simple food in unchanging backstreet pub, a throwback to the 1940s, serving ale from the jug, with coal fires, a cast-iron range and big cases of stuffed birds and fish; children and dogs welcome, pretty, secluded garden *(01509) 674814*

7. ✕ ⌂ KIMBERLEY
Nelson & Railway *(1.7 miles off M1 **junction 26**; at exit roundabout take A610 towards Ripley, then signed Kimberley, pub in Station Rd)*
£46.95; cheery and spotless beamed Victorian pub with well kept ales from the Hardys & Hansons brewery opposite, good value straightforward and satisfying bar food (12-6 Sun), no smoking area, traditional furniture, pub games; children allowed in restaurant, dogs in bar, good-sized cottagey garden, open all day, *(0115) 938 2177*

8. ❀ UNDERWOOD
Felley Priory Garden *(0.8 miles off M1 **junction 27**; on left of A608 westbound)*
Developed over the last 25 years or so around a romantic old house (not open) dating back over 400 years, these richly planted hillside gardens have several areas nicely broken up by thick hedges, rose and clematis pergolas, and old masonry. They span styles from medieval to high Victorian and later, and are filled with mainly old-fashioned plants, often rare; there's a rose garden with over 90 varieties. Plants sales (all grown here), tearoom, disabled access; best to phone for limited opening times; *(01773) 810230*; £2.50. The Red Lion (Church Lane) has good value family food.

9. ☞ WORSBROUGH
Worsbrough Country Park *(2.5 miles off M1 **junction 36** via A61 NE; Park Rd)*
Hard to believe this was once a busy industrial area; the only sign of those days is the working corn mill, now the Worsbrough Mill Museum but still producing stoneground flour. Snacks, shop, some disabled access; usually cl Mon (exc bank hols), Tues, Mon-Sat Nov, Dec and Mar and all Jan-Feb; *(01226) 774527*; car park £1. About a mile away, Wigfield Farm is a hit with children, with traditional and rare breeds. Café and picnic area, shop (where you can buy their flour), disabled access; cl 2 wks Christmas-New Year; *(01226) 733702*; £2. The peaceful 200 acres also include nature trails.

10. ☞ WAKEFIELD
Yorkshire Sculpture Park *(1.3 miles off M1 **junction 38**; A637 N – West Bretton)*
Major contemporary and modern sculpture carefully and imaginatively displayed in 500 acres of 18th-c landscaped parkland and gardens. Also three indoor galleries, a new underground gallery and a visitor centre. Meals, snacks, shop, disabled access; cl 24-25 and 31 Dec; *(01924) 830302*; parking £3.

11. ☞ LEEDS
Temple Newsam House *(2.1 miles off M1 **junction 46**; A63 W, then after A6120 roundabout turn left into Colton Rd)*
Capability Brown designed the wonderful two square miles of landscaped parkland and gardens in which this house stands, an extraordinary asset for any city. Recently reopened after extensive restoration and damp-proofing, the house itself dates from Tudor and Jacobean times, and contains the city's very good collections of decorative and fine art, as well as an exceptional assemblage of Chippendale furniture; they do free tours on Tues. Rare breeds and a working organic farm in the grounds, picnic and play areas. Shop, disabled access (with a lift now); grounds open daily (free, £1.50 car park), house cl Mon, 25-26 Dec; *(0113) 264 7321*; house £3, house and farm £5.

M2

12. 🏃 FAVERSHAM
***Brogdale Orchard** (1.7 miles off M2 **junction 6**; A251 into town, left on A2, then 2nd left into Brogdale Rd)*
This large fruit farm, home to the National Fruit Collection, with over 4,000 different varieties of fruit (2,300 different apples alone), is set in 150 acres of beautiful Kent countryside. The shop sells, in season, cherries, plums, apples, pears, medlars, quinces, soft fruit and, throughout the year, fruit trees. Free access to shop, teashop, disabled access. Open all year. Guided tours Mar-Nov. *(01795) 552863. £4.*

13. ✕ 🛏 FAVERSHAM
***Read's** (1.4 miles off M2 **junction 7**; A2 into town – Macknade Manor, Canterbury Rd)*
£130; restaurant-with-rooms in Georgian manor house with neat surrounding gardens that provide home-grown vegetables and herbs for the kitchen; exceptionally good innovative english cooking including fine fish dishes and lovely puddings, a marvellous wine list, and neat young staff; cl Sun, Mon; disabled access *(01795) 535344*

14. 🏃 BOUGHTON
***Farming World** (1.2 miles off M2 **junction 7**; A229 towards Ramsgate, then signed from first exit)*
Friendly farm with traditional and rare breeds and heavy horses, tractor and waggon rides, nature trails, adventure playgrounds inc a new indoor one, walled garden, and seasonal fruit and veg. A hawking centre has daily flying displays and bird handling (summer only), and an incubation and conservation room where you can see baby birds hatching, and there's a new glass-fronted bee-keeping exhibition room. Meals, snacks, farm shop, disabled access (sensory garden specially designed for the disabled); ring for winter opening times; *(01227) 751144; £5.50.* The White Horse at Boughton Street has decent food all day.

M3

15. ✕ WEST END
*Inn at West End (2.4 miles from M3 **junction 3**; A322 S, on right)*
Open-plan roadside dining pub with constantly changing, consistently good food inc lots of fresh fish, and friendly efficient service; smart line of dining tables, crisp linen, attractive modern prints on canary yellow walls, also chatty bar area with plenty of pale woodwork and woodburner, tiled garden room and pleasant garden; good drinks inc espresso machine and good value champagne by the glass (landlord is a wine merchant, and can also supply by the case), daily papers; children over 5 *(01276) 858652*

16. ⌂ BAGSHOT
*Pennyhill Park (2.3 miles off M3 **junction 3**; A322, left on to A30 then right into Church Rd and College Rd)*
£260, plus special breaks; 123 individually designed luxury rms and suites. Impressive Victorian country house in 120 acres of well kept gardens and parkland inc a 9-hole golf course, tennis courts, outdoor heated swimming pool, clay pigeon shooting, archery, fishing, and an international rugby pitch; friendly courteous staff, wood-panelled bar with resident pianist, comfortable two-level lounge and reading room, very good imaginative food in two restaurants, jazz Sun lunchtime, and terraces overlooking the golf course; disabled access; dogs in bedrooms and some other areas *(01276) 471774*

17. ✕ WINCHESTER
*Black Boy (1 mile from M3 **junction 10** northbound, via B3403 towards city then left into Wharf Hill, but car park 220 metres further along B3403; rather further and less easy from **junction 9**)*
Splendidly eccentric décor with masses to look at in several different boldly painted areas, enjoyable home-made food (Tues evening to Sun lunchtime) from sandwiches and hearty lunches to more soigné evening dishes, local ales and decent wines, two log fires, friendly staff; well chosen and reproduced music, traditional games; dogs and children allowed, attractive secluded terrace *(01962) 861754*

M4

18. 🏛 WINDSOR
*(2 miles from M4 **junction 6**, via A355)*
Just a short way off the motorway, Windsor has plenty of variety, to fill anything from an hour or so to the best part of a day. It's dominated by its famous castle, the largest inhabited one in the world. The little streets to the S have many pretty timber-framed or Georgian-fronted houses and shops. The High St, by contrast, is wide and busy (the Guildhall here, completed by Sir Christopher Wren, is worth a look – open 10-2 Mon, or Tues after a bank hol – free). You can walk by the Thames (for example, from Home Park, beyond the station). Windsor Great Park has miles of well maintained and peaceful parkland, so sensitively landscaped that it takes the occasional surprising find (statues, even a totem pole) to remind you that it's not natural. The Two Brewers in pretty Park St is a good food pub. In the quieter nearby Thames-side village of Old Windsor the Union has good bar food, and the café at the Windsor Farm Shop (Datchet Rd) is good value.

19. ✕ 🏛 ETON
Gilbeys Bar and Restaurant *(1.5 miles from M4 **junction 6**: A355 towards Windsor, Eton signed off left on B3026; turn right into High St (B3022))*
Bustling wine bar with an airy and relaxed bar overlooking the High St, a restaurant and conservatory with bookable tables and friendly helpful staff, an elegant private dining room, imaginative modern food, and a super wine list; cl 1 wk over Christmas; disabled access. Sister restaurants in Old Amersham and in Ealing, West London. For a longer break from the traffic, it's well worth looking around the small town: so close to Windsor it's pretty much part of it, this has a restrained and decorous High St with a mix of interesting old shops and houses. Its glory is Eton College, the famous public school, whose stately Tudor and later buildings in graceful precincts are marvellously calm during the school's holidays. The Chapel is an outstanding late Gothic building in the Perpendicular style, and a museum tells the story of the school from its foundation in 1440 up to the present, with fascinating videos on life for pupils here today. Bizarre information is turned up by the various

historical documents – in the 17th c, for example, smoking was compulsory for all scholars as a protection against bubonic plague. The Brewhouse Gallery has some good changing exhibitions, and next door is a collection of egyptian antiquities. Shop, some disabled access; cl am in term-time, and all Oct-Mar; *(01753) 671177;* from £3.70 (guided tours from £4.70) *(01753) 854921*

20. ✕ ⇔ BRAY
*Waterside Inn (2.3 miles off M4 **junction 8/9**; A308 towards Windsor, then left at Bray sign on to B3028, then right on Ferry Rd)*
£160; in a lovely setting by the Thames, this enormously – and justifiably – popular restaurant is a very special place, and for many, the perfect dining experience; impeccable, classic french cooking beautifully presented inc superb puddings, wonderful petits fours, cosseting and helpful service, and a fine french wine list; a lovely place to stay, too; cl Mon, Tues (but open Tues evening during June, July, Aug); children over 12; disabled access *(01628) 620691*

21. ✕ BRAY
*Crown (1.7 miles off M4 **junction 8/9**; A308 towards Windsor, then left at Bray sign on to B3028; High St)*
14th-c, with plenty of standing timbers and very low beams, enjoyable food (not Sun or Mon evenings) in partly panelled bar and restaurant, well kept ales and decent wine choice, oak tables, leather-backed armchairs, three log fires, good service; provision for children and dogs, tables in sheltered flagstoned courtyard and big back garden *(01628) 621936*

22. 🧒 SHINFIELD
*Magpie & Parrot (2.6 miles from M4 **junction 11**, via B3270; A327 just SE of Shinfield – heading out on Arborfield Rd, keep eyes skinned for small hand-painted green Nursery sign on left, and Fullers 'bar open' blackboard)*
Unique place for a relaxing break: a comfortable fireside chat, something to drink (they do a real ale, as well as a good choice of soft drinks – and malt whiskies), peanut bowls on each table, a fine mix of individualistic seats and bric-a-brac, a most hospitable landlady – and as it's also a nursery, good value plants to buy, too; dogs but no children allowed inside, summer hog roasts, terrace tables by immaculate back lawn; open 12-7 (12-3 Sun) *(0118) 988 4130*

MOTORWAY BREAKS

23. ⌘ WOOTTON BASSETT
*Marsh Farm Hotel (2.5 miles off M4 **junction 16**; A3102 towards Wootton, then at A3102/B4042 roundabout turn right towards Hook; hotel on left)*
£70, plus special breaks; 50 rms. Handsome Victorian farmhouse in landscaped grounds with particularly warm and friendly atmosphere, comfortable lounge, convivial bar, and enjoyable food in conservatory restaurant; cl 25-31 Dec; disabled access *(01793) 848044*

M5

24. ☼ WYCHBOLD
*Webbs Garden Centre (1.1 miles off M5 **junction 5**; A38 N towards Bromsgrove)*
One of the best in the country, attractively laid out with two acres of riverside gardens, a massive choice of things to buy, and events throughout the year. Meals, snacks, disabled access; cl 25-26 Dec and Easter Sun; *(01527) 860000*; free.

25. ✗ CROWLE
*Old Chequers (2.5 miles off M5 **junction 6**; A4538 S towards Pershore, then first left to Crowle Green)*
This smoothly run much-modernised dining pub rambles extensively around an island bar, with pubby furniture, lots of pictures for sale at the back, and a coal-effect gas fire at one end; there's a big square extension on the right with more tables; popular generous food (all home-made) includes good value imaginative light lunches plus more substantial dishes, prompt, friendly service, well kept real ales, and picnic-sets on the grass behind; cl Sun pm, 25-26 Dec, 1 Jan; no children; disabled access *(01905) 381275*

26. ☼ TEWKESBURY
*(1.5 miles off M5 **junction 9**; A438 into town)*
Severnside town, site of the last battle in the Wars of the Roses in 1471, still full of attractive half-timbered medieval buildings in a maze of little alleyways. Most impressive is the abbey, its massively confident Norman tower one of the finest in existence. Also splendid vaulting,

8

some 14th-c stained glass, and regular concerts; guided tours available, phone for details; *(01684) 850959*. In Church St, the attractive John Moore Countryside Museum commemorates the work of the local naturalist/writer. Shop, usually open Tues-Sat and bank hols (exc 1-2pm) Apr-Oct; *(01684) 297174*. The historic Bell Hotel is useful for lunch.

27. 🕸 FRAMPTON ON SEVERN
Frampton Court *(2.8 miles off M5 **junction 13**; A38 S, then right on B4071)*
Elegant Georgian house family home of the Cliffords, with original furniture, porcelain, tapestry and paintings, and fascinating garden. Disabled access to garden; B&B all year, personal tours by appointment; *(01452) 740267*; £5. The village green is said to be the longest in the country (with 18th-c orangery – now self-catering holiday accommodation – and dutch ornamental canal). The cheerful Three Horseshoes does good lunchtime sandwiches and ploughman's, opening its lounge/dining room for evening meals. Just outside the village the Gloucester & Sharpness Canal passes grand colonnaded lock keepers' houses by pretty swing bridges.

28. ✕ ⇋ ALMONDSBURY
Bowl *(1.2 miles off M5 **junction 16** (so quite handy for M4 **junction 20**); from A38 towards Thornbury, first left signed Lower Almondsbury, then first right down Sundays Hill, then at bottom right again into Church Rd)*
£71; bustling prettily set pub, long and comfortable, with beams, stripped stone and big log fires, enjoyable food inc interesting salads and smaller helpings for children, well kept ales; children and dogs welcome, popular tables outside, bdrm annexe, open all day Sun *(01454) 612757*

29. 🕸 WESTON-SUPER-MARE
Helicopter Museum *(2.5 miles off M5 **junction 21**; A370 then A371 towards Banwell, forking right into B3146 Locking Moor Rd)*
An unexpected find, with over 70 helicopters inc the World Speed Record holder, spectacular helicopters from the Queen's Flight and Russian Gunship; can see the restoration projects in the workshops, take a helicopter experience flight, and let the under 12s stage a rescue in the Lynx helicopter play area; café and shop; disabled access; cl Mon and Tues (exc summer and bank hols), and 25-26 Dec, 1 Jan; *(01934) 635227*; £4.95.

MOTORWAY BREAKS

30. ✕ TAUNTON
Hankridge Arms *(0.7 miles off M5 **junction 25**; A358 towards city, then right at roundabout, right at next roundabout into Hankridge Way, Deane Gate (nr Sainsbury))*
16th-c former farm reworked as well appointed old-style dining pub in modern shopping complex, buoyant atmosphere and quick friendly service, good value generous food from interesting soups and sandwiches up in bar and largely no smoking restaurant, Badger real ales and decent wines, big log fire; piped music; plenty of tables outside *(01823) 444405*

31. ☸ UFFCULME
Coldharbour Mill Working Museum *(2.8 miles off M5 **junction 27**, via A38 eastbound, B3181 and B3440)*
You can watch every stage in the production of wool at this well restored 18th-c mill building. It was operated as a woollen factory by the same family for almost 200 years. Meals, snacks, shop, disabled access; cl Christmas; *(01884) 840960*; £5.50.

32. ⌂ CULLOMPTON
Upton House *(2.5 miles off M5 **junction 28**; B3181 into Cullompton, where fork left down Cockpit Hill into Duke St; turn left after crossing motorway and river)*
£56; 3 rms. Big, pink-washed 300-year-old farmhouse in large garden and surrounded by 180 acres of organic farm and lots of horses (the owners breed racehorses); careful renovation has revealed beamed ceilings, panelling, and huge stone fireplaces, and there's a woodburning stove and fine furniture in sitting room, oak-panelled dining room and sunny conservatory, good breakfasts served around a big table, and welcoming hosts; pubs and restaurants nearby; cl Christmas/New Year; children over 12 *(01884) 33097*

33. ✕ TOPSHAM
Bridge Inn *(2.3 miles off M5 **junction 30**: Topsham signed from exit roundabout; in Topsham follow signpost '(A376) Exmouth' on Elmgrove Rd, into Bridge Hill)*
Utterly unspoilt, relaxed and old-fashioned, run by same friendly family for over a century, with fine old traditional layout and furnishings (true country workmanship), log fire, simple tasty bar food such as pasties,

good sandwiches and ploughman's, excellent local hand-fried crisps; provision for children and dogs, riverside picnic-sets *(01392) 873862*

34. ✕ ⛴ TOPSHAM
*Georgian Tea Room (2 miles off M5 **junction 30**; A376 towards Exmouth then almost immediately first turn right on to Clyst Rd; High St)*
£50; 18th-c house with pretty embroidered tablecloths and fresh flowers, and good food all day – breakfasts, morning coffee, snacks, lunchtime meals inc a popular roast on Tues, Thurs and Sun, cream teas with home-made cakes and cookies, and a wide range of teas and coffees with home-made lemonade; no smoking bdrms; cl Weds, 25-26 Dec; partial disabled access *(01392) 873465*

35. 🐾 CLYST ST MARY
*Crealy Adventure Park (2.4 miles off M5 **junction 30**,*
via A376/A3052)
There's plenty to amuse children of all ages at this bustling family complex. The Magical Kingdom, a delightfully constructed area aimed mostly at under-7s, has play areas and a soaring gondola swing, while among the attractions for older children are bumper boats, go-karts and a farm where you can milk the cows, and meet baby animals. Many of the attractions are indoors, inc some of the animals, and a good varied adventure playground. There's also a family roller-coaster, swingboat, a new carousel and log flume, toddlers' garden play area, multicolour meadow, splash zone, pony rides and lakeside walks (with an embryonic arboretum); lots of special events and activities. Meals, snacks, shop, disabled access; *(0870) 116 3333*; cl Mon and Tues during term-time Nov-18 Mar, 24-26 Dec and 1 Jan; **£7.95**. If you don't want to eat in the park, the Half Moon is good value.

M6

36. ✕ LICHFIELD
*Boat (2.7 miles from M6 Toll **junction T6**: B5011 S, then left on A5, then at Muckley Corner roundabout head SW on A461 Walsall Rd)*
Well run modern pub with café furniture, cheerfully light area dominated by big floor-to-ceiling food blackboards opening straight on to the kitchen doing good choice of interesting well prepared food (all day Sun), pleasant carpeted area, real ales *(01543) 361692*

MOTORWAY BREAKS

37. 🍴 BARTHOMLEY
White Lion (a mile from M6 junction 16; from exit roundabout take B5078 N towards Alsager, then Barthomley signposted on left)
Timeless 17th-c black and white thatched pub, open all day (cl Thurs till 5 (01270) 882242), with a blazing open fire, heavy oak beams dating back to Stuart times (mind your head), attractively moulded black panelling, and thick wobbly old tables. At lunchtime, friendly and efficient staff serve good value sandwiches, as well as bargain simple hot dishes. Well kept Burtonwood and guest ales, no noisy games machines or music. Outside, seats and picnic-sets on the cobbles have a charming view of the charming village with all its thatch and black and white timbering. The early 15th-c red sandstone church of St Bertiline across the road is well worth a visit.

38. 🛏 SANDBACH
Old Hall (1.2 miles from M6 junction 17, via A534 towards Crewe; High St)
£70, plus special breaks; 11 comfortable rms. Fine Jacobean timbered hotel with lots of original panelling and fireplaces, relaxing lounge, friendly welcome, and popular, attractive restaurant; disabled access; dogs in bedrooms *(01270) 761221*

39. 🍴 TABLEY
Cuckoo Land (1.4 miles from M6 junction 19; A556 towards Northwich; Old School House, Chester Rd, Nether Tabley)
The friendly owners will take you on a guided tour of this huge collection of cuckoo clocks, all made in the Black Forest. They currently have over 550 rare and beautiful clocks, most of them working; five working historic fairground organs are among the other mechanisms on show, as well as a collection of vintage motorcycles. Phone for an appointment; snacks, shop, disabled access; *(01565) 633039*; £5. A mile or so further, the Smoker at Plumley is a popular 16th-c thatched pub with open fires and comfortable sofas in three well decorated connecting rooms, good swiftly served food, a wide choice of whiskies, well kept real ales, and friendly service; big garden; disabled access.

M6

40. 🕍 LEYLAND
British Commercial Vehicle Museum *(1.4 miles off M6 **junction 28** via B5256, bearing left into Churchill Way then Golden Hill Lane; turn right into King St)*
Jazzed up with sound effects, this has over 90 perfectly restored british waggons, buses, trucks, vans, fire engines and even a Popemobile, shining so much you'd think they were new. Snacks, shop, disabled access; open Sun, Tues-Thurs and bank hols Apr-Sept, Sun only Oct; *(01772) 451011*; £4. The Midge Hall (Midge Hall Lane, about 2m W of here) is a popular food pub. Leyland also has a pleasant little town trail, and the medieval church has some fine stained glass.

41. 🕍 SAMLESBURY
Samlesbury Hall *(2.5 miles off M6 junction 31, via A59 E and A677)*
Well restored half-timbered 14th-c manor house, with good changing exhibitions and craft demonstrations, and sales of antiques. Meals, snacks, disabled access to ground floor only; cl Sat, 25-26 Dec, and 1 Jan; *(01254) 812010*; £3. There's a good farm shop at Huntley Gate Farm (A59), with around 46 different flavours of home-made ice-cream; cl Mon (exc bank hols). The New Hall Tavern (B6230) has enjoyable food.

42. ✕ BAY HORSE
Bay Horse *(1.2 miles off M6 **junction 33**: A6 S, then off on left)*
More civilised country restaurant than pub, with delicious imaginative food using lots of fresh local ingredients (not Sun evening, snacks only 1-2pm Sat) in rambling series of small no smoking dining areas – red décor, beams, good log fires, soft lighting, comfortably padded seating; friendly staff, good tea and coffee, TV for racing and cricket in bar; children welcome, tables in garden behind, cl Mon *(01524) 791204*

43. 🕍 CARNFORTH
*(2.2 miles off M6 **junction 35**; A6 into town, turn right into Market St and keep on to station)*
The station (once voted the worst in England) at this otherwise unremarkable little town starred in *Brief Encounter* in 1945. A £1.75m project to restore it to its cinematic heyday has been completed (and the famous clock is working again), the restaurant and bar have been refurbished with 1945 furniture and décor, and a new heritage centre

MOTORWAY BREAKS

has opened with exhibitions on the town's history. Ask at the visitor centre about maps for self-guided walks around Carnforth; shops, disabled access (and facilities); *(01524) 720333*. A mile or so N are the ruins of a 14th-c manor house, Warton Old Rectory, and the County Hotel (A6) has reliable traditional food.

44. ✕ TEBAY
Tebay Services (on M6 just N of junction 38)
Unique in being run by a small firm set up by locals (a farmer and baker); all the usual motorway services, open 24 hrs, but with much more individuality, and obviously strong local roots, using genuine local produce for its good snacks and meals; attractive waterside surroundings, friendly helpful service, even an on-site farm shop *(01539) 624511*

45. ✕ YANWATH
*Gate Inn (2.3 miles from M6 junction 40; A66 towards Brough,
then right on A6, right on B5320, then follow village signpost)*
Good inventive restaurant-quality food from a shortish menu plus 2-course lunches, well kept real ales, obliging service, log fire, and no smoking dining room; cl Mon pm *(01768) 862386*

46. ☸ PENRITH
*The best fudge in the world (1.1 miles off M6 junction 40;
A592 into town, to The Toffee Shop, 7 Brunswick Rd)*
Unmissable if you've a sweet tooth, this fudge, hand-made here for nearly a century, with world-wide devotees, melts in the mouth with a deliciously unique taste.

M8

47. ☸ GLASGOW
*House for an Art Lover (0.8 miles off M8 junction 23; Helen St S, left
on A761, doubling back at next roundabout to enter Bellahouston Park)*
Built to uplifting 1901 designs by Charles Rennie Mackintosh, with an exciting array of decorative rooms, and contemporary art exhibitions. Meals, snacks, shop, disabled access; usually cl pm Thurs-Sun, but opening times in Oct-Mar vary; *(0141) 353 4770*; £3.50. The Empire

Exhibition of 1938 was held in this spreading park, whose lovely gardens include a Victorian walled garden and sweeping lawns.

M9

48. ✗ LINLITHGOW
*Four Marys (2 miles off M9 **junction 3** eastbound, via A803 into town – 65 High St; if going E use **junction 2 or 4** – both rather longer)*
Lots of interesting Mary, Queen of Scots memorabilia, temptingly priced food (all day in summer) in bar and restaurant, good changing real ales and friendly service; children in restaurant, open all day *(01506) 842171*

49. ✗ ⇌ LINLITHGOW
*Champany Inn (1 mile off M9 **junction 3** westbound; A803 N, right on A904; use **junction 2** going E)*
£125; wonderful aberdeen angus beef as well as lovely fresh fish (they also have their own smoke-house), home-made ice-creams, and good wines; cheaper bistro-style meals in their Chop and Ale House next door; main restaurant cl Sun (bistro open all week), 25-26 Dec and 1-2 Jan; disabled access; children over 8 in restaurant *(01506) 834532*

M11

50. ☵ HASTINGWOOD
*Rainbow & Dove (just off M11 **junction 7**; Hastingwood signed after Ongar signs at exit roundabout)*
Good value food from tasty sandwiches to steaks and fresh fish, well kept ales, good quick service even when it's bustling, fires in all three homely little rooms off the main bar area, low beams and stripped brick; children in eating area, picnic-sets out on the grass

51. ☵ HATFIELD FOREST
*(2.9 miles off M11 **junction 8**; A120 E, then after nearly 2 miles first turn right in Takeley)*
This NT medieval Royal hunting forest is an unexpected survivor, with

MOTORWAY BREAKS

ancient mainly hornbeam woodland, not on quite the same scale as Epping Forest but still extensive enough, with nature trails, cycle paths, and a lake where you can fish (mid-June to mid-Mar; around £4.50 – phone to check). Look out for the unusual shell grotto built in the 1750s by the family that once owned the forest. The new boardwalk around the forest makes for easy clean walks. Information centre and café *(01279) 870678*

52. ✕ BIRCHANGER
Three Willows (0.8 miles off M11 junction 8: A120 towards Bishops Stortford, then almost immediately right to Birchanger Village; don't be waylaid earlier by the Birchanger Services signpost!)
Good fresh fish is the top draw in this roomy and comfortable pub, alongside a wide choice of other straightforward food (not Sun evening) from lunchtime sandwiches to steaks; friendly attentive staff, decent wines and well kept ales, plenty of cricket memorabilia; dogs allowed, picnic-sets out on heated terrace and lawn with play area (no children allowed inside) *(01279) 815913*

53. 🏛 DUXFORD
Imperial War Museum Duxford (just off M11 junction 10, via A505 westbound)
Unmissable for anyone interested in aviation and great for families too, this big WWI airfield is home to Europe's best collection of military and civil aircraft (nearly 200, 50 of which regularly fly) from flimsy-looking bi-planes to the current state-of-the-art front-line fighters, notably the SR-71 Blackbird spyplane. Children can clamber into the cockpits of some, pick up helmets and gunpacks, and there`s an adventure playground. They also have a huge collection of tanks and military vehicles, a naval collection inc midget submarines and helicopters, and changing exhibitions. The American Air Museum, a collection of US combat aircraft, is in a remarkable building by Norman Foster. The site covers about a mile (a bus can take you between the different bits) and much of it is preserved as it was during the early 1940s, including the hangars and the Battle of Britain Operations Room. Each year they have several dramatic air shows (extra charge), and some planes still fly on other days. A free bus runs every hour from and to Cambridge Station; it takes about 20 minutes. Meals and snacks (and plenty of space for pic-

nics), shop, good disabled access; cl 24-26 Dec; *(01223) 835000*; £12, children free. The Green Man close by at Thriplow is an interesting place for lunch.

54. ⌂ DUXFORD
Duxford Lodge *(under 2 miles from M11 **junction 10**; A505 eastbound, then first right turn into Hunts Rd; Ickleton Rd)*
£105; 15 good-sized, warm rms, 2 with four-posters. Carefully run late Victorian hotel in an acre of neatly kept landscaped gardens, with a welcoming, relaxed atmosphere, individually chosen modern paintings and prints, a restful little lounge, decent wines, enjoyable modern cooking in the airy no smoking restaurant, and good breakfasts; partial disabled access; dogs in some bedrooms *(01223) 836444*

55. ✕ HINXTON
Red Lion *(2 miles off M11 **junction 9** northbound; take first exit off A11, A1301 N, then left turn into village – High St; a little further from **junction 10**, via A505 E and A1301 S)*
Leather chesterfields in dusky bar, high-backed padded settles in informal dining area, smart no smoking restaurant, enjoyable food from familiar lunchtime bar dishes to more unexpected things, friendly efficient service, decent ales and wines; children and dogs allowed, attractive garden with terrace and picnic-sets *(01799) 530601*

56. ✕ MADINGLEY
Three Horseshoes *(2.1 miles off M11 **junction 14**; local road off northbound exit ramp, turning left into The Avenue; also quickly reached off A14, via A428; High St)*
Thatched dining pub, smart and well run, with a relaxed and civilised atmosphere, open fire in the charming bar, and an attractive conservatory; very good imaginative food, well kept real ales, a thoughtful, but fairly priced wine list (many by the glass inc champagne), and efficient attentive service; pretty summer garden; cl Sun pm *(01954) 210221*

M20

57. ⌂ WEST MALLING
Scott House *(1.8 miles off M20 **junction 4**; A228 S, right on to A20 then first left into High St)*
£79; 5 pretty little rms. No smoking Georgian town house (from which the family also run an antiques and interior design business) with big comfortable lounge, good breakfasts in dining room, a friendly atmosphere, and helpful owners; cl Christmas/New Year; children over 10. In the same attractive conservation village, the Swan (Swan St; *(01732) 521910)* is a stylish modern brasserie with good contemporary food *(01732) 841380*

58. ※ MAIDSTONE
Museum of Kent Life *(just off M20 **junction 6**; brown signs off A229 Sandling roundabout Maidstone side of motorway)*
The story of the Kent countryside, entertainingly told over 28 acres, taking in farming tools, crafts, gardens, animals, and the county's last coal-fired oast house; also, a 1950s house and a 19th-c chapel. There are also two historic cottages, rescued from the path of the Channel Tunnel rail link at Lenham Heath; Old Cottage tells the story of the rescue, while Waterstreet Cottage has been reconstructed in World War II style. Children's play area, barrel-making at the new cooper's shop, and lots of special events; dogs allowed on lead. Meals, snacks, shop, disabled access; cl Nov-Feb; *(01622) 763936*; £5.50. Nearby, the well restored 17th-c Tyland Barn on Bluebell Hill is the HQ of Kent Wildlife Trust, with information on the area's nature reserves; cl 22 Dec-beginning Feb; *(01622) 662012*; free. The 16th/17th-c Kings Arms in the pretty neighbouring village of Boxley has decent food (all day Sun), with pleasant walks nearby.

59. ※ LEEDS
Leeds Castle *(1.2 miles off M20 **junction 8**; A20 towards Ashford then right on B2163)*
Long renowned as one of the loveliest castles in the country, perfectly placed on two little islands in the middle of a lake in nearly a square mile of landscaped parkland. It dates from the 9th c, and was converted

into a Royal residence by Henry VIII. Lots of paintings, furniture and tapestries, and a unique dog-collar. The enormous grounds have gardens (inc a mediterranean one), a maze and grotto, duck enclosure and aviary (well liked by readers), and a golf course. It's a busy place, not quite as idyllic as it appears from a distance, but very satisfying for a day out. Special events from food and wine festivals to open-air concerts. Meals, snacks, shop, good disabled access; cl 25 June, 2 July, and 25 Dec; *(01622) 765400*; around £13, but seasonal changes to prices. The Windmill at Eyhorne Street is good value for lunch.

60. ✗ HOLLINGBOURNE
Windmill *(1 mile off M20 junction 8: A20 towards Ashford (away from Maidstone), then left into B2163 – Eyhorne Street village)*
Chatty old-world timbered dining pub with low and heavy black beams, huge inglenook fireplace and snug separate areas, well kept ales and good choice of reasonably priced wines, wide choice of enjoyable food (all day wknds) inc good daily specials and plentiful fresh veg, quick friendly service, no smoking dining room; children very welcome, neat sunny garden with play area; the village has a good many handsome ancient buildings *(01622) 880280*

M25

61. 🐾 GODSTONE
Godstone Farm *(1.6 miles from M25 junction 6; B2235 into village, then bear left past the White Hart (a sound beamed and timbered Beefeater dining pub) on B3226, forking off right on to Tilburstow Hill Rd)*
Friendly small 40-acre working farm; children are encouraged to touch the animals, and even climb in with some of them; good play areas. Meals, snacks, shop, disabled access; cl 25-26 Dec; *(01883) 742546*; £5.50 per child (accompanied adults free).

62. 🐾 CHESSINGTON
Chessington World of Adventures *(2.5 miles off M25 junction 9, on A243)*
This is the place to head for unadulterated family fun. The park is full of great rides and attractions for under 12s including Land of the Dragons,

MOTORWAY BREAKS

a whole themed land for mini-sized adventurers, with rides, an indoor adventure play house and puppet theatre; don't miss the amazing animal encounters. Meals, snacks, shop, some disabled access; open 16 March-30 Oct with some mid-week closed days off peak – best to check *(0870) 4447777*; £28 and with every adult ticket purchased, a child under 12 goes in free. The Star down towards the M25 is a good value food stop.

63. ✗ OTTERSHAW

Castle *(2.6 miles off M25 junction 11 via A320 S; after A319 roundabout pass church on right, then after another 350 yards or so take sharp left turn into Brox Rd)*

Welcoming and relaxed, with wide range of popular home-made pubby food (not Sun evening) from good value sandwiches up, half a dozen well kept changing ales, good winter log fires, horse tack and rustic paraphernalia, no smoking dining area and small side conservatory; dogs welcome, sheltered garden with tables in little bowers, open all day wknds *(01932) 872373*

64. ✗ DENHAM

Swan *(0.7 miles off M25 junction 16, or M40 junction 1; follow Denham Village signs)*

Civilised and buoyant dining pub in charming village street, beautifully presented up-to-date good food, nice wines by the glass, real ales, excellent courteous staff, old or antique tables and chairs, carefully chosen pictures, heavy drapes and colour scheme, open fires and fresh flowers; children and dogs welcome, extensive floodlit garden, open all day *(01895) 832085*

65. ✗ CHENIES

Red Lion *(2 miles off M25 junction 18; A404 towards Amersham, then village signed on right; Chesham Rd)*

Bustling unpretentious traditional pub with great choice of inventive good value food (lots of the dishes come in two sizes), well kept ales inc one brewed for them locally; dogs allowed (no children inside), picnic-sets on small side terrace *(01923) 282722*

66. 🚶 LONDON COLNEY
Willows Farm Village *(0.7 miles off M25 **junction 22**; take first exit off roundabout on N side of motorway (Barnet Rd), turning right into Lowbell Lane)*
Busy working farm with boat trips, lakeside walks, shire horses, loads of sheep, pigs and other traditional animals and the usual farmyard activities. Also trampolines, mini tractors, old-fashioned fairground rides and bouncy haystacks. A decent play area has spiral slides and climbing frames, and under-5s have a separate one. A busy schedule of well thought out events includes falconry displays, duck trials and sheep racing (both repeated several times during the day). There's an indoor theatre during holidays and at wknds, and in summer they grow a maize maze. Younger children enjoy meeting the baby animals in their animal nursery, and the guinea-pig village is splendid, with 300 very friendly residents. Many of the main attractions are under cover. Meals, snacks, shop, disabled access; cl Nov-Mar; £8.95 (all inc); *(01727) 822444*.

67. 🚶 LONDON COLNEY
De Havilland Aircraft Heritage Centre *(1 mile off M25 **junction 22**; next to Salisbury Hall, off B556)*
The Mosquito aircraft were developed here in secret from 1939, and the site houses a collection of 20 different De Havilland aircraft, as well as engines and other memorabilia, and a display outlining the history of the aircraft company. Snacks in verandah-style area in main hangar, shop, disabled access; open pm Tues, Thurs and Sat, all day Sun and bank hols from first Sun in Mar to last Sun in Oct; *(01727) 822051*; £5. The Green Dragon (Waterside) has good value food, and there are pretty riverside gardens nearby.

68. 🚶 EPPING FOREST
*(1.7 miles off M25 **junction 26**; heading towards Loughton, turn right at the first crossroads – this takes you to the Forest Information Centre)*
A magnificent survival, an expansive tract of ancient hornbeam coppice, mainly tucked between the M25 and outer London; the 6,000 acres have remained free from developers since 1878. There are miles of leafy walks (and rides – you can hire horses locally), with some rough grazing, and occasional distant views; they've recently introduced Longhorn cattle. There are so many woodland paths that getting lost is part of the experience; the long-distance Forest Way is however well marked. On

MOTORWAY BREAKS

the W side is a pleasant diversion to High Beach, from where a few field paths lead SW; the Owl at Lippitts Hill is a useful refreshment stop.

69. ✕ POTTERS CROUCH
Holly Bush (2.3 miles off M25 junction 21A: A405 towards St Albans, then first left, then after a mile turn left (ie away from Chiswell Green), then at T-junction turn right into Blunts Lane; can also be reached fairly quickly, with a good map, from M1 exits 6 and 8 (and even M10))
Welcoming and relaxing country pub kept spotless, fresh flowers and candles, antique dressers, cushioned settles, carefully lit pictures, daily papers, good Fullers ales, calm efficient service, fairly short choice of fresh straightforward food (lunchtimes only, not Sun); no children inside, pleasant tree-sheltered garden behind *(01727) 851792*

M27

70. ☸ OWER
Paultons Park (2 miles off M27 junction 2; brown signs from junction)
Agreeable family leisure park with over 50 attractions and rides, gardens, birds and wildfowl, as well as model dinosaurs in marshland, a 10-acre lake with working waterwheel, hedge maze, animated *Wind in the Willows* scenes, and unique Romany Experience with the sights, sounds and smells of traditional gypsy life. The mini log flume and digger ride for younger children join rides such as the Raging River log flume, swingboat, tea-cups, and go-karts (the only thing with an extra charge), roller-coaster and several good play areas, many ideal for toddlers. Meals, snacks, shop, disabled access; cl wkdys Nov and Dec (exc Christmas specials), and all Jan to mid-Mar; *(023) 8081 4455*; £14.50

M40

71. ✕ HEDGERLEY
White Horse (2.4 miles off M40 junction 2; at exit roundabout take Slough turnoff, then first left on Hedgerley Lane alongside M40; after 1.5 miles turn right at T-junction into Village Lane)
Jolly country local with splendid range of real ales tapped from the cask

M40

behind a tiny hatch counter, good farm cider and belgian beers too; cottagey bar with lots of beams and stripped brick, log fire, cheerful friendly service, enjoyable lunchtime bar food; dogs welcome, children in canopy extension, tables outside, open all day wknds *(01753) 643225*

72. ✕ LEWKNOR
Olde Leathern Bottel *(0.5 miles off M40 **junction 6**; just off B4009 towards Watlington – High St)*
Low heavy beams, open fires, well liked home-made food with good puddings in bar and restaurant, well kept ales and eight wines by the glass; dogs and children welcome, no smoking family room, attractive garden with plenty of picnic-sets and play area *(01844) 351482*

73. ⌨ GREAT MILTON
Manoir aux Quat' Saisons *(2 miles off M40 **junction 7** via A329 SW; right into Church St)*
£275, plus winter breaks; 32 opulent rms. Luxurious Jacobean manor in 27 acres of parkland and lovely gardens with an impeccable kitchen garden; sumptuous lounges with fine furniture, beautiful flowers and open fires, conservatory, exquisitely presented superb food (at a price), and exemplary service; residential cookery courses; disabled access *(01844) 278881*

74. ✕ GAYDON
Malt Shovel *(1.2 miles off M40 **junction 12**, via B4451 SW, crossing B4100 (left then right), then bear left into Church Rd)*
Popular bar with a good relaxed atmosphere, log fire, milk churns and earthenware containers in a loft above the bar, steps up to a snug area with comfortable sofas, and busy dining room with a mix of pubby and dining tables; enjoyable unpretentious food cooked by the chef-landlord, real ales, and friendly efficient staff *(01926) 641221*

75. ⚑ GAYDON
Heritage Motor Centre *(2.5 miles off M40 **junction 12**; B4451 SW, then first right on B4100 Banbury Rd; then signed off left)*
Busy centre with the world's biggest collection of classic british cars – 200 in all, and around 150 are on display, starting with an 1895 Wolseley. Also hundreds of drawings, photographs, trophies and

MOTORWAY BREAKS

models, hi-tech displays and video shows. There's a 4-wheel-drive off-road experience, go-kart track (for the over 8s), miniature roadway, nature trail and play area. The design of the building is incredible, especially inside. Meals, snacks (lunchtimes only), shop, disabled access; *(01926) 641188*; £8. The Malt Shovel has good value food.

76. BISHOP'S TACHBROOK
*Mallory Court (2.7 miles off M40 **junction 13** northbound (a bit further off **junction 14** southbound); keep on B4087 past village, turning right into Harbury Lane)*
£195, plus special breaks; 29 comfortable rms. Fine ancient-looking house – actually built around 1910 – with elegant antiques and flower-filled day rooms, attentive staff, and excellent food using home-grown produce in oak-panelled restaurant; ten acres of lovely gardens with outdoor swimming pool, tennis, and croquet; children over 9; disabled access; dogs in bedrooms by prior arrangement *(01926) 330214*

77. SHERBOURNE
*Old Rectory (0.7 miles off M40 **junction 15**; A46 towards Stratford then second left into Vicarage Lane)*
£85; 7 rms with hand-carved four-posters and brass beds. Charming 17th-c country house with cosy sitting room, big log fire in inglenook fireplace, beams, flagstones and elm floors, honesty bar, and enjoyable breakfasts; cl Christmas and New Year; no children; dogs in Stable Block rooms only *(01926) 624562*

78. HOCKLEY HEATH
*Nuthurst Grange (1 mile off M40 **junction 16** southbound; A3400 N, then first left)*
£165, plus special breaks; 15 comfortable, spacious rms with lots of extras. Red brick, creeper-clad Edwardian house in landscaped gardens, with light, airy and prettily decorated public rooms, lovely fresh flowers, enjoyable modern british cooking using home-grown produce, good breakfasts, and pleasant helpful staff; cl Christmas; disabled access; dogs in bedrooms by prior arrangement *(01564) 783972*

M45

79. 🚶 WATERPERRY
Waterperry Gardens *(1.9 miles off M40 junction 8A;
first left off A418 E)*
Colourful 80-year-old gardens with herbaceous borders, formal rose garden with new and old roses, medieval knot and alpine gardens, and a pleasant river walk; there's a Saxon church with original windows, a little agricultural museum (cl am, and Mon), and a craft gallery with changing exhibitions (cl Mon). Snacks, garden shop with interesting plants, disabled access; cl 25 Dec-1 Jan, and around 14-17 July for an arts and crafts festival; *(01844) 339226*; £4. The Rising Sun in Wheatley has enjoyable food.

M42

80. 🚶 BODYMOOR HEATH
Kingsbury Water Park *(2.7 miles off M42 junction 9; A4097 NE, then
at next roundabout turn first left, bearing left on to Bodymoor Heath Lane)*
30 lakes and pools, created by gravel excavations, in 620 landscaped acres. Waterside and woodland walks, nature trails (maps and leaflets at the visitor centre), and two play areas. You can fish (from £1.90, under-16s fish for free during open season at Mitchell's Pool). Meals, snacks, shop, good disabled access (mobility scooters available free); cl 25 Dec; *(01827) 872660*; free, £2.50 for parking. The park also contains **Broomey Croft Children's Farm**; all the usual farm animals for children to feed, plus tractor rides (wknds and school hols), and play and picnic areas. Snacks, shop, disabled access; cl Sept-Easter exc wknds and usually half-terms; *(01827) 873844*; £3.90. The canalside Dog & Doublet has decent food.

M45

81. ✕ 🛏 DUNCHURCH
Dun Cow *(1.3 miles off M45 junction 1: on junction of A45 and A426)*
£59.95; reasonably priced food all day in well run and handsomely oak-beamed Vintage Inn with friendly staff, nice house wines, two no smoking areas, log fires, rugs on wooden and flagstone floors, country pictures and bric-a-brac, and farmhouse furniture; children welcome,

MOTORWAY BREAKS

tables in sunny coachyard and on sheltered lawn, open all day, well equipped bdrms

M50

82. ⌂ BROMSBERROW HEATH
Grove House *(1.6 miles off M50 **junction 2**, via A417 towards Ledbury, first left after just under a mile)*
£79.50; 3 spacious rms with bowls of fruit and home-made biscuits, 2 with four-posters. Wisteria-clad 15th-c manor house with dark panelling, open fires, beams, fresh flowers and polished antiques, and good evening meals at huge dining table using home-grown produce; 13 acres of fields and garden, hard tennis court, and neighbour's outdoor swimming pool; cl Christmas *(01531) 650584*

83. ✕ UPTON BISHOP
Moody Cow *(2 miles from M50 **junction 3** westbound (or **junction 4** eastbound), via B4221; continue on B4221 to rejoin at next junction)*
In a quiet village, this cheerful and friendly pub has several snug separate areas, a pleasant medley of stripped country furniture, a big log fire, no smoking rustic candlelit restaurant and second small dining room, a good choice of enjoyable food, and well kept beers; children must be well behaved; partial disabled access *(01989) 780470*

M53

84. ☸ ELLESMERE PORT
Boat Museum *(just off M53 **junction 9**; South Pier Rd)*
Set in a picturesque historic dock complex, a huge floating collection of canal boats, as well as steam engines, a blacksmith's forge, workers' cottages, stables, big indoor exhibitions (inc one about the families that lived and worked on the waterways), and boat trips. Shop, mostly disabled access; cl Thurs and Fri Nov–Mar, and a few days over Christmas; *(0151) 355 5017*; £5.95. Parts of the surrounding dock have been redeveloped with craft workshops and the like. The Woodlands (Chester Rd) is a useful pub/restaurant (with its own bowling green).

M54

85. 🕸 ELLESMERE PORT
Blue Planet (1.1 miles from M53 junction 10, via A5117 and B5332 (Longlooms Rd))
One of Britain's most stunning aquariums, this includes a dramatic 233-ft viewing tunnel through sharks, stingray, and nearly 16,000 tons of water; a moving walkway lets you trundle along gawping. Knowledgeable staff (many of them marine biologists) are on hand to answer questions, and they give talks throughout the day. Good shows in the Aquatheatre, where you can watch divers feeding the creatures; they use underwater microphones to chat with the audience. The main displays re-create water environments from around the world, and touch-pools give children the chance to handle starfish and the like. As well as fish they have reptiles, insects, and now otters too; their encounter sessions can introduce you to everything from toads and hissing cockroaches to toxic frogs. Also several film and slide shows, and free face painting. Meals, snacks, shop, good disabled access; cl 25 Dec; *(0870) 4448440*; £8.50 adults. Nearby is the huge factory outlet shopping village, Cheshire Oaks, a great place to pick up bargains.

86. 🛏 HOOLE
Hoole Hall (just off M53 junction 12; off A56 towards Chester)
£94.90, plus special breaks; 97 well equipped rms, some no smoking. Extended and attractively refurbished 18th-c hall with five acres of gardens, good food in two restaurants, and friendly service; good disabled access; dogs in downstairs bedrooms with doors to terrace *(01244) 408800*

M54

87. 🕸 WOLVERHAMPTON
Moseley Old Hall (1.9 miles off M54 junction 1; A460 S, then at next roundabout turn right on Moseley Rd; Moseley Old Hall Lane is then on right)
Tudor house famed as a hiding place for Charles II after the Battle of Worcester. The façade has altered since, but the furnishings and atmosphere in its panelled rooms don't seem to have changed much, and there's a 17th-c knot garden. Readers particularly enjoy the guided tours. Teas, shop, limited disabled access; cl am, also Mon (exc

MOTORWAY BREAKS

bank hols), Tues, Thurs-Fri, and mid-Dec-late-Mar; *(01902) 782808*; £4.80; NT.

88. ⊨ WREKIN
Buckatree Hall *(1.4 miles off M54 junction 7; S on minor rd towards the Wrekin, then first left)*
£80; 62 rms, several with own balconies and many with lake views. Comfortable former hunting lodge dating from 1820, in large wooded estate at the foot of the Wrekin; extended and modernised with comfortable day rooms, enjoyable food in the Terrace Restaurant, and helpful attentive service; dogs welcome in bedrooms *(01952) 641821*

89. ⊨ WROCKWARDINE
Church Farm *(1.7 miles off M54 junction 7, via Drummery Lane (first right, heading W on B5061 from exit))*
£58, plus special breaks; 5 individual well equipped rms, most with own bthrm. Friendly Georgian farmhouse on very ancient site overlooking the attractive garden and church; a relaxed atmosphere, particularly good caring service, beams and log fire in lounge, and good daily changing food in traditionally furnished dining room; children over 10; dogs in certain bedrooms *(01952) 244917*

M55

90. ✕ KIRKHAM
Cromwellian *(2.3 miles off M55 junction 3; A585 S, left at roundabout on to B5192, bearing left on it into Poulton St)*
Tiny evening restaurant in 17th-c house with consistently good interesting food from a fixed-price menu – thoughtful wine list, too; cl Sun, Mon, 2 wks Jan, 2 wks Oct *(01772) 685680*

M56

91. 🕸 LITTLE BOLLINGTON
(2 miles from M56 junction 7 – A56 towards Lymm, then first right at Stamford Arms into Park Lane; use A556 to get back on to M56 westbound)

M57

This peaceful hamlet gives strolls by the Bridgewater Canal and in Dunham Hall deer park. The beamed Swan With Two Nicks is a very pleasant refreshment stop, full of brass, copper and bric-a-brac, with some antique settles. It has a log fire, good choice of generous above-average food from filling baguettes up, well kept ales such as Boddingtons, Greene King Old Speckled Hen and Timothy Taylors Landlord, decent wines, and cheerful helpful staff; tables outside, open all day.

92. 🕅 ALTRINCHAM
Dunham Massey Hall, Garden and Park (3 miles off M56 junction 7; B5160 left off A56)
Early Georgian manor house extensively remodelled in the early 20th c, with impressive collections of walnut furniture, silverware, paintings, and restored kitchen, pantry and laundry. The largely unaltered grounds have plenty of deer, formal avenues of trees, and a working Elizabethan saw mill. Friendly staff give free tours daily. Meals, snacks, shop, disabled access to ground floor of hall; open Sat-Weds April-Oct, house cl am; *(0161) 941 1025*; £6.50 house and garden, £3.80 garden only; NT.

93. ✗ DARESBURY
Ring o' Bells (1.5 miles off M56 junction 11; A56 N, then right on B5356)
Relaxing Chef & Brewer with good wheelchair access and nice range of places to sit from down-to-earth and homely to more of a library style; good choice of well liked food all day (two no smoking dining rooms), lots of wines by the glass and well kept ales; children welcome, long partly terraced garden, open all day *(01925) 740256*

M57

94. 🕅 PRESCOT
Knowsley Safari Park (1.2 miles off M57 junction 2, via A57 E; park signed off left)
Five-mile drive through very natural-looking reserves of lions, tigers, rhinos, monkeys and other animals; they have the biggest herd of

MOTORWAY BREAKS

african elephants in Europe. There's a roller-coaster and a pirate ship ride (not included in admission); also pets' corner, miniature railway, and an information centre. Meals, snacks, shop, disabled access; cl 25 Dec; *(0151) 430 9009*; £9.50. If you have to pass through the town, the museum (Church St) has an interesting collection relating to the area's former clock-making industry; cl 1-2pm, Sun am, Mon (inc bank hols), Good Fri, 25 Dec-1 Jan; *(0151) 430 7787*; free. The Clock Face (Derby St) is a pleasant old mansion-house pub here.

M60

95. 🕉 STOCKPORT
Hat Works *(1 mile off M60 **junction 1**; Wellington Mill on A6 S (Wellington Rd))*
This is the UK's only museum dedicated to the hatting industry, hats and headwear; two floors of interactive exhibits that take you through the history of the town's once thriving hatting industry; there's something for all ages, guided tours, and a programme of events and activities ranging from creative workshops for adults and children to performances and themed talks; open all year; *(0161) 355 7770*; £3.95.

96. 🕉 MANCHESTER
Manchester United Museum *(2.5 miles off M60 **junction 6**; A56 towards centre, then left on Sir Matt Busby Way, Old Trafford)*
Purpose-built football museum, covering the club's history from its foundation in 1878 to the more recent glory days. Hundreds of exhibits (changing almost as frequently as their strip) and tours of the ground (must book in advance, not match days, and limited on the days before). Meals, snacks, shop (not unjustifiably they call it a megastore), disabled access; cl a few days over Christmas; *(0870) 442 1994*; £9 tour and museum, £6 museum only.

M61

97. ✘ WHEELTON
Dressers Arms *(2.1 miles off M61 **junction 8**; A674 towards Blackburn,*

*then in Wheelton fork right into Briers Brow; 3.6 miles off M65 **junction 3**, also via A674)*
Good home-made bar food (all day wknds) using local supplies and good range of beers (at least one from their own microbrewery) in cosy low-beamed little rooms full of old oak and traditional features, with two no smoking areas; children and dogs welcome, chinese restaurant upstairs, lots of picnic-sets on front terrace, open all day *(01254) 830041*

M66

98. ✕ BURY
Lord Raglan *(2 miles off M66 northbound, **junction 1**; A56 S then left in Walmersley on Walmersley Old Rd/Bury Old Rd, up cobbled lane to Mount Pleasant, Nangreaves; if coming from N, stay on A56 S instead of joining M66, and turn left in Walmersley as above)*
18th-c pub high on the moors overlooking Bury, with tasty food from open sandwiches to steaks in cosy bar or big panelled restaurant, and brewing its own interesting beers; beams, bric-a-brac and antique clocks, huge log fire, splendid view; children and dogs welcome, open all day wknds *(0161) 764 6680*

M77

99. 🐾 GLASGOW
Pollok House *(1.5 miles off M77 **junction 2**, via B762 E; Pollok Country Park, Pollokshaws Rd)*
Treasures here include silver, ceramics and porcelain, but it's the paintings (for which the house was largely redesigned 100 years ago) that stand out, with a collection of spanish masters such as Goya and El Greco cannily acquired in the mid-19th c when they were greatly undervalued. Meals, snacks, gift and food shops; disabled access; cl 25-26 Dec, 1-2 Jan; *(0141) 616 6410*; £8.

MOTORWAY BREAKS

100. 🎨 GLASGOW
Burrell Collection *(1.5 miles off M77 **junction 2**, via B762 E; Pollok Country Park, Pollokshaws Rd)*
A couple of miles out in the suburbs, but not to be missed – and rarely too crowded. Splendidly and imaginatively housed in a modern building created to show its different parts to perfection, the huge collection – far too much to see at one go – includes egyptian alabaster, chinese jade, oriental rugs, remarkable tapestries, medieval metalwork and stained glass, even medieval doorways and windows set into the walls, as well as paintings by Degas, Manet and Rembrandt among others. Good meals and snacks, shop, disabled access; cl 25-26 Dec, 1-2 Jan; *(0141) 287 2550*; free (parking £1.50).

M90

101. ✕ KELTY
Butterchurn *(0.5 miles off M90 **junction 4** via B914 W)*
In the courtyard of a farm, this popular restaurant has fine views over Loch Leven, and serves morning coffee, lunch, afternoon teas, snacks, and traditional high teas using fresh local ingredients; they also sell their own products to take away and have a craft and gift centre, farmyard pets for children, and walks and cycle trails; cl Sun-Thurs pms, 25-26 Dec and 1-2 Jan; disabled access *(01383) 830169*

102. ✕ PERTH
Let's Eat *(2.5 miles off M90 **junction 11**; A85 N, then left over second bridge, bearing right on Charlotte St; 77 Kinnoull St)*
Very popular restaurant in what was the Theatre Royal; relaxed friendly atmosphere, enjoyable modern cooking inc proper old-fashioned puddings, and short selective wine list; cl Sun-Mon, 2 wks Jan, 2 wks July; disabled access *(01738) 643377*

M180

103. 🚶 ELSHAM
Elsham Hall Country & Wildlife Park *(1.8 miles off M180 junction 5; local rd direct from exit roundabout)*
Arboretum, lakeside gardens, animal farm, farming museum, adventure playground, carp and trout lakes with carp feeding jetty, and newly refurbished Falconry Centre with flying displays; lovely new contemporary walled garden with lots to inspire children, gardeners and art lovers alike; entertainment on bank hols and other events all year in courtyard; tearoom/restaurant and delicatessen; cl Mon and Tues (exc bank and school hols), and all mid-Sept to Mar; *(01652) 688698*; £5.

A1

104. ✕ ⇌ LEMSFORD
Auberge du Lac (2 miles off A1(M) junction 5; from Lemsford Village Rd bear right on to B653)
£170, 18th-c former hunting lodge on a lake, in the magnificent parkland of Brocket Hall; big windows give charming views of the water and terrace, tables are beautifully set, innovative modern cooking is based on classical french principles (lunch is particularly good value), and service is courteous and professional; bdrms in Melbourne Lodge, the former stables for Brocket Hall; cl Sun pm, all Mon; disabled access *(01707) 368888*

105. ⇌ SANDY
Highfield Farm (off A1 S-bound carriageway just S of Tempsford flyover)
£65; 10 rms (some in charmingly converted barn). Neatly kept whitewashed house (no smoking) set well away from A1 and surrounded by attractive arable farmland with plenty of room; warmly friendly, helpful owner, open fire in comfortable sitting room, and breakfasts in pleasant dining room; disabled access; dogs in bedrooms *(01767) 682332*

106. ⅍ ST NEOTS
(just off A1)
Pleasant town next to the River Ouse with a large market place and a pleasant landscaped park; the medieval church of St Mary's is worth a look, and the Chequers near it has good value food. An interesting little museum (New St), in a former police station and Magistrate's Court, has a rare example of a 1907 cell block; other displays include the story of St Neot, local crafts and trades, and changing exhibitions by local artists, with new interactive displays; shop, disabled access; open Tues-Sat (cl during Jan school hols), best to check *(01480) 388788*

107. ✕ ⇌ STILTON
Bell (1 mile off A1, via B1043 (High St))
£96.50; 22 rms. Elegant, carefully restored coaching inn with attractive rambling bars, big log fire, generous helpings of good food using the famous cheese (which was first sold from here), and seats in the sheltered cobbled and flagstoned courtyard; cl 25 Dec *(01733) 241066*

108. ✕ ⋈ WANSFORD
Haycock (just off A1, highly visible just S of A47)
£115, plus special breaks; 50 individually decorated rms. 16th-c golden stone inn with relaxed, comfortable and carefully furnished lounges and pubby bar; pretty lunchtime café, smart restaurant with good food, excellent wines and efficient friendly service; garden with boules, fishing and cricket; disabled access. The little village it dominates is attractive, with a fine bridge over the Nene, and a good antiques shop; dogs in some bedrooms *(01780) 782223*

109. 🕍 STAMFORD
(just off A1)
Many would support John Betjeman's verdict that this is England's most attractive town. Within the medieval walls are no less than 500 listed buildings, inc a good number of attractive medieval churches – particularly All Saints in the centre, St George's with excellent 15th-c stained glass, and St Mary's nearby. There are riverside strolls and quite a few craft and antiques shops. The George, one of the town's grandest buildings with some parts going back to Saxon times, is excellent for lunch (and has food all day); the Crown (All Saints Pl) does traditional english country dishes.

110. ✕ STRETTON
Jackson Stops (under a mile off A1, at B668 (Oakham) exit; follow village sign, turning off Clipsham road into Manor Road, pub on left)
Smart thatched dining pub with good inventive modern food (not Sun evening) in appealingly light and airy main restaurant, attentive service, thoughtful wine list, good real ales, nicely old-fashioned traditional bar and second stripped-stone dining room; cl Mon *(01780) 410237*

111. ⋈ STRETTON
Ram Jam Inn (0.2 miles off A1; just off B668 towards Oakham)
£74.10; 7 comfortable and well equipped rms. Actually on the A1, this civilised place has a comfortable airily modern lounge bar, a café bar and bistro, good interesting food quickly served all day from open-plan kitchen, and useful small wine list; large garden and orchard; cl 25 Dec; dogs welcome in bedrooms *(01780) 410776*

MOTORWAY BREAKS

112. 🕸 WOOLSTHORPE
***Woolsthorpe Manor** (0.8 miles off A1; Woolsthorpe Rd right off B6403)*
Birthplace and family home of Isaac Newton, who conducted some of his most famous experiments here. Farm buildings, orchard with the famous apple tree, and interactive science discovery centre. Snacks, shop, disabled access to ground floor and science centre; open 1-5pm Weds-Sun and bank hol Mon, April-Sept, Good Fri and wknds March and Oct; (01476) 860338; £4.20; NT.

113. 🕸 NEWARK
***Newark Air Museum** (1.4 miles off A1; A46 towards Lincoln, then return along A46 from next roundabout, to The Airfield, Winthorpe)*
Over 70 aircraft and cockpit sections from across the history of aviation inc transport, training and reconnaissance aircraft, helicopters, and diverse jet fighters and bombers inc two russian MiGs; half the exhibits are under cover, so fine all year round. Snacks, shop, disabled access; (01636) 707170; £5.50.

114. ✕ SIBTHORPE HILL
***Mussel & Crab** (0.3 miles off A1 via B1164 from A57 Markham Moor roundabout N of Tuxford)*
Friendly, well run dining pub with spacious lounge bar, a mediterranean-style restaurant leading off, most enjoyable food with a strong emphasis on fish, a thoughtful wine list (quite a few inc champagne by the glass) with helpful notes, and two outside terraces; good disabled access (01777) 870491

115. 🕸 BRODSWORTH
***Brodsworth Hall and Gardens** (2.2 miles off A1(M) junction 37; A635 W then first right)*
Grand house vividly illustrating life in Victorian times; the family that lived here closed off parts of the house as their fortunes waned, inadvertently preserving the contents and décor exactly as they were (right down to the billiard score-book). Richly furnished rooms, lots of marble statues, and busily cluttered servants' wing; a new exhibition covers the use of chintz in english country houses. The family commissioned some of the largest and fastest yachts of the Victorian era, and an exhibition charts the history of these splendid vessels. The marvellous formal gardens and parkland are gradually being restored. Meals, snacks,

shop, disabled access; cl am, Mon (exc bank hols), and all Nov-Mar (exc gardens open wknds); *(01302) 722598*; £6.60; EH.

116. 🛏 MONK FRYSTON
Monk Fryston Hall (2.5 miles off A1 via A63 E (may be a little further when new section of A1(M) opens here))
£116, plus special breaks; 29 comfortable rms. Benedictine manor house in 30 acres of secluded gardens with lake and woodland, an oak-panelled lounge and bar with log fires, antiques, paintings and fresh flowers, good honest food, and friendly helpful staff; disabled access; dogs in bedrooms and public areas (not restaurant) *(01977) 682369*

117. ✕ 🛏 ALDBOROUGH
Ship (1.3 miles off A1(M) junction 48; heading towards Boroughbridge from exit roundabouts, take first right)
£49; 3 rms. Friendly and neatly kept 14th-c pub nr ancient church and Roman town, with coal fire in stone inglenook and old-fashioned seats in heavily beamed bar, ample food, separate restaurant, good breakfasts, well kept real ales, and seats on spacious lawn; cl 24-26 Dec *(01423) 322749*

118. ✕ 🛏 BOROUGHBRIDGE
Black Bull (1.6 miles off A1(M) junction 48; St James Sq)
£54; attractive 13th-c inn with big stone fireplace and brown leather seats in main bar area (served through an old-fashioned hatch), a cosy, traditional snug, well liked interesting bar food, well kept real ales, enjoyable wines (with nine by the glass), and afternoon teas; friendly and attentive service; bdrms; disabled access *(01432) 322413*

119. 🗝 NORTON CONYERS
Norton Conyers (2 miles off A1; heading N, left turn 1.3 miles after A61 interchange, into Hollins Lane, then right and left to pass Wath)
The same family have lived in this late medieval house (with Stuart and Georgian additions) for around 380 years, and the furniture and pictures reflect this long connection. Charlotte Brontë used the building as a model for Thornfield Hall, and a recently uncovered blocked staircase fuelled speculation about a mad woman confined in the attic. Look out for the hoofprint on the stairs. Attractively planted 18th-c walled garden. Seasonal pick-your-own fruit, shop (with unusual hardy plants),

MOTORWAY BREAKS

limited disabled access; open pm bank hols Sun and Mon Easter-29 Aug, pm daily 27 June-3 July, garden also open Thurs all year and am during the above times, phone to check; *(01765) 640333*; house £5, garden free. The Bull and Bruce Arms in West Tanfield are useful for lunch.

120. ✕ ⌂ PICKHILL
Nags Head *(2.1 miles off A1 Masham turnoff; village signed off B6267 in Ainderby Quernhow)*
£70; deservedly popular old inn run for 30 years by two brothers, with a nice mix of customers, busy tap room, smarter lounge, no smoking restaurant, particularly good food inc interesting daily specials and lovely puddings, friendly efficient staff, a fine wine list and well kept real ales; bdrms; disabled access *(01845) 567391*

121. ✕ CARTHORPE
Fox & Hounds *(2.2 miles off A1, S of Leeming Bar, via B6285 through Burneston)*
Pretty little extended village house with two log fires and some evocative Victorian photographs of Whitby, an attractive high-raftered, no smoking restaurant with lots of farm and smithy tools, enjoyable interesting food (fine daily specials and puddings inc yummy home-made ice-creams), decent wines, and helpful, friendly service; cl Mon, first wk Jan; disabled access *(01845) 567433*

122. ✕ AYCLIFFE
County *(1.2 miles off A1(M) **junction 69**; A167 N. then in High St fork off right to The Green)*
Stylish pub with furnishings in the extended bar and no smoking bistro that are light and modern, definitely geared to dining; minimalist décor, a friendly and civilised atmosphere, exceptionally good and very popular high quality cooking using local produce, a good choice of wines by the glass, and four well kept real ales; swift service by friendly young staff *(01325) 312273*

123. ⌂ CHESTER-LE-STREET
Lumley Castle *(1.8 miles off A1(M) **junction 63**; A167, then left on B1284, then next left into Ropery Lane)*
£160, plus special breaks; 59 wonderfully atmospheric rms. Splendid 14th-c castle with Norman origins standing above the river Wear;

plenty of gothic character in atmospheric rooms, tapestries, rugs and statues, carved wood and chandeliers, dimly lit corridors and spiral staircases, billiards room and library, good modern cooking in vaulted no smoking restaurant (they hold Elizabethan banquets), and 9 acres of grounds; cl 24-26 Dec, 1 Jan; partial disabled access *(0191) 389 1111*

124. ◨ GATESHEAD
Eslington Villa (1.5 miles off A1; one approach is by B1426 from A692 exit, then third exit from next roundabout on to Kingsway North, then left at next roundabout on to Eastern Ave, then left on to Station Rd)
£84.50, plus wknd breaks; 18 rms. Comfortable, extended Edwardian house in quiet residential area with some original features, a lounge with comfortably modern furniture and bay windows overlooking garden, good food in conservatory restaurant, and a friendly atmosphere; cl 4 days over Christmas; disabled access; dogs welcome in bedrooms *(0191) 487 6017*

125. ✕ STANNINGTON
Ridley Arms (just off A1 S of Morpeth)
Extended dining pub well arranged in separate relaxing carefully lit areas, mainly no smoking and some with comfortable armchairs, generous tasty unpretentious food all day, good choice of real ales and wines by the glass; sensible prices, children welcome, good disabled access *(01670) 789216*

126. ✕ ◨ NEWTON-ON-THE-MOOR
Cook & Barker Arms (0.4 miles off A1 S of Alnwick)
£65; beautifully prepared imaginative food in bustling stone pub's unfussy, long beamed bar, with partly panelled walls, a coal fire and coal-effect gas one, and a couple of no smoking areas; changing real ales, decent whiskies and 12 wines by the glass; cl 25 Dec pm; disabled access *(01665) 575234*

127. 🛦 ALNWICK
(1 mile off A1)
Busy town at the heart of prosperous farming country (farmers' market last Fri of month), with some attractive old streets nr the market square – it was used in the film *Elizabeth*. The hillside church of St Michael and All Angels above the river is a perfect example of a

MOTORWAY BREAKS

complete Late Gothic building. A new local history museum in a former church, Bailiffgate, has a mix of interactive and more traditional displays; shop, disabled access; cl Mon Nov-Easter and 24 Dec-1 Jan; *(01665) 605847*. An impressive number of second-hand books are on sale in the converted Victorian station, and the Market Tavern has bargain food. Hulne Park, a couple of miles out on the B6346, is excellent for gentle parkland walks; dogs not allowed. Don't miss the whimsical Brizlee Tower and hermit's cave, also some abbey and priory remains.

128. 🕅 ALNWICK
Alnwick Castle (1.3 miles off A1, via A1068 and B6346)
The 'Windsor of the North' dates back to the 11th c, the second-largest inhabited castle in the country. Stone soldiers stand guard on the battlements, and inside all is Renaissance grandeur, with a magnificent art collection taking in works by Titian, Van Dyck and Canaletto, and an outstanding Claude. Also a famous collection of Meissen china, Roman remains, refurbished museum with displays on the Duke of Northumberland's own private army and local archaeology, and children's playground. Exciting for gardeners, the rapidly developing new 12-acre sloping walled garden is a magnificent partnership of water, topiary, and precision plantings, designed by the Wirtz family of Belgium. Water displays, ornamental garden, water tower walk, rose garden, and woodland walks. Meals, snacks, shop; disabled access (garden, part of castle); castle open Apr-Oct, garden cl 25 Dec; *(01665) 510777*; £7.95 castle, £6 garden.

129. ✕ WARENFORD
Warenford Lodge (just off A1 S of B6348/B1341)
Very individual old (though rather modern-feeling) dining pub with stripped stonework, a big stone fireplace, comfortable extension with woodburner, really good attractively presented imaginative food, and decent wines; children in evening dining room only; cl Mon, Tues-Fri am (all day winter Tues), all Jan; limited disabled access *(01668) 213453*

130. 🕅 PAXTON
Paxton House (2 miles off A1 from Berwick; B6461 W)
Fine 18th-c Palladian country house with Adam interiors and Chippendale furniture. 12 period rooms and the largest picture gallery in a

Scottish country house, with over 70 paintings from the National Galleries of Scotland. 80 acres of gardens, woodland and riverside walks, squirrel hide, adventure playground, and picnic areas. Meals, snacks, shop, disabled access; house open daily Easter-end Oct; *(01289) 386291*; £6, £3 gardens only. Cantys Brig towards Berwick has good food.

131. 🕸 BERWICK-UPON-TWEED
(1.7 miles off A1 bypass)
Captured or sacked 13 times before it finally came under English rule for good in 1482, the town's quieter more recent centuries have left it largely unspoilt, with some handsome 18th-c buildings and a fine 17th-c church. In Marygate, the handsome Georgian town hall with its soaring spire houses the Cell Block Museum; unusual in being upstairs, the gaol here was used between 1761 and 1849. Hour-long guided tours leave 10.30 and 2pm Easter-end Sept; *(01289) 330900*; £1.50. Most people who come here seem to while away at least a bit of time watching the swans on the River Tweed, or alternatively, look out over the sea from the Rob Roy restaurant (Spittal Rd), which has good local fish. Other places we can recommend for food are Barrels (Bridge St) and Foxtons (Hide Hill). The town has an impressive track record for hospitality: in the early 19th c it boasted a formidable total of 59 pubs and three coaching inns. Today, a more striking feature is its extraordinary trio of bridges, best appreciated by walking along the Tweed: there are paths on both banks, starting from the East Ord picnic site by the A1 road bridge. The town ramparts, impressively intact, were a masterpiece of 16th-c military planning. Partly grassed over and easy to walk, they give good views (though stick to the path – there are sudden drops).

132. 🕸 MUSSELBURGH
Newhailes House *(0.8 miles off A1; A6095 into Musselburgh)*
Once home to the influential Dalrymple family, this 17th-c house with its impressive rococo interiors and fine furnishings has been carefully conserved 'as found' rather than restored, leaving textiles faded and paint chipped. Once the largest in Scotland, the library drew praise from Dr Johnson. The 80-acre grounds are being restored too, and an old stable block has a visitor centre (free). Snacks, shop, disabled access; cl ams, Tues-Weds and Nov-Mar; *(0131) 653 5599*; pre-booked guided tours; NTS.

MOTORWAY BREAKS

133. ✗ EAST LINTON
Drovers (0.5 miles off A1 on B1377; Bridge St)
Comfortable 18th-c inn with prints and pictures for sale, cosy armchairs, a basket of logs by the woodburner, hops around the bar, very good interesting food (more elaborate in the evening), a good range of real ales, and partly no smoking upstairs restaurant *(01620) 860298*

A2

134. ⌑ DOVER
Churchill (0.7 miles off A2; from A20 after terminal roundabout take first left into Marine Parade waterside rd, and on into Waterloo Cres)
£102, plus special breaks; 66 comfortable rms, several with balconies. Above the harbour, this Regency terrace hotel has a congenial bar, sun lounge and terrace, friendly staff, and enjoyable food (lots of fresh fish) in brasserie-style restaurant overlooking the Channel; health club; disabled access *(01304) 203633*

135. ※ DOVER
Dover Castle (Best to take A258 from A2 roundabout N of town)
Not to be missed, an excellently preserved magnificent Norman fortress with its original keep, 242-ft well, and massive walls and towers. There's a lot to see inc the atmospheric complex of underground tunnels that played a vital role in World War II, and an exhibition which dramatically re-creates an early 13th-c siege. Also included are the Pharos Tower (a Roman lighthouse using a 4th-floor flaring brazier as a guide-light), and a restored Saxon church. A walk round the battlements gives bird's-eye views of the comings and goings down in the harbour (something which captivates small children); the audioguide (a small extra cost) adds interest to your stroll. Meals, snacks, shop, disabled access; cl 24-26 Dec, 1 Jan, and every Tues and Weds in Nov, Dec, Jan; *(01304) 211067*; £8.95; EH.

136. ※ HERNHILL
Mount Ephraim Gardens (1.5 miles off A2 at Boughton Street; turn into Bull Lane at W end of The Street, then right into Staple Street)
Eight acres of pleasant gardens, with japanese-style rock garden, topiary garden, water garden, woodland walk, a rose garden, and a developing

grass maze; good views. Teas, shop; cl am, Mon (except bank hols), Tues and Fri and Oct-Easter; *(01227) 751496*; £4. There's a craft centre on Sun pm. By the church and small green of this charming village, the ancient Red Lion has decent food.

137. 🏛 COBHAM
(1.8 miles off A2, a mile or so before start of M2)
An attractive village, with a good mix of unspoilt buildings from various centuries – an excellent place to walk round (as Dickens liked to do). The partly 13th-c church is worth examining, with its magnificent brasses and tombs, as is the 14th-c New College, like a miniature Oxford college but far less known to visitors (open daily, disabled access; *(01474) 812503*; free). The Leather Bottle has decent food, interesting Dickens memorabilia and a good garden.

A3

138. ✕ COMPTON
Tea Shop (0.5 miles off A3 just SW of A31 interchange; Down Lane, off B3000)
Well liked cottagey teashop doing morning coffee, light lunches and afternoon tea, home-made cakes, scones and jams, free-range eggs, a wide range of drinks inc interesting juices, seltzers, and fruity mineral waters, lots of indian, chinese, herbal and fruit teas, and different coffees; cl 24 Dec-6 Jan; partial disabled access *(01483) 811030*

139. ✕ ⛨ EASHING
Stag (0.3 miles off A3 southbound, S of Hurtmore turn-off; or pub signed off A283 just SE of exit roundabout at N end of A3 Milford bypass)
£55; partly 15th-c pub tucked away by converted mill buildings, charming old-fashioned bar on the right, and cosy room beyond with dark-wallpapered walls, stag's head and big stag print, cookery books on shelves by the log fire, and an extensive, rambling, similarly furnished area on the left with a big woodburner in a huge fireplace; enjoyable food from big blackboard lists, well kept real ales, 15 wines by the glass, attentive and chatty neatly dressed staff, and a table of daily papers; tables out among mature trees *(01483) 421568*

MOTORWAY BREAKS

140. ✕ ROWLAND'S CASTLE
Castle Inn (2.8 miles off A3(M) junction 2, via B2149; Finchdean Rd, by Redhill Rd/Woodberry Lane junction)
Chatty pub with sturdy country furnishings in two appealing eating rooms, enjoyable popular food all day (not after 3pm on winter Sun and Mon), well kept ales and country wines; disabled access and facilities are good *(023) 9241 2494*

141. ✕ CHALTON
Red Lion (1.4 miles off A3, opposite Clanfield turn-off)
Hampshire's oldest pub extended from obviously ancient heavy-beamed core, popular food (not Sun evening), good beer, wine and whisky choice, pretty garden *(023) 9259 2246*

A5

142. ※ DUNSTABLE DOWNS
(1.8 miles from A5: B489 towards Tring from Dunstable, then left on B4541)
Very popular with kite-fliers and gliders at wknds or in summer; there's a countryside centre (open Apr-Oct, plus wknds Nov-Mar), three car parks, and lots of space to run around. The downs give great views from a spectacular escarpment path, amid ancient grasslands. They can be linked to a circuit incorporating Whipsnade village and the nearby Tree Cathedral – the best walk in Beds. Five Knolls is an important Bronze Age burial mound, excavated by Agatha Christie's husband Sir Max Mallowan and Gerald Dunning. The Horse & Jockey (A5183) is a useful family food pub.

143. ※ BLETCHLEY
Bletchley Park (2.8 miles off A5, at B4034/A4140 roundabout; turn off B4034 at Eight Bells pub, then right into Wilton Ave)
Victorian mansion where 10,000 men and women worked cracking german codes during World War II. It's a fascinating story, told here in meticulous and intriguing detail: too technical perhaps for younger children. Around the grounds are carefully preserved wartime huts and vehicles, collections of wartime fire engines, uniforms and vintage toys,

a fascinating exhibition tracing the development of computers, and children's trails, with recorded commentaries. It's a genuine, untouristy place, staffed by dedicated volunteers. Excellent guided tours 11am and 2pm. Meals, snacks, shop, disabled access; *(01908) 640404*; £10, children under 8 free.

144. PAULERSPURY
***Vine House** (0.4 miles off A5 N of Milton Keynes; 100 High St)*
£85; 6 individually decorated rms. 300-year-old building with carefully preserved original features, a relaxed welcoming atmosphere, cosy bar with open fire, and very good modern English cooking (inc home-made bread and petits fours) in attractive restaurant; pretty cottage garden; cl 1 wk over Christmas; partial disabled access *(01327) 811267*

145. SHREWSBURY
***Fitz Manor** (2.7 miles off A5 NW of Shrewsbury, via Forton just
N of River Severn)*
£60; 3 rms, shared bthrm. Lovely black and white timbered 15th-c manor house with oak panelling and log fire in comfortable sitting room, a big dining room with antiques, paintings and parquet flooring, good evening meals, big breakfasts, and friendly owners; outdoor heated swimming pool *(01743) 850295*

146. KNOCKIN
***Top Farmhouse** (2 miles W off A5 via B4396/B4397; turn left in village)*
£50; 3 pretty rms. Most attractive Grade I listed black and white timbered house dating back to the 16th c, with friendly owners, lots of timbers and beams, a log fire in the restful comfortable drawing room, good breakfasts in the large dining room, and an appealing garden; grand piano; children over 12; dogs in bedrooms *(01691) 682582*

147. OSWESTRY
***Park Hall** (0.9 miles off A5; A495 NE, then second left into Burma Rd)*
Looks at past, present and future farming techniques and countryside activities, in restored Victorian farm buildings (80% is under cover), with vintage farm machinery inc a working gas engine. The new Victorian classroom and museum gives insight into the life of a Victorian child. A play barn houses a bouncy castle and pedal tractor

MOTORWAY BREAKS

circuit, and there's a soft play area and computer centre; also a collection of rare cars and bikes. Animals inc shire horses, rare breeds of cattle, pigs, sheep and poultry, and more cuddly creatures in the pets' corner. There's also a woodland area with unusual tree carvings and adventure playground, children's driving school (chances to test drive electric vehicles), and quad bikes. With milking demonstrations (by hand or machine) at 1pm, tractor-drawn carriage rides and various activities, it's a good half-day's fun for families with smaller children. Meals, snacks, shop, good disabled access; cl 25-26 Dec and Mon-Thurs except during school hols and 1-24 Dec; *(01691) 671123*; £5.35.

148. 🦙 CHIRK
Chirk Castle (2 miles off A5 via B5070 town rd; signed off W)
One of the lucky few of Edward I's castles to survive as an occupied home rather than fall to ruin. The exterior is still much as it was when built 700 years ago, with its high walls and drum towers, though there have been lots of alterations inside: most of the medieval-looking decorations were by Pugin in the 19th c, the elegant stone staircase dates from the 18th c, and the Long Gallery is 17th-c. The wrought-iron entrance gates are particularly fine, and the formal gardens are magnificent. Meals, snacks, shop, some disabled access; cl Mon, Tues (exc bank hols) Nov-Mar; *(01691) 777701*; £6.40, garden only £4; NT. It's right by a well preserved stretch of the earthworks of Offa's Dyke.

149. 🦙 LLANGOLLEN
Llangollen Railway (just off A5 via A539, turning left on A542 over river; Abbey Rd)
Runs eight miles, with steam and diesel trains from the pleasantly preserved station of Llangollen to the village of Carrog up the Dee, where the Grouse in a lovely setting above the river does reasonably priced food all day; special events inc santa specials. Snacks, shop, special coach for the disabled (you have to book); cl mid-Oct to mid-Apr; *(01978) 860951* for talking timetable; £8 full return fare, less for shorter trips.

150. 🦙 LLANGWM
Ewephoria (1 mile off A5, 4 or 5 miles NW of A494)
As well as seeing the sheepdogs put through their paces at these enjoyable shows, you can watch shearing demonstrations, and learn about a

dozen or more different breeds of sheep in their ram parade. The best time to visit is spring when there are lots of baby lambs (you may be able to feed them); picnic and indoor play areas. Meals, snacks, shop, dogs welcome on a lead, disabled access; *(01490) 460369*; cl Mon (exc bank hols), Sat, and all Nov-Easter; £4.20.

151. ⌂ BETWS-Y-COED
Ty Gwyn (on A5 (and A470))
£64, plus special breaks; 13 pretty rms, most with own bthrm. Welcoming and well run 17th-c coaching inn with interesting old prints, furniture and bric-a-brac, good food and friendly service; pleasant setting overlooking river and a very good base for the area; children free if sharing parents' room; cl Mon-Weds in Jan; disabled access; dogs in bedrooms *(01690) 710383*

152. ✕ ⌂ CAPEL GARMON
White Horse (2 miles off A5 just S of Betws-y-coed, on Capel Garmon link to A470)
£66, plus midweek off-season breaks; 6 simple rms (those in newer part are quietest). Comfortable, homely, low-beamed inn with friendly atmosphere, winter log fires, very good home-made food in bar and cosy no smoking restaurant (some traditional welsh meals), magnificent views, delightful surrounding countryside; cl 24-25 Dec; children over 12 *(01690) 710271*

153. ✕ LLANGOLLEN
Corn Mill (just off A5 via A539 – then last left turn before bridge)
Stunning conversion of big watermill, handsomely refitted inside with several uncluttered levels of new pale pine flooring, a striking open stairway with gleaming timber and tensioned steel rails, mainly stripped stone walls, and quite a bit of the old mill machinery; a great waterwheel turns between the building and external decking cantilevered over the River Dee, and a terrace has lots of good teak tables and chairs, and a superb view over the river; a lively bustling chatty feel, quick service from plenty of neat young staff, nicely chosen pictures (many to do with water), good changing food, well kept real ales, and careful choice of wines *(01978) 869555*

A6

154. ✕ STREATLEY
Chequers *(just off A6 at Streatley roundabout; Sharpenhoe Rd, via Church Rd)*
Popular partly panelled open-plan L-shaped local, mix of chairs and table sizes, old-fashioned prints and old local photographs, good value food inc some inventive dishes, doorstep sandwiches and omelettes till late, Greene King IPA, Abbot, Old Speckled Hen and Ruddles County, cheerful staff, open fire in public bar; nostalgic piped music, Tues quiz night; garden with Sun lunchtime jazz. For a sunny-day picnic alternative, the Sharpenhoe Clappers just N (a mile off A6) are steep-sided downland with chalkland flora and butterflies, crowned with a fine beechwood and Iron Age hill fort; the area is owned by the National Trust and is laced with paths.

155. ✕ SILSOE
Star & Garter *(just off A6; High St)*
Smart pub by village church, large bar and raised no smoking dining area, enjoyable usual bar food from sandwiches and baked potatoes up, low prices, efficient service, evening restaurant, well kept ales such as Adnams, B&T Shefford and Black Sheep; nice good-sized terrace. Just outside the village is Wrest Park House & Gardens: inspired by french chateaux, the 19th-c house has a few ornately plastered rooms open to visitors, but the enormous formal gardens are the main attraction. They go on for over 90 acres and give a good example of the changes in gardening styles between 1700 and 1850. Perhaps best of all is the Great Garden, designed by the Duke of Kent between 1706 and 1740 and later modified by Capability Brown, with lovely views down the water to the baroque pavilion. Snacks, shop, disabled access to grounds only (can be tricky in the grassy gardens); open wknds and bank hols Apr-Oct; *(01525) 860152; £4;* EH.

156. ✕ MILTON ERNEST
Strawberry Tree *(almost on A6; 3 Radwell Rd)*
18th-c thatched cottage with low beams and open fires, very good interesting lunchtime and evening food using the best ingredients from

a sensibly short menu in the no smoking dining room; cl Sat am, Sun, Mon, Tues, 2 wks winter, 2 wks summer *(01234) 823633*

157. ⇔ BLETSOE
***North End Barns** (1 mile off A6, just N of Milton Ernest; follow The Avenue towards Riseley)*
£50; 8 rms. 16th-c farmhouse with carefully converted barn on a working arable and sheep farm; fine barn beams, cheerful décor, a wide choice of breakfast dishes eaten around a large communal table in the farmhouse, and nearby pubs for evening meals; no smoking; disabled access *(01234) 781320*

158. ✕ THORPE LANGTON
***Bakers Arms** (1.7 miles off A6 (from 1.5 miles SE of B6047 junction))*
Extended thatched pub with a warm friendly welcome, simple country furnishings, well presented interesting food changing daily (need to book well ahead), helpful service, well kept beer, an extensive wine list, and no smoking snug; cl wkdy lunchtimes, Sun and Mon pm; children over 12 *(01858) 545201*

159. ✕ ⇔ EAST LANGTON
***Bell** (1.5 miles off A6; village signed off B6047 Melton Rd)*
£59.50; pretty creeper-covered inn with a warm inviting atmosphere, a log fire and plain wooden tables in the long stripped stone bar, monthly changing imaginative food, and a no smoking dining room; own-brewed beers, decent wines, and friendly efficient service; cl 25 Dec; partial disabled access *(01858) 545278*

160. ⇔ ROTHLEY
***Rothley Court** (1.2 miles off A6 N of Leicester; go straight through village via Town Green St into Westfield Lane)*
£110; 32 rms (the ones in the main house have more character). Mentioned in the Domesday Book, this carefully run manor house with its beautifully preserved 13th-c chapel has some fine oak panelling, open fires, a comfortable bar, conservatory, and courteous staff; seats out on the terrace and in the garden; disabled access *(0116) 237 4141*

MOTORWAY BREAKS

161. 🛉 ELVASTON
Elvaston Castle Country Park *(1.5 miles off A6, via London Rd (old A6) from roundabout E of Derby, then left on B5010)*
200 acres of lovely 19th-c landscaped parkland, with formal and Old English gardens, wooded walks, and wildfowl on the ornamental lake. Snacks, shop, disabled access; *(01332) 571342*; car park 80p wkdys, £1.40 wknds.

162. 🛉 BELPER
Derwent Valley Visitor Centre *(just off A6; A517 (Bridge Foot))*
Though it looks quite simple from the outside, this early 19th-c cotton mill was the most technically advanced building of its time, and is now a World Heritage Site. New exhibitions inside trace the evolution of the machines which developed the factory system with examples from hand spinning wheels and a spinning jenny right up to 20th-c machines of mass production. You can find out more about the Belper man who took Britain's industrial plans to America, and they've a fine collection of silk and cotton stockings. Shop, disabled access; open pm Weds-Sun and bank hol Mon, Nov-Feb wknds only; cl 25 Dec; *(01773) 880474*; £2. The Holly Bush over in Makeney has just the right sort of atmosphere.

163. ✕ ⊨ ALDERWASLEY
Bear *(2.2 miles off A6 in Ambergate, via Holly Lane and Jackass Lane on high back rd towards Wirksworth)*
£70; enchantingly unspoilt pub in peaceful setting with a delightful interior, several small dark rooms with low beams and bare boards, a great variety of old tables and seats, log fires in huge stone fireplaces, candles galore, plenty of Staffordshire china ornaments, several grandfather clocks, and canaries, talkative cockatoos, an african grey parrot and budgies; enjoyable daily changing food (all day) using the best local ingredients, fine range of interesting wines, well kept real ales, and peaceful country views from well spaced picnic-sets out on the side grass *(01629) 822585*

164. 🛉 CROMFORD
(just off A6)
A good example of an 18th-c cotton-milling village, little developed after its original building, and rewarding to stroll through. Carefully

A6

preserved North St (1777) is the first true industrial street in Derbyshire, and in Mill Lane Cromford Mill is the world's first successful water-powered cotton mill; the 1771 start of the factory age, it's now a World Heritage Site. Meals, snacks, shops, limited disabled access; cl 25 Dec; *(01629) 824297*; site free, tours £2. The old-fashioned Boat Inn has good value basic food. The canal is a quiet and attractive early Industrial Revolution setting with a restored steam-powered pumping house and a fine aqueduct over the river.

165. 🕊 MATLOCK BATH
Heights of Abraham (just off A6 (brown signs); Upperwood Rd)
Cable cars up to 60-acre hilltop country park with dramatic views and two stunning show caverns; multi-media explanatory show, nature trails, nicely laid out woodland walks, the Prospect Tower to climb, and a few play areas (inc a maze, and a playground aimed at the under-5s); usually special events in summer. Good restaurant and café, limited disabled access; cl Nov-15 Feb and wkdys 8-23 March; *(01629) 582365*; £7.50.

166. ✕ ⛌ ROWSLEY
Peacock (on A6)
£125, plus special breaks; 16 comfortable rms. Smart 17th-c country house hotel by River Derwent (private fishing in season), with well kept gardens, friendly staff, interesting and pleasant old-fashioned inner bar, spacious and comfortable lounge, and very popular restaurant; it's a lovely place just to stop for coffee (with excellent shortbread), too. Just W of here is a good craft centre (cl Jan wkdys) around working water-turbine Cauldwell's Mill; dogs in bedrooms, £5 *(01629) 733518*

167. 🕊 ROWSLEY
Peak Village (just off A6 (Chatsworth Rd))
Shopping village in the heart of the Peak District with 26 factory outlets, craft and other shops. A historic toy exhibition includes a life-size Chitty Chitty Bang Bang. Meals, snacks, disabled access; *(01629) 735326*; free.

168. 🕊 HADDON HALL
Haddon Hall (on A6)
One of the most perfectly preserved medieval manor houses in England, still with its 12th-c painted chapel, 14th-c kitchen, and

51

MOTORWAY BREAKS

banqueting hall with minstrels' gallery. Perhaps because nothing's been added to the original furniture and tapestries, some rooms can seem rather bare; a bright spot is Rex Whistler's painting of the house in the silver-panelled long gallery. It's a particularly pretty location in summer when the long terraced rose gardens are in full bloom. Several films and TV adaptations have had scenes shot here in recent years. Meals, snacks, shop; cl 2-3 July, Mon-Weds in Oct, and all Nov-Mar; *(01629) 812855*; £7.25. The Lathkil Hotel up in Over Haddon is good for lunch.

169. ✕ BAKEWELL
Byways (just off A6 via A6I9; Water Lane)
Olde-worlde tearoom with several separate areas, roaring log fire, well presented good value food from snacks and morning coffee or afternoon teas to meals, and warmly friendly staff *(01629) 812807*

170. ⋈ ASHFORD IN THE WATER
Riverside Country House Hotel (0.3 miles off A6; Fennel St, in village)
£125, plus special breaks; 15 individually decorated pretty rms. Creeper-covered Georgian house in delightful village with attractive riverside gardens, a relaxed house-party atmosphere, antiques and log fires in cosy sitting rooms, good modern English cooking, and professional service; no children; disabled access *(01629) 814275*

171. ⋈ MONSAL HEAD
Monsal Head Hotel (1.6 miles off A6 in Ashford, via B6465)
£50, plus special breaks; 7 very good rms, some with lovely views. Comfortable and enjoyable small hotel in marvellous setting high above the River Wye, with horsy theme in bar (converted from old stables), freshly prepared decent food using seasonal produce, and good service; cl 25 Dec. This winding Monsal Dale is the outstanding place for walks in the central part of the White Peak area, its pastoral quality emphasised by the disused limestone cotton mills along the way. It's especially lovely in May and June with wild flowers enriching the pastures along the broader stretches. Don't expect to have it to yourself. There's also good access from the A6 a couple of miles towards Buxton from Ashford in the Water; dogs in bedrooms and part of pub *(01629) 640250*

A7

172. 🐾 CHAPEL-EN-LE-FRITH
Chestnut Centre *(0.4 miles off A6, via A625)*
Warmly recommended conservation park, concerned especially with breeding otters and barn owls, but other animals and birds of prey too; good observation platforms. Snacks, shop; cl wkdys Jan and Feb; *(01298) 814099; £5.95.*

173. 🐾 TORRS RIVERSIDE PARK
(brown signs off A6 Buxton Rd)
This deep gorge below New Mills is a good place to potter among the ivy-covered remains of former mills and other industrial relics; the canal basin has been largely restored over at Buxworth – the Navigation here is an enjoyable pub. The Goyt Way is a track heading N towards and beyond Marple, partly following the Peak Forest Canal – a pretty walk.

174. ✕ ⚑ BIRCH VALE
Waltzing Weasel *(2.7 miles off A6, via A6015 New Mills rd)*
£78; 8 lovely rms. Attractive traditional inn with open fire, some handsome furnishings, daily papers and plants in quiet civilised bar, very good food using the best seasonal produce in charming back restaurant (fine views), excellent puddings and cheeses, obliging service; children over 7 in restaurant; disabled access; dogs in bedrooms and bar *(01663) 743402*

A7

175. ✕ ⚑ MELROSE
Burts *(2.9 miles off A7 via A6091 and B6374; Market Sq – handy for A68 too)*
£98, plus special breaks; 20 rms. Welcoming 18th-c family-run hotel close to abbey ruins in delightfully quiet village; coal fire in bustling bar, residents' lounge, consistently popular imaginative food, exceptional breakfasts; cl 24-26 Dec; dogs in bedrooms and lounge only *(01896) 822285*

176. 🐾 MELROSE
Melrose Abbey *(2.9 miles off A7 via A6091 and B6374)*
The ruins are among the finest in the country – best in moonlight, as Scott says (though he admitted he never saw them thus himself). Look

53

MOTORWAY BREAKS

out for the wonderful stonework on the 14th-c nave (and the pig playing the bagpipes). Archaeological investigations now leave little doubt that this was the burial place of Robert the Bruce's heart. Shop; limited disabled access; *(01896) 822562*; £4; HS. Just opposite are good views of the abbey and Eildon Hills from Harmony Garden (St Mary St), a tranquil walled garden around an early 19th-c house.

177. 🏛 MELROSE
Abbotsford House *(1.1 miles off A7; A6091 E, then B6360 at next roundabout)*
Set grandly on the River Tweed, this was the home of Sir Walter Scott until his death in 1832. You can still see his mammoth 9,000-volume library, and several of the historical oddities he liked to collect, like Rob Roy's sporran. Snacks, shop, disabled access; cl Nov to mid-Mar; *(01896) 752043*; £4.75.

A9

178. 🏛 STIRLING
Stirling Castle *(0.9 miles off A9/A84 roundabout, straight up Union St then well signed)*
Provides magnificent views from its lofty hilltop site. It became very popular with the Royal Family in the 15th and 16th centuries, and most of the buildings date from that period. It's great fun to visit, from the flame-lit medieval kitchen to the splendid Chapel Royal built by James VI (and I of England), and the Great Hall of James V's Renaissance palace. A huge new hammerbeam roof has been crafted here from 350 oak trees, and the restoration of the castle's lavish early 16th-c furnishings continues with on-site tapestry weaving. Snacks, shop; cl 25-26 Dec; *(01786) 450000*; £7.50 inc Argyll's lodging, parking £2; HS. There's a good visitor centre in a restored building next door, and Whistlebinkies (St Mary's Wynd), formerly part of the ancient castle stables, has decent food.

179. 🛏 EAST HAUGH
East Haugh House *(1 mile off A9 just S of Pitlochry, on Old Military Rd parallel to A9)*

£138, inc dinner, plus special breaks; 13 rms, 5 in converted bothy, some with four-posters and one with open fire. Turreted stone house with lots of character, delightful bar in cream and navy with a fishing theme, house-party atmosphere and particularly good food inc local seafood, game in season cooked by chef/proprietor, and home-grown vegetables in new restaurant; excellent shooting, stalking and salmon and trout fishing on surrounding local estates; cl 20-27 Dec; disabled access to one room; dogs in ground-floor bedrooms with direct access outside *(01796) 473121*

180. AVIEMORE
Lynwilg House *(off A9 just S)*
£60; 3 rms. Attractive, quietly set 1930s-style house in four acres of landscaped gardens with open fire in spacious lounge, lovely breakfasts with their own free-range eggs and home-baked bread, super dinners using home-grown produce, and charming owners; plenty to do nearby; cl Nov-Dec, Jan; children over 5; dogs in one bedroom *(01479) 811685*

181. GOLSPIE
Dunrobin Castle *(on A9)*
Splendid castle – a gleaming elegantly turreted structure with views out to sea, and gardens modelled on those at Versailles. The family home of the Earls and Dukes of Sutherland for longer than anyone can remember, the site was named after Earl Robin in the 13th c; he was responsible for the original square keep. Drastically renovated and enlarged to cope with a hugely bigger family in the 19th c, it has fine collections of furnishings and art, and a unique collection of Pictish stones; falconry. Snacks, meals, shop; cl 16 Oct-31 Mar, gardens open all year; *(01408) 633177*; **£6.50**. The Ben Bhraggie has good value food in a pleasant conservatory (on Weds you may find the pipe band practising outside).

A10

182. ELY
(just off A10)
This busy little market town with good shops and some lovely old

MOTORWAY BREAKS

buildings well repays a leisurely stroll. The cathedral is one of England's most striking, its distinctive towers dominating the skyline for miles. Its façade, covered in blind arcading, is fantastic, but most remarkable perhaps is the Octagonal Tower, over 400 tons suspended in space without any visible means of support; it looks especially impressive from inside. The Lady Chapel has the widest medieval vault in the country, and the walls are carved with hundreds of tiny statues (all brutally beheaded in the Reformation). The splendid Norman nave seems even longer than it really is because it's so narrow. It's worth trying to catch the evensong here, 5.30pm daily exc Weds (Sun at 3.45pm). Meals, snacks, shop, disabled access to ground floor; (01353) 667735; £4.80. The cathedral's stained glass museum (extra charge) is interesting, and a bonus is the unusual view over the cathedral. Other high points are Oliver Cromwell's House, and a good museum. The Old Fire Engine House next to the cathedral (01353) 662582 has good hearty english cooking inc nice puddings, an interesting wine list, simple furnishings and a relaxed atmosphere; large walled garden, also an art gallery; cl Sun pm, bank hols, 25 Dec-6 Jan. **£95**; The Lamb (Lynn Rd; 31 comfortable rms, (01353) 663574) is a pleasant, neatly kept old coaching inn, newly refurbished, also near the cathedral, with two smart bars, enjoyable food in an attractive restaurant, very friendly staff, and good car parking – a bonus here.

183 ✕ STOW BARDOLPH
Hare Arms (just off A10; old Lynn Rd)
Pretty, creeper-covered pub with old advertising signs, fresh flowers, plenty of tables around its central servery, and a good log fire in welcoming bar; maybe two friendly ginger cats and a sort of tabby; spacious, heated and well planted no smoking conservatory, good interesting food, well kept real ales, a decent range of wines, and quite a few malt whiskies; pretty garden with picnic-sets and wandering peacocks and chickens; cl 25-26 and 31 Dec; children in conservatory and family room only (01366) 382229

A11

184. ⌂ SIX MILE BOTTOM
Swynford Paddocks (1 mile from A11, via A1304)
£135; 15 individually furnished rms with good bthrms. Gabled country

house in neat grounds overlooking stud paddocks; carefully furnished rooms with fresh flowers and log fires, bar decorated with Brigadier memorabilia (a tribute to the great racehorse who is buried in the hotel grounds), conservatory Garden Room, a relaxed atmosphere, good food, and friendly service; tennis, putting and croquet; disabled access; dogs welcome in bedrooms *(01638) 570234*

185. ⌂ WORLINGTON
Worlington Hall *(1.4 miles off A11; Old Newmarket Rd towards Barton Mills then first left into Golf Links Rd, to B1102)*
£80; 9 comfortable rms with decanter of sherry and fruit. 16th-c former manor house in five acres with a 9-hole pitch and putt course, comfortable panelled lounge bar with log fire, good food in relaxed candlelit bistro, and friendly staff; dogs in bedrooms and lounge *(01638) 712237*

A12

186. ☸ WRITTLE
Hylands House and Gardens *(2.1 miles off A12; B1007 towards Stock, then left into Ship Rd; Hylands Park)*
Neo-classical villa set in 570 acres of parkland. Nine recently restored rooms inc a Georgian entrance hall, gilded Victorian drawing room and the sumptuously ornate Banqueting Room. Further restoration to be completed in 2006 will inc the Grand Staircase and Repton Room, with views over the restored landscape. Full disabled access to the house; cl Tues-Sat, guided tours by arrangement; *(01245 496800)*; £3.20; free to park and garden.

187. ☸ COPFORD
Copford church *(1.5 miles off A12 at A120 junction; B1408 towards Colchester, then second right into School Rd)*
Originally built around AD1130, and worth a visit particularly for its well restored 12th-c wall paintings.

MOTORWAY BREAKS

188. ✕ DEDHAM
Milsom's (1 mile off A12; Stratford Rd, W of village)
Stylish place with ties to le Talbooth country house; scrubbed wooden tables on wooden floors in two dining areas, contemporary bistro-style food, a good wine list, and smart, casual staff; open for morning coffee; disabled access *(01206) 322795*

189. ⌂ HIGHAM
Old Vicarage (1.1 miles off A12 at Stratford St Mary, via School Lane into Higham Rd)
£70, plus special breaks; 3 rms, 2 with own bthrm. Charming Tudor house nr quiet village with very friendly owners, pretty sitting room with fresh flowers, log fire and antiques, and enjoyable breakfasts in attractive breakfast room; play room with toys for children, grounds and fine gardens with river views (they have boats), tennis court, trampoline, and heated swimming pool; dogs welcome *(01206) 337248*

190. ✕ WOODBRIDGE
Captain's Table (0.9 miles off A12 on B1079; Quay St)
16th-c cottage with three interlinked beamed rooms, cheerful décor, enjoyable interesting food inc plenty of fresh fish, helpful service, and a thoughtful wine list; cl Sun pm, Mon (except bank hols), 1st 2 wks Jan; disabled access *(01394) 383145*

191. ⚐ WOODBRIDGE
(0.7 miles off A12 via B1079)
Quietly attractive and rather dignified market town, with many fine buildings, both a windmill and (on its busy quay) a tidal mill, and interesting book and antiques shops, and a church of great style and interest. The Anchor (Quay St), Bull and Kings Head (Market Hill) and Old Mariner and Olde Bell & Steelyard (New St) all do decent bar lunches.

192. ⌂ CAMPSEY ASH
Old Rectory (1.4 miles off A12 via B1078 E)
£85; 7 comfortable, pretty rms. Very relaxed and welcoming no smoking Georgian house by church, with charming owner and staff, log fire in comfortable and restful drawing room, quite a few Victorian prints, first-class food from a set menu in summer conservatory or two other

dining rooms with more log fires, a good honesty bar, a sensational wine list with very modest mark-ups on its finest wines, and sizeable homely gardens; dogs in bedrooms *(01728) 746524*

193. ✗ ⇌ SNAPE
Crown *(2.5 miles off A12 via A1094, then right on B1069)*
£70; unspoilt smugglers' inn with a relaxed and warmly friendly atmosphere, old brick floors, beams, big brick inglenook and nice old furnishings; particularly good interesting well presented food served by smiling staff, pre- and post-concert suppers, a thoughtful wine list (16 by the glass inc champagne), well kept real ales, and tables in pretty garden; cl 25 Dec, 26 Dec pm; no children; partial disabled access *(01728) 688324*

194. ✗ KELSALE
Harrisons *(just off A12)*
White-painted 16th-c thatched cottage housing a pretty, two-storey timbered dining room offering modern and traditional cooking using the best local produce; a short well priced wine list, and friendly efficient service; cl Sun, Mon, from 24 Dec pm for 2 wks *(01728) 604444*

195. ✗ BRAMFIELD
Queens Head *(2 miles off A12 via A144)*
Popular pub with pleasantly relaxed high-raftered lounge bar, a good log fire in impressive fireplace, no smoking side bar, family room, and wide choice of very good interesting food inc organic dishes (super puddings also); well kept real ales, good wines, and maybe home-made elderflower cordial; cl 26 Dec *(01986) 784214*

196. 🦌 BLYTHBURGH
Blythburgh church *(just off A12)*
Magnificent building known as the Cathedral of the Marshes, in a lovely setting above the Blyth estuary; the White Hart opposite is a good family dining pub open all day, with robust pocket-friendly food, spacious lawns looking down on tidal marshes, and bedrooms.

197. 🦌 KESSINGLAND
Suffolk Wildlife Park *(just off A12 S of Lowestoft)*
Attractively set in almost 100 acres of coastal parkland, this very

MOTORWAY BREAKS

committed place looks after mainly animals from Africa, many of which you won't be able to see anywhere else in the country. Some of the residents are from critically endangered species, and the staff are proud of their breeding successes. Everything children most like to see is here: from lions, cheetah and giraffes, to snakes, flamingoes and meerkats, and they've very rare white rhinos (shown off to great effect in their spectacular rhino house). There are plenty of feeding displays and talks spread throughout the day; also play areas inc a separate section for under-5s, and perhaps extra activities in the summer hols. A train makes it easier to get round the site. Meals, snacks, shop, disabled access; cl 25-26 Dec; *(01502) 740291*; £9.95.

A13

198. ✕ ⌂ HORNDON-ON-THE-HILL
Bell (1.3 miles off Stanford-le-Hope bypass; B1007 into North Hill, bearing left into village)
£65; bustling 15th-c inn with a heavily beamed bar, polished oak floorboards and flagstones, carefully prepared imaginative food, seven real ales, good choice of wines; restaurant; cl 25-26 Dec, bank hol Mon; disabled access *(01375) 673154*

A14

199. ⌂ BURSTALL
Mulberry Hall (2.2 miles off A14 Sproughton exit; Sproughton Rd, crossing B1113 (left and right) into Burstall Lane)
£56; 2 comfortable rms. Once owned by Cardinal Wolsey, this lovely old farmhouse has a fine garden, an inglenook fireplace in the big beamed sitting room, excellent food (ordered in advance) in pretty dining room, very good breakfasts with home-baked bread and preserves, and helpful friendly owners; tennis and croquet; cl Christmas-New Year *(01473) 652348*

200. 🏛 STOWMARKET
Museum of East Anglian Life (1 mile off A14 eastbound; A1308 into town, right on Station Rd then first left; Iliffe Way, opp Asda; 2.8 miles off A14 westbound via A1120/A1308)

Excellent 70-acre open-air museum. Children look at the reconstructed buildings with a genuine sense of astonishment, and even the 1950s domestic room settings seem prehistoric to fresher eyes. Most of the buildings have been removed from their original settings and rebuilt here; the oldest is a splendid 13th-c timber barn, now housing a collection of horse-drawn vehicles. Among the rest are an old schoolroom, a smithy, chapel, windpump, and a very pretty watermill. They're quite spread out, so a fair bit of walking is involved. Also wandering around are various traditional farm animals, and on some Suns they have demonstrations of local crafts and skills like wood-turning and basket-making; their occasional event days are usually around the spring and summer bank hols. There's a decent rustic-style adventure play area, and it's great for a picnic. Meals, snacks, shop, disabled access; cl Nov-Mar; *(01449) 612229*; £6.50.

201. ⌂ BEYTON
Manorhouse (0.3 miles off A14 at Beyton exit; The Green)
£60; 4 large pretty rms, 2 in house, 2 in barn conversion. Overlooking the village green, this charming no smoking 15th-c longhouse has lots of beams in the sitting/dining room, fresh flowers, antiques and paintings by the friendly owner's mother, super breakfasts, enjoyable dinners (occasionally), and large garden; cl Christmas; no children *(01359) 270960*

202. ✕ ⌂ BURY ST EDMUNDS
Angel (1 mile off A14/A143/A134 junction, following town centre signs; Angel Hill)
£120, plus special breaks; 75 individually decorated rms. Thriving creeper-clad 15th-c country-town hotel with particularly friendly staff, comfortable lounge and relaxed bar, log fires and fresh flowers, and good food in elegant restaurant and downstairs medieval vaulted room (Mr Pickwick enjoyed a roast dinner here); disabled access; dogs welcome in bedrooms *(01284) 714000*

203. ✕ FEN DRAYTON
Three Tuns (0.9 miles off A14 eastbound (a little longer westbound); High St)
Pretty thatched inn with two inglenook fireplaces and heavy Tudor beams and timbers in its unpretentious and cosy bar; well kept real

MOTORWAY BREAKS

ales, generous helpings of good reasonably priced food, and a neat back garden with children's play equipment; children until 8pm; disabled access *(01954) 230242*

204. 🕺 HEMINGFORD GREY
(1 mile off A14 eastbound, rather longer (via A1096 St Ives rd) westbound; High St)
Charming village with a manor house lived in for nearly 900 years (said to be the oldest continuously inhabited house in Britain). There's a peaceful view of the church over the willow-bordered river (the odd church tower is the result of its spire being lopped off by an 18th-c storm); the Cock is a dining pub with really good food and quick service; and nearby Hemingford Abbots is also pretty.

205. ✕ ⇔ HUNTINGDON
Old Bridge *(just off A14; High St (ring rd just off B1044 entering from easternmost Huntingdon slip rd))*
£150, plus wknd breaks; 24 excellent rms with CD stereos and power showers. Creeper-covered Georgian hotel with pretty lounge, log fire in panelled bar, imaginative british cooking and extensive wine list in the no smoking restaurant and less formal lunchtime room (nice murals), and quick courteous service; riverside gardens; partial disabled access; dogs in bedrooms, bar, and lounge *(01480) 451591*

206. ⇔ CRANFORD
Dairy Farm *(1.7 miles off A14 at **A510 junction**; turn right off High St into Grafton Rd, then next right into St Andrews Lane)*
£50; 4 comfortable rms. Charming 17th-c manor house of great character on an arable and sheep farm, with oak beams and inglenook fireplaces, good homely cooking using home-grown fruit and vegetables, kind, attentive owners, and garden with charming summer house and ancient dovecote; no smoking; cl Christmas; partial disabled access; dogs in annexe *(01536) 330273*

A15

207. ⊨ BOURNE
Cawthorpe Hall (0.3 miles off A15 N of Bourne)
£70; 4 rms, most with own bthrm. Georgian house surrounded by three acres of rose fields from which Mr Armstrong produces english rose oil and water; huge studio extension leading off grand entrance hall with wicker armchairs, sofas and big contemporary artwork; interesting furniture, a very relaxed atmosphere, charming friendly owners, and enjoyable breakfasts and afternoon tea; pubs nearby for evening meals; cl Christmas; partial disabled access *(01778) 423830*

208. ✕ ⊨ DYKE
Wishing Well (0.5 miles off A15 N of Bourne; village signed)
£65; 12 rms with showers. Long rambling bar with heavy beams, dark stone, brassware, candlelight and a big fireplace; good value food, no smoking restaurant, helpful service, friendly atmosphere; gardens and grounds with play area; disabled access *(01778) 422970*

A16

209. ⊨ SPALDING
Cley Hall (1.2 miles off A16; 22 High St (B1172))
£75; 12 smart rms, 8 in annexe. Handsome Georgian manor house overlooking the River Welland with attractive back gardens, comfortable seating areas, very good, popular food in the no smoking Garden Restaurant and more informal bistro, and friendly, helpful staff; dogs welcome in bedrooms *(01775) 725157*

210. ❀ SPALDING
Springfields Gardens (just off A16, A151 towards centre then first right into Camel Gate)
Home of the UK flower bulb industry since 1966, they've now extensively remodelled the gardens (features include gardens designed by celebrity gardeners, woodland walks and a carp lake), and a smart factory outlet shopping village has around 40 shops (inc a garden centre);

MOTORWAY BREAKS

indoor and outdoor play areas, and regular special events. Meals, snacks, disabled access; *(01775) 724843*; free.

211. 🕸 BOSTON
(on A16 and A52)
Once the country's second-largest seaport, this little town has a number of pretty spots and handsome historic buildings. Most famous is the Boston Stump, the graceful tower of the magnificent 14th-c church St Botolph's. Climb to the top for far views over this flat landscape – it's the second tallest parish church in the country (the tallest is in Louth); the inside is spectacular too. Another prominent feature of the skyline is the waterside Maud Foster Mill, the tallest working windmill in the country, and one of the most photogenic (you can climb all seven floors); café (specialising in vegetarian food), shop with organic flour; open Weds, Sat and pm Sun, plus Thurs and Fri Jul-Aug; *(01205) 352188*. Goodbarns Yard (Wormgate) is a popular central pub/restaurant, and the Eagle (West St) has good value food. The surroundings (and the Lincolnshire coast generally) are too flat for driving to be very interesting around here, and side roads which look clear on a map can turn out to be tryingly slow in practice, with muddy agricultural vehicles trundling along; the B1183 and B1192 aren't bad.

212 ✗ HALTON HOLEGATE
Bell *(1.2 miles off A16; B1195 E of Spilsby)*
Timeless village pub, simple but comfortable and consistently friendly, with wide choice of decent generous home-made food cooked by landlord inc Sun lunches and outstanding fish and chips, tempting prices, well kept local ales, Lancaster bomber pictures, back family eating area (with tropical fish tank) and restaurant *(01790) 753242*

213. ✗ LOUTH
Chuzzlewits *(1 mile off A16 via B1200; turn right into Upgate (B1520))*
Family-run no smoking tearoom with a civilised atmosphere, little glass chandeliers, dining chairs around pretty print glass-covered table-clothed tables, potted palms, and big shop-front windows; wide choice of speciality teas and coffees, home-made cakes, pastries and biscuits, a good range of interesting snacks and light meals, and young waitresses in long black dresses with white frilly aprons and little lacy white caps; cl Sun, Mon and Tues; disabled access *(01507) 611171*

214. 🚶 LOUTH
Louth church *(1.4 miles off A16, via B1200; left turn into Church St)*
Elegant 16th-c building with the tallest spire of any parish church in Britain. The tower can be climbed on summer afternoons; hundreds of steps for a fabulous view. The market town is a pleasant stop, with lots of bustle on Weds, and some interesting shops; besides Chuzzlewits, the Masons Arms (Cornmarket) has enjoyable food.

A17

215. 🚶 LONG SUTTON
Butterfly & Wildlife Park *(1.5 miles off A17; Little London, via Roman Bank off B1359)*
Much more at this well organised place than simply the butterflies: they have everything from goats and pigs through llamas and wallabies to snakes and crocodiles. The walk-through tropical house is one of the country's biggest, with hundreds of butterflies flying free, and outside are lots of pretty wildflower walks to attract native species. The Reptile House is fun, as is the splendid collection of insects and creepy-crawlies. They have the only UK colony of breeding possums, and a birds of prey centre has twice-daily flying displays (weather permitting). Many of the farmyard animals can be stroked, inc the new water buffalo. There's also an adventure playground, a separate area for toddlers, and mini golf and tractor rides (extra charges). Snacks, shop, disabled access; open Easter-Oct; *(01406) 363833*; £5.50. This small town is pleasant to potter around, especially on market day (Fri).

216. ✖ GEDNEY DYKE
Chequers *(1.7 miles off A17, via B1359)*
Spotlessly kept and welcoming fenland pub with an open fire in the bar, a no smoking dining conservatory, no smoking restaurant, very good home-made food, well kept real ales, a decent wine list, and friendly staff; pretty bdrms; cl Sun pm, Mon am *(01406) 362666*

217. ⌂ HOLBEACH
Pipwell Manor *(0.3 miles off A17 (N of A151); Washway Rd)*
£50; 3 comfortable rms. Handsome 18th-c farmhouse, welcoming and

MOTORWAY BREAKS

spotless, with log fire in comfortable sitting room, pretty panelled dining room, afternoon tea with home-made cakes on arrival, good breakfasts with their own eggs and home-made preserves, and a conservatory; miniature railway in large gardens, and free bikes; no smoking; cl 23 Dec-2 Jan; children over 10 *(01406) 423119*

A21

218. ⌂ BATTLE
Little Hemingfold Hotel (2.2 miles off A21 just N of Hastings, via A2100 (NB it's S of Battle))
£92, plus special breaks; 12 rms, 6 on ground floor in adjoining Coach House. Partly 17th-c, partly early Victorian farmhouse in 40 acres of woodland, with trout lake, tennis, gardens, and lots of walks (the two labradors may come with you); comfortable sitting rooms, open fires, restful atmosphere and very good food using home-grown produce at own candlelit table; children over 7; cl 2 Jan-10 Feb; dogs in bedrooms *(01424) 774338*

219. ✕ SALEHURST
Salehurst Halt (0.5 miles off A21; village signed E off roundabout at N end of Robertsbridge bypass)
Beamed and partly flagstoned, tucked quietly by 14th-c church, with enjoyable lunchtime bar food and some more elaborate evening dishes, good real ales and wines, charming suntrap back garden; children and dogs welcome; cl Mon, no food Sun evening *(01580) 880620*

220. ෴ BEDGEBURY
Bedgebury Pinetum (0.9 miles off A21, signed on to B2079 just N of Flimwell)
Lakeside landscaped valley established in 1925 with walks through renowned collection of magnificent conifers. Dogs welcome on leads, snacks (not Mon); shop; open all year round; *(01580) 211781*; **£4**

221. ෴ LAMBERHURST
Scotney Castle Garden (just off S end of new A21 bypass)
Beautiful 19th-c gardens surrounding the ruins of a small 14th-c moated

castle, with impressive rhododendrons, azaleas and roses – a really romantic place. Shop, some disabled access (they recommend a strong pusher); open Weds-Sun and bank hols 18 Mar-Oct (exc Good Fri), castle open same hours May to mid-Sept, but best to check; *(01892) 891081*; £4.80; NT. A public footpath strides through the estate's woods and pastures, which can form a basis for circular walks from Kilndown to Lamberhurst and back. The Brown Trout, on B2169, has good fish. The attractive village has at last gained its sorely needed bypass.

A22

222. ✗ EAST HOATHLY
Foresters Arms (just off A22 Hailsham—Uckfield (take south-easternmost of the two turn-offs); South St)
Good rather interesting food in simply furnished small two-room bar and snugly charming library-style dining room, well kept Harveys, decent wines and good coffee, informal helpful service, good wheelchair access; children and dogs welcome *(01825) 840208*

A23

223. 🚶 HANDCROSS
Nymans Garden (0.4 miles off A23/A279 interchange; B2114 S)
Perhaps the most romantic of all Wealden gardens, rewarding at any time, with excellent well marked woodland walks. Rare trees inc magnificent southern beeches and eucryphias, as well as fine camellias, rhododendrons and magnolias, countless other interesting flowering shrubs, a secluded sunken garden, and an extensive artfully composed wilderness. Meals, snacks, plant sales, shop, disabled access; cl Mon (exc bank hols), Tues, and wkdys Nov-Feb; *(01444) 400321*; £6.50; NT. The Wheatsheaf (B2110 W) has good food.

A24

224. ☛ SHIPLEY
Goffsland Farm *(1.3 miles off A24, from roundabout at S end of Southwater bypass; Mill Straight towards Southwater, then second left on to Shipley Rd; handy for A272 too)*
£44; 2 rms inc 1 family rm with own access. 17th-c Wealden farmhouse on 260-acre family farm with good breakfasts, and a friendly welcome; horse-riding and plenty of surrounding walks; children over 5; dogs welcome *(01403) 730434*

225. ✕ BLACKBROOK
Plough *(1.2 miles off A24; just under a mile S from A25 roundabout fork left on Chart Lane)*
Popular pub with award-winning hanging baskets and window boxes, a no smoking red saloon bar and public bar with a formidable collection of ties, old saws on the ceiling, and flatirons and bottles, and generous helpings of good imaginative food inc popular curry evenings; very friendly service from smart staff, 16 wines by the glass, and well kept real ales; pretty cottagey garden with Swiss play house for children; cl Sun pm, 25-26 Dec, 1 Jan; limited disabled access *(01306) 886603*

226. ☒ BOX HILL
(1.5 miles off A24 N of Dorking; Zig Zag Rd, off B2209)
Surrey's most popular viewpoint, with a summit car park and walks on its steep juniper and boxwood slopes: wild orchids and butterflies in early summer, perhaps field mushrooms in early autumn.

227. ✕ MICKLEHAM
King William IV *(just off A24 Leatherhead—Dorking; Byttom Hill, steep track up by partly green-painted restaurant – public car park down here is best place to park)*
Relaxed and unpretentious pub cut into the hillside with fine views from the snug front bar, a spacious back bar with log fires and fresh flowers, wide range of interesting daily specials inc good vegetarian choice, well kept ales, lovely terraced garden, and nice walks; cl 25 Dec, 26 Dec pm and 31 Dec; children over 12 *(01372) 372590*

A26

228. ⌂ UCKFIELD
Horsted Place (on A26 S, just S of A22 junction)
£165, plus special breaks; 20 fulsomely decorated spacious rms. Stately Victorian country house on extensive estate, with antiques, flowers and log fires in luxurious drawing rooms, delicious food and good wine list in no smoking dining room, and croquet and tennis; reduced green fees at East Sussex National Golf Club; cl first wk Jan; children over 7; disabled access *(01825) 750581*

A27

229. ※ ALFRISTON
Drusillas Park (just off A27 by Alfriston turn-off)
They keep only animals that they can provide with everything they'd have in the wild, so no lions, tigers or elephants, but plenty of smaller and arguably more entertaining creatures. You watch the meerkats through a little dome, there's a walk-through fruit bat enclosure, and Penguin Bay has underwater viewpoints. Elsewhere is everything from snakes and other creepy-crawlies to a splendid range of monkeys. There's a farmyard area, and Pet World gives younger visitors a chance to get close to rabbits, chinchillas and perhaps even a cockroach. The play areas are good, and they've recently added an interactive frog pond; a jolly little railway chuffs its way around the park, and there's a paddling pool with a large plastic whale that squirts water. Some of the extras have an additional charge: an activity centre open at wknds and in school holidays costs from £1.50; also £3 for face-painting, £1 for jungle adventure golf, £2 to pan for gold, and £1.50 for penguin plunge (the bouncy slide). Good meals and snacks, picnic areas, shops, excellent disabled access (there's also a sensory trail); cl 24-26 Dec; *(01323) 874100*; £11.

230. ※ ALFRISTON
(1.4 miles off A27)
In a sheltered spot below the downs, and with inviting paths along the

MOTORWAY BREAKS

Cuckmere River, this is one of the south-east's most appealing villages – at quieter times of year (in high summer the ice-cream eaters, teashops and curio shops somewhat blunt its appeal). It has thatched, tiled and timbered houses, and a fine church built on a Saxon funeral barrow, by a large green just off the single main street. One of the most engaging buildings in the village is the Star Inn, with some intricate painted 15th-c carvings among its handsome timbering. The George and Olde Smugglers are good for lunch.

231. ✗ ALCISTON
Rose Cottage (0.3 miles off A27 just W of Alciston)
In the same family for over 30 years, this charming little wisteria-covered cottage is full of harnesses, traps, ironware and bric-a-brac; Jasper is the talking parrot (mornings only); very good promptly served food (esp the simply cooked fresh fish) using organic vegetables and their own eggs, well kept real ales, decent wines and a good range of other drinks like kir and Pimms, a small no smoking evening restaurant, and seats outside; cl 25-26 Dec; children over 10 *(01323) 870377*

232. ⌨ LEWES
Shelleys (1.3 miles off A27 W roundabout; the A277 takes you straight to it, on the High St)
£185, plus special breaks; 19 pretty rms. Once owned by relatives of the poet, this stylish and spacious 17th-c town house is warm and friendly, with good food, nice breakfasts and bar lunches in elegant dining room, and seats in the quiet back garden; limited disabled access; dogs in bedrooms *(01273) 472361*

233. ✗ BURPHAM
George & Dragon (2.4 miles off A27 just E of Arundel; Warningcamp turn-off, and follow road up and up)
Smartly comfortable dining pub with splendid views down to Arundel Castle and river; good promptly served food with unusual specials inc good vegetarian dishes, elegant restaurant – worth booking; no food Sun pm and cl Sun pm during winter; children over 8; disabled access *(01903) 883131*

234. ☜ ARUNDEL
Wildfowl & Wetlands Trust (nearly 2 miles off A27 bypass roundabout; Mill Rd)
Over 60 acres of well landscaped pens, lake, and paddocks, home to over a thousand ducks, geese and swans from all over the world inc rare species; hides overlook the various habitats. They've recently added a children's discovery trail, reed bed boardwalk, and a wildlife art gallery; children's activities in school hols and as we went to press they were building a new environmentally friendly education centre, due for completion in August; they also hope to offer boat trips around the reserve this summer. Meals, snacks, shop, disabled access; cl 25 Dec; *(01903) 883355*; £5.95. The lane past the Trust ends at a little cluster of houses by an isolated church and former watermill. On the way to the Trust, the Black Rabbit (open all day, with lots of outside tables, and summer boat trips) has a superb location and does food.

235. ☜ ARUNDEL
Arundel Castle (0.3 miles off A27, from roundabout at either end of bypass)
Seat and home of the Dukes of Norfolk and their ancestors for nearly a thousand years – a magnificent sight, a great spread of well kept towers and battlements soaring above the town and the trees around it. The keep and the curtain wall are the oldest parts; the rest dates mainly from the 19th c, and seven restored Victorian bedrooms are now on view (£1 extra). Excellent art collection, inc portraits by Van Dyck, Gainsborough and Canaletto, as well as 16th-c furniture, and personal possessions of Mary, Queen of Scots; the library is a highlight, and there are Victorian flower and vegetable gardens. Meals, snacks, shop, limited disabled access; cl am, Sat (except bank hol wknds) and all Nov-Mar; *(01903) 883136*; £11.

236. ☜ FONTWELL
Denmans Garden (1 mile off A27; A29 S, first right, then right again into Denmans Lane)
Colourful series of vistas over 3½ acres, inc exuberantly oriental-feeling areas with a gravel stream, ornamental grasses, bamboos and flowering cherries, as well as a beautiful richly planted walled garden. Meals, snacks, plant sales, disabled access; cl Nov-Feb; *(01243) 542808*;

MOTORWAY BREAKS

£3.75. In the pretty nearby village of Eartham there is a small but charming church; the George there, open all day summer wknds, is an enjoyable dining pub.

237. 🕊 TANGMERE
Military Aviation Museum (0.9 miles off A27 E of Chichester)
Good collection of flying memorabilia based around the former RAF Battle of Britain station from which SOE agents flew to France. Displays include a De Havilland Sea Vixen and an English Electric Lightning fighter. Snacks, shop, disabled access; cl Dec-Jan; *(01243) 775223*; £5. The nearby Bader Arms has more memorabilia; and the 16th-c thatched Gribble at Oving is an attractive place for lunch.

238. 🕊 FISHBOURNE
Roman Palace (1.9 miles off A27 from W end roundabout of Chichester bypass; A259 W, then right on Salthill Rd)
This magnificent villa with its 100 or so rooms was occupied from the 1st to the 3rd c, and is the largest known residence from the period in Britain. Some archaeologists now think the Romans first landed here (and not in Kent as was originally supposed), to reinstate the recently evicted king. They probably built his successor this palace. You can see 25 mosaic floors (some are quite remarkable, and it's a bigger collection than anywhere else in Britain), and a garden has been laid out according to its 1st-c plan. Much of the palace is buried beneath nearby housing. Snacks, shop, disabled access; cl wkdys mid-Dec to Jan; *(01243) 785859*; £5.40. The Bulls Head has good food.

239. ✕ ⊨ EAST ASHLING
Horse & Groom (1.9 miles off A27 W of Chichester; B2146 N, then right on B2178)
£60; charming country pub with nice scrubbed trestle tables on old pale flagstones and woodburner in big inglenook in the proper front bar, big blackboard listing the changing choice of good food, and extensive back dining area (entirely no smoking); well kept real ales, a fine choice of wines by the glass, efficient but friendly and informal service, french windows to garden with picnic-sets; comfortable bdrms in adjoining barn conversion *(01243) 575339*

240. ✕ LANGSTONE
Royal Oak (0.8 miles off A27; off A3023 just before Hayling Island bridge; Langstone High St)
Charmingly placed waterside food pub, now completely no smoking, good pub food inc all-day snacks, real ales and good wine choice, spacious flagstoned bar and linked dining areas, open fires; looks out over the thousands of acres of silted harbour, swans and boats at high tide, with oystercatchers and droves of darting dunlins on the low-tide mud flats; interesting walks along the old sea wall *(023) 9248 3125*

A30

241. ✕ ⋈ STOCKLAND
Kings Arms (2.4 miles off A30 in Yarcombe; village signposted)
£65; 3 rms. Cream-faced thatched pub with elegant rooms, open fires, first-class food in bar and evening restaurant (esp fish), and interesting wine list; skittle alley, live music Sat, Sun pm; cl 25 Dec; dogs in bedrooms *(01404) 881361*

242. ⋈ GITTISHAM
Combe House (2 miles off A30 at W end of Honiton bypass)
£138, plus winter breaks; 15 individually decorated pretty rms with lovely views. Peaceful, Grade I listed, Elizabethan country hotel in gardens with 400-year-old cedar of Lebanon, and walks around the 3,500-acre estate; elegant sitting rooms with fine panelling, antiques, portraits and fresh flowers, a happy relaxed atmosphere, very good food in restaurant and faithfully restored Georgian kitchen, and fine wines; dogs welcome away from restaurant *(01404) 540400*

243. ✕ ⋈ LIFTON
Arundell Arms (a mile off A30, at A388 turn-off)
£136, plus special breaks; 27 well equipped rms, 5 in annexe over the road. Carefully renovated old coaching inn with 20 miles of its own waters – salmon and trout fishing and a long-established fly-fishing school; comfortable sitting room, log fires, super food in both bar and elegant restaurant, carefully chosen wines, and kind service from local

MOTORWAY BREAKS

staff; new eating area in attractive terraced garden; cl 3 nights over Christmas; disabled access; dogs allowed away from restaurant *(01566) 784666*

244. ℳ ✕ ALTARNUN
Rising Sun *(2.5 miles from A30; in Altarnun keep on towards Camelford)*
Cheerful 16th-c traditional pub on edge of Bodmin Moor, low beams and flagstones, good fires, thriving local atmosphere, hearty home cooking and well kept ales in variety, decent house wines; tables outside, open all day wknds, *(01566) 86636*. In the village itself, the altarless church (hence the name) is well worth a look, with an enchanting set of 16th-c carved bench ends – much humanity and humour.

245. ℳ LANHYDROCK
Lanhydrock House *(1.6 miles off A30; first right turn off A38)*
This splendid old house has a staggering 50 rooms to look at; the highlight is the Long Gallery, with its magnificently illustrated Old Testament scenes – it's one of the few original 16th-c parts left, as a disastrous fire in the 19th c resulted in major changes and refurbishments. Do leave time to explore the pretty formal gardens (glorious around May) and grounds with Victorian coach house stables; it's a lovely walk down to the river and back through the woods. Good meals and snacks, shop and plant sales, disabled access; house cl Mon (exc bank hols) and Nov-Mar; *(01208) 265950*; £7.90, £4.40 grounds only (free Nov to mid-Feb); NT. The Crown down at Lanlivery is most enjoyable for lunch, in a Jane Austen village setting.

246. ℳ NEWLYN EAST
Lappa Valley Steam Railway and Leisure Park *(2 miles off A30 near Mitchell; follow brown signs)*
15-inch gauge steam line through pretty countryside to an old lead mine. It's surrounded by parkland with lakes, woodland walk, a maze, and play areas; a section of the old branch line leads to a nine-hole golf course. Meals, snacks, shop, some disabled access; cl Nov-Easter, and some days in April and Oct – best to check train times; *(01872) 510317*; £7, covers fare and all attractions exc golf and bikes.

A31

247. ✗ ⋈ MITCHELL
Plume of Feathers *(0.4 miles off A30, signed from A3076 exit roundabout)*
£75; Popular food pub, open all day, with friendly licensees, attractive bars, stripped old beams, an enormous open fire, pastel-coloured walls, plenty of seats for either a drink or a meal, and a natural spring well that has been made into a glass-topped table; no smoking restaurant with interesting paintings; nice garden; good, interesting and well presented food, well kept real ales, a comprehensive wine list, and fresh italian coffees; well liked bdrms *(01872) 510387*

248. ⋈ HAYLE
Paradise Park Wildlife Sanctuary *(2.8 miles off A30, from A3074 roundabout; follow brown signs)*
The World Parrot Trust's HQ, with some of the beautiful and sometimes rare residents shown to spectacular effect in the huge Parrot Jungle, a splendid mix of waterfalls, swamps and streams; it has a feeding station for their hyacinthine macaws from Brazil. You can try feeding lorikeets in the walk-through Australian aviaries (nectar for sale in the shop), there's a toucan aviary, and lots of other exotic birds and numerous animals inc miniature horses, pygmy goats, alpacas, miniature sheep, red pandas and a lemur, some of which you can feed at the Fun Farm. Daily free-flying bird show (usually at 12.30), summer bird of prey displays (not Sat exc July-Aug), entertaining penguin and otter feeding shows, children's quiz trails, big play area, indoor play centre, and a narrow-gauge railway gently rattling through the park. Adults may prefer the tropical plants in the Victorian walled garden, or the Bird in Hand pub that brews its own Wheal Ale. Meals, snacks, shop (and plant sales), mostly disabled access; *(01736) 751020*; £7.95.

A31

249. ✗ BENTLEY
Bull *(right by A31 SW of Farnham; can be reached directly from both carriageways, but rather tricky westbound)*
Welcoming and relaxing little low-beamed two-room refuge from the trunk road, good choice of good well presented food from memorable

MOTORWAY BREAKS

sandwiches to some enterprising main dishes, log fire, good coffee and other drinks, lots of local photographs; a few picnic-sets in garden with pretty raised terrace (pleasant despite the traffic noise) *(01420) 22156*

250. ✕ ⌑ MINSTEAD
Trusty Servant *(0.5 miles off A31 W of Cadnam, just over a mile past M27 junction 1; turn left to village green)*
£60; nicely varied choice of very good generous food all day, from sandwiches and traditional favourites to trend-setters, in big airy dining room and relaxed two-room Victorian bar, quick friendly service, well kept changing ales, decent house wines and country wines; provision for children and dogs, simple comfortable bdrms with good breakfast, open all day *(023) 8081 2137*

251. ❀ MINSTEAD
Furzey Gardens *(0.5 miles off A31 W of Cadnam, just over a mile past M27 junction 1; School Lane)*
Eight peaceful acres, with developing young arboretum, sensory garden and lake, around charming 16th-c thatched cottage and local craft gallery (open Mar-Oct and wknds Nov-mid-Dec). Snacks, plant sales, limited disabled access; *(023) 8081 2464*; £3.80. The village is quiet and pretty, with a fine old church at the top of the hill.

252. ❀ STAPEHILL
Knoll Gardens *(1.3 miles off A31; from B3073 roundabout take Wimborne Rd (away from Wimborne!), then first right into Stapehill Rd)*
Rare and exotic plants in various colourfully themed well developed informal gardens, with over 6,000 different well labelled species, many of which can be bought in the expanding nursery (which specialises in grasses and hardy perennials); a focal point is the formal Dragon Garden to which they've added a mediterranean-style gravel garden, and meadow garden. Snacks, disabled access; cl Mon and Tues, and 4 weeks over Christmas; *(01202) 873931*; £4. They maintain a good working relationship with adjacent Trehane Nurseries (noted for a great range of camellias), and the Angel at Longham (A348) has good value food.

253. ⌂ WIMBORNE MINSTER
Beechleas *(1 mile off A31, via B3073; Poole Rd)*
£99, plus special breaks; 9 attractive, comfortable rms. Carefully restored Georgian house with open fires in cosy sitting room and charming dining room, airy conservatory overlooking walled garden, enjoyable Aga-cooked food using organic produce, nice breakfasts, and friendly helpful owners; lots to do and see nearby; cl 24 Dec-mid-Jan; partial disabled access; dogs in bedrooms by arrangement *(01202) 841684*

254. ✗ WIMBORNE MINSTER
Cloisters *(1.1 miles off A31, via B3073 or B3078; East St)*
Friendly restaurant with pleasant décor and enjoyable food inc breakfast with home-made marmalade, lunchtime snacks and meals, and afternoon tea; cl 4 days over Christmas; disabled access *(01202) 880593*

A33

255. ≋ STRATFIELD SAYE
Stratfield Saye House *(1.5 miles off A33; from B3349 roundabout in Heckfield, take local rd (Welsh Lane) opp B3349)*
Bought for the Duke of Wellington after Waterloo, this 17th-c house has recently reopened after restoration work. Perhaps surprisingly, the Duke had a taste for french furniture, lots of which is still here, as is his splendid funeral carriage. Snacks, shop, disabled access; phone for very limited opening times, admission by guided tour only, £6; *(01256) 882882*. There are pleasant walks on Heckfield Heath E of the estate, and Wellington Country Park in Berks is nearby.

A34

256. ✗ OLD BURGHCLERE
Dew Pond *(0.6 miles off A34 about 6 miles S of Newbury)*
Beautiful 16th-c country house with log fires, friendly atmosphere, and imaginative attractively presented evening meals using fresh local produce on a frequently changing small menu – good game, fish and lovely

MOTORWAY BREAKS

puddings; no smoking; cl Sun, Mon, 2 wks Jan/Aug; no under-5s; disabled access *(01635) 278408*

257. ⊨ STOCKCROSS
Vineyard *(0.7 miles from A34/A4 roundabout; off B4000)*
£317, plus special breaks; 31 lovely big elegant rms or suites with garden views. Old hunting lodge with lots of modern art out in the grounds and in the public rooms, opulent country house-style furnishings, plants, lovely flower arrangements, newspapers and books, excellent food in restaurant, two exceptional wine lists, and kind staff; indoor swimming pool and gym *(01635) 528770*

258. ※ SCHOLAR GREEN
Rode Hall Gardens *(1.5 miles off A34, just N of Kidsgrove; Church Lane)*
In a Repton landscape, this fine house has been in the same family since it was first built in the early 18th c (though it's been extensively remodelled inside since then); the large gardens include a stylish rose garden, a working Victorian walled kitchen garden, and a grotto and ice-house. Snacks, poor disabled access (steps up to house, pebbled walkways in garden); house open pm Weds and bank hols, garden open pm Tues-Thurs and bank hols during Apr-Sept (also 3 wks in Feb for snowdrops); *(01270) 873237*; £5 house and garden, £3 garden only.

259. ※ ASTBURY
(just off A34 S of Congleton)
This is a delightful village, and its church is well worth a look – graceful detached spire, spectacular roofing, rich carving. The partly 16th-c Egerton Arms, open all day, is a charming pub, with well kept Robinsons ales and good value food from sandwiches up, inc OAP lunches Mon-Thurs. Their bedrooms are also good value; *(01260) 273946.*

260. ※ CAPESTHORNE
Capesthorne Hall *(A34, just S of A537)*
18th-c family home of the Bromley-Davenports, who have lived on the site since Domesday; fine paintings include Lowry's unusual interpretation of the house's striking exterior, and there's a good collection of Roman and Greek busts and vases. Also lovely Georgian chapel and

60 acres of gardens and woodland. Snacks, disabled access; open pm Weds, Sun and bank hols Apr-Oct; *(01625) 861221*; £6.50, £4.00 garden and chapel only.

A35

261. ✕ CHRISTCHURCH
Ship in Distress *(0.7 miles off A35; B3059, keeping straight ahead towards Mudeford at Purewell Cross (next roundabout), into Stanpit)*
Friendly and cottagey pub, homely bar with entertaining clutter of more or less nautical bric-a-brac, appealingly cheerful restaurant, well kept ales, good wines by the glass, and some excellent food (all day in summer) – they bake their own bread, and the seafood is especially good; open all day from 10 *(01202) 485123*

262. ✕ EAST MORDEN
Cock & Bottle *(0.6 miles off A35, via B3075)*
Popular dining pub with several beamed communicating areas, a nice mix of old furnishings, good log fire, enjoyable food inc interesting daily specials with plenty of fish and seasonal game, well kept beers and good wines; cl 25-26 Dec; disabled access *(01929) 459238*

263. ⚞ ATHELHAMPTON
Athelhampton House and Gardens *(1.5 miles off A35; brown signs)*
This magnificent 15th-c house is built on the legendary site of King Athelstan's palace. The great hall has a fantastic roof, and throughout are beautiful furnishings and contents, with some fine panelling. An added bonus is the acres of wonderful formal and landscaped gardens with rare plants, topiary and fountain pools. Meals, snacks, shop, disabled access; open daily (exc Fri-Sat) Mar-Oct, and Sun only (cl 1-2pm) Nov-Feb; *(01305) 848363*; £8 house and gardens, £5.75 garden only (voucher admits two adults for the price of one). The young Thomas Hardy helped design the church across the road. The Martyrs at Tolpuddle has decent home cooking.

MOTORWAY BREAKS

264. ⋈ LOWER BOCKHAMPTON
Yalbury Cottage (1.3 miles off A35, E of Dorchester)
£94, plus special breaks; 8 rms overlooking garden or fields. Very attractive family-run 16th-c thatched house with a relaxed friendly atmosphere, and low beams and inglenook fireplaces in comfortable lounge and dining room; carefully cooked often imaginative food, good wines, and attractive mature garden; dogs in bedrooms *(01305) 262382*

265. ⋈ DORCHESTER
Casterbridge (1 mile off A35, B3150 from E roundabout; High East St)
£80, plus wknd breaks; 14 individually decorated, pretty rms with neat little bathrooms. Particularly well run and friendly small Georgian hotel in town centre, with attractive, cosy sitting room, a useful small library/bar, nicely decorated breakfast room with light and airy attached conservatory, very good breakfasts using top quality local produce, and charming, helpful staff; no evening meals (lots of nearby restaurants); best to book early as they are very popular; cl Christmas; disabled access *(01305) 264043*

266. ⋈ DORCHESTER
Maiden Castle (0.5 miles off A35, from A354 S; no access from bypass)
Europe's most famous Iron Age fort, a series of massive grassy ramparts covering 47 acres, and once home to some 200 families; the Romans captured it after a particularly bloody battle. It's so vast that the tour of its grassy ramparts almost qualifies as a fully fledged walk; free.

267. ✕ ⋈ DALWOOD
Tuckers Arms (1.1 miles off A35; village signed 2 miles W of Axminster)
£59.50; Delightful thatched medieval longhouse with fine flagstoned bar, lots of beams, log fire in inglenook, woodburner, a good mix of dining chairs, window seats and wall settles, huge collection of miniature bottles, well prepared enterprising bar food and lots of colourful hanging baskets; disabled access *(01404) 881342*

268. ⋈ DALWOOD
Burrow Farm Gardens (half a mile or so off A35; turn off at Taunton Cross sign)
Part of this 10-acre site has been created from an ancient Roman clay

pit, with spacious lawns, borders and unusual shrubs and trees, as well as a woodland garden, pergola walk with old-fashioned roses, and super views; also a rill garden, and a wildlife lake. Cream teas, snacks, nursery, some disabled access; cl Oct-Mar; *(01404) 831285*; £3.50.

A36

269. ⋈ SALISBURY
Stratford Lodge (0.6 miles off A36 via A345 N; third left into Park Lane)
£75, plus special breaks; 8 rms. Warmly friendly and relaxed Victorian house with antique furnishings, fresh flowers, generous helpings of very good carefully prepared evening food, super breakfasts in conservatory, and quiet garden; children over 5 *(01722) 325177*

270. ⋈ WILTON
Wilton House (just off A36)
Particularly satisfying to visit; the original house was damaged by a fire in 1647, and superbly redesigned by John Webb and Inigo Jones, the latter responsible for the magnificent Double Cube room, considered by many to be one of the country's finest surviving rooms from this period; it's full of splendid works by Van Dyck. The Tudor kitchen and Victorian laundry have both been well restored to give a good impression of their original use. The furnishings and art are exquisite, and a doll's house re-creates some parts of the house in miniature. The 21-acre grounds inc an adventure playground, water and rose gardens, restful cloister garden, a striking Palladian bridge, and woodland walks; plenty of space for picnics. Meals, snacks, shop, disabled access; cl Nov-Mar and Sat; *(01722) 746720*; £9.75; grounds only £4.50. The ornately italianate 19th-c church incorporates all sorts of treasures, esp its magnificent medieval continental stained glass and 2,000-year-old marble pillars. Wiltons (Market Pl) is good for lunch, and the charming Victoria & Albert in nearby Netherhampton is nicely off the tourist track, with a pleasant riverside walk into Salisbury.

271. ⋈ LITTLE LANGFORD
Little Langford Farmhouse (1.6 miles off A36; take the Langfords exit, cross River Wylye and turn left)

MOTORWAY BREAKS

£57; 3 spacious rms with period furniture. Victorian gothick farmhouse with turreted entrance hall and plenty of original features, sitting room with open fire, friendly owners, a baby grand, billiards room, light suppers if arranged beforehand, and big garden; can observe the working farm (dairy and arable), and there are plenty of downland walks; no smoking; cl Nov-Feb; children over 12 *(01722) 790205*

272. ✕ ⋈ HEYTESBURY
Angel (0.6 miles off A36; village signed from roundabout at E end of Warminster bypass)
£75; 8 comfortable light rms. 16th-c coaching inn with armchairs, sofas, and a good fire in cosy homely lounge, a long chatty beamed bar, and good service from friendly staff; wide choice of consistently good food in charming back dining room that opens on to secluded garden; disabled access; dogs in bedrooms, if small and well behaved *(01985) 840330*

273. ⋈ WARMINSTER
Bishopstrow House (1.5 miles off A36 from Heytesbury roundabout at E end of bypass; B3414)
£199, plus special breaks; 32 sumptuous rms, some with jacuzzi. Charming ivy-clad Georgian house in 27 acres with heated indoor and outdoor swimming pools, indoor and outdoor tennis courts, fitness centre and beauty treatment rooms, and own fishing on River Wylye; very relaxed friendly atmosphere, log fires, lovely fresh flowers, antiques and fine paintings in boldly decorated day rooms, and really impressive food; disabled access; dogs in bedrooms, *(01985) 212312*

274. ⋈ WARMINSTER
Old Bell (1.2 miles off A36 bypass; Market Pl (B3414))
£60, plus special breaks; 15 comfortable rms. 14th-c country-town hotel with traditional bar food, popular Sunday carvery, restaurant, good choice of wines, pretty central courtyard, and friendly service; cl Christmas; lots to do nearby *(01985) 216611*

275. ⋈ BECKINGTON
Pickford House (0.2 miles off A36; Bath Rd)
£45; 5 rms, some with river view and most with own bthrm. Honey-

coloured hilltop stone house, with open fire in sitting room, bar, delicious evening meals (by arrangement) and breakfasts, a relaxed friendly atmosphere, helpful courteous owners and friendly collie; big garden with swimming pool; you can take over the house with a group of friends for a gourmet wknd; partial disabled access; dogs in some bedrooms, depending on size of dog *(01373) 830329*

276. ⌨ HINTON CHARTERHOUSE
Homewood Park (just off A36 S of Bath)
£150, plus winter breaks; 19 lovely rms. Charming Victorian hotel on the edge of Hinton Priory and in ten acres of gardens and woodlands; flowers, oil paintings and fine furniture in graceful relaxing day rooms, and an elegant restaurant with very good imaginative food (honey from their own bees – you can help them collect it); tennis, croquet, and outdoor swimming pool; disabled access *(01225) 723731*

A37

277. ⌨ YETMINSTER
Manor Farmhouse (2.3 miles off A37; High St)
£70; 4 rms. Fine, carefully modernised, no smoking 17th-c building, with beams and oak panelling, inglenook fireplaces, homely sitting room, helpful owners, and good fresh traditional cooking; cl 24 Dec-6 Jan; disabled access; children over 12 *(0800) 0566761*

278. ⌨ BARWICK
Little Barwick House (0.4 miles off A37 Keyford roundabout, via Church Lane E)
£120, plus special breaks; 6 attractive rms. Carefully run listed Georgian dower house in 3½ acres 2m S of Yeovil, and thought of as a restaurant-with-rooms; lovely relaxed atmosphere, log fire in cosy lounge, excellent food using local produce, a thoughtful wine list, super breakfasts, nice afternoon tea, and particularly good service; cl 2 wks Jan; dogs in bedrooms *(01935) 423902*

279. ✗ LOVINGTON
Pilgrims Rest (1.6 miles off A37, via B3153 E towards Castle Cary)

MOTORWAY BREAKS

Quietly placed and civilised country bar/bistro with particularly good interesting food cooked by the landlord, using fresh ingredients; chatty and relaxed, with sunny modern prints, settees and easy chair by cosy inner area's big fireplace, snug heavy-beamed eating area with candles on its american-clothed tables, and no smoking dining room; nice wines by the glass, well kept ales from the nearby brewery, daily papers, some tables outside; cl Sun pm, Mon and Tues am, 10 days Jan *(01963) 240597*

280. ⌂ SHEPTON MALLET
***Charlton House and Mulberry Restaurant** (0.5 miles off A37; A361 E)*
£165, plus special breaks; 25 attractive and stylish rooms with nice extras, and large bthrms. Substantial Georgian hotel in landscaped grounds; bare-boarded rooms with oriental rugs, dark red walls with lots of old photographs and posters, and show-casing the owners' Mulberry style of informal furnishings; smart dining room and 3-bay conservatory, restored 18th-c orangery dining room, exceptionally good modern cooking, interesting wines, and helpful, efficient uniformed staff; seats on the back terrace overlooking a big lawn, and croquet; health spa; they are kind to children; disabled access; dogs in one room only *(01749) 342008*

281. ✕ SHEPTON MALLET
***Blostins** (0.5 miles off A37 via B3136 (Bath Rd) from N of town, into Waterloo Rd)*
Friendly little candlelit evening bistro with consistently good interesting food inc lovely puddings, and fairly priced wines; cl Sun-Mon, 1 wk Jan, 1 wk Easter and 2 wks Aug *(01749) 343648*

282. ✕ DOULTING
***Waggon & Horses** (1.3 miles off A37 N of Shepton Mallet; pub signed E along Mendip ridge just S of **A367 junction**, from Beacon Hill crossroads)*
18th-c inn with stone-mullioned latticed windows, a rambling bar with interesting pictures for sale, two no smoking rooms, a choice of enjoyable bar food, decent house wines, cocktails, real ales, and a lovely big walled garden with various fancy fowl (they sell the eggs), a goat and horses; big raftered gallery for art shows and classical music; cl 25 Dec; children must be very well behaved; disabled access *(01749) 880302*

283. ⊨ STON EASTON
*Ston Easton Park (off A37 just S of **A39 junction**)*
£150; 22 really lovely rms. Majestic Palladian mansion of Bath stone with beautifully landscaped 18th-c gardens and 26 acres of parkland; elegant day rooms with antiques and flowers, an attractive no smoking restaurant with good food (much grown in the kitchen garden), fine afternoon teas, library and billiard room, and extremely helpful, friendly and unstuffy service; children over 7 in dining room; dogs in bedrooms at manager`s discretion *(01761) 241631*

284. ⊨ HUNSTRETE
Hunstrete House (1.5 miles off A37 from Chelwood via A368 E)
£185, plus special breaks; 25 individually decorated rms. Classically handsome, mainly 18th-c country-house hotel on the edge of the Mendips, in 92 acres inc lovely Victorian walled garden and deer park; comfortable and elegantly furnished day rooms with antiques, paintings, log fires, fresh garden flowers, a tranquil atmosphere, excellent service, and very good food using home-grown produce when possible; croquet lawn, heated outdoor swimming pool, all-weather tennis court, and nearby riding; limited disabled access; dogs in bedrooms *(01761) 490490*

285. ✕ ⊨ STANTON WICK
Carpenters Arms (1 mile off A37; village signed off A368 just W, then bear right)
£89.50; 12 rms. Warm and attractively furnished tile-roofed inn, converted from a row of miners' cottages, in peaceful countryside; big log fire and woodburner, stripped stone and beams, a wide choice of good food inc generous breakfasts, well kept beers, and friendly efficient staff; pianist Fri and Sat pms; cl 25-26 and 31 Dec *(01761) 490202*

A38

286. ⊨ ROLLESTON ON DOVE
Brookhouse Hotel (1.7 miles N off A38 from A5121 junction E of Stretton, via Claymills Rd and Dovecliff Rd, leading into Station Rd)
£115, plus wknd breaks; 19 comfortable rms with Victorian brass or four-poster beds. Handsome ivy-covered William & Mary brick building in five

MOTORWAY BREAKS

acres of lovely gardens with comfortable antiques-filled rooms, and good food using seasonal local produce in elegant little dining room; children over 12; disabled access; dogs welcome in bedrooms *(01283) 814188*

287. ✕ ⇥ KEMPSEY
Walter de Cantelupe (on A38; Main Rd)
£77; popular roadside pub with friendly relaxed bar, quite a mix of furniture, flowers and candles on tables, a good big fireplace, interesting food, well kept real ales, a good choice of wines by the glass, and hardworking landlord; cl Mon exc bank hols, no food Sun pm and second half of Jan; no children after 8.15pm *(01905) 820572*

288. ⇥ SALTASH
Erth Barton (2 miles off A38 in Notter, via Trematon; Elmgate)
£80; 3 rms. Lovely old manor house with its own chapel, peaceful rooms with lots of books, pictures and big fireplaces, good enjoyable food, bird-watching in the surrounding estuaries, and riding (you can bring your own horse); children over 12; dogs welcome in bedrooms *(01752) 842127*

289. ⇥ LISKEARD
Well House (2.6 miles off A38, on minor rd S from A390 roundabout to – and past – St Keyne station)
£115, plus special breaks; 9 individually designed rms with fine views. Light and airy Victorian country house, recently redecorated, with warm, friendly owners, courteous staff, comfortable drawing room, cosy little bar, and particularly good food and fine wines in dining room overlooking terrace and lawns; three acres of gardens with hard tennis court, swimming pool and croquet lawn; children over 8 in evening restaurant; dogs welcome away from reception areas and restaurant *(01579) 342001*

A39

290. 🕸 INSTOW
Tapeley Park (2 miles off A39; turn off B3233, passing Westleigh Inn)
The very pretty italianate garden with rococo features and walled kitchen garden is the main draw, though there's also a pets' corner,

play area, and woodland walk. Lovely views down to the sea. Teas and snacks in period dairy, plant sales, some disabled access; cl Sat, and Nov-Mar; (01271) 342558; £4 (house tours £2.50 – you need to give a week's notice).

291. ✕ ST KEW
St Kew Inn (1.3 miles off A39 N of Wadebridge; village signed)
Handsome stone-built pub, open all day July/Aug, with welcoming owners, nice old-fashioned furnishings in neatly kept bar, good popular food, well kept St Austell ales and good wine list, and big peaceful garden; lovely church next door *(01208) 841259*

292. ⌂ LITTLE PETHERICK
Old Mill House (2.7 miles from A39; A389 towards Padstow)
£75; 7 rms. 16th-c corn mill in lovely riverside gardens with waterwheel and other original features, enjoyable breakfasts in beamed dining room, bar and lounges, and attentive service; good evening meals; cl Dec-Jan; no children *(01841) 540388*

A40

293. ⌂ OXFORD
Cotswold House (0.4 miles off A40 via A4165 into town; 363 Banbury Rd)
£80; 7 comfortable rms with showers. Beautifully kept modern no smoking Cotswold stone house with particularly helpful owners, residents' lounge, very good breakfasts, pretty flowers throughout, and neat back garden; children over 6; disabled access *(01865) 310558*

294. ✕ GODSTOW
Trout (1.1 miles off A40, from A44 roundabout N of Oxford; Godstow Rd)
Olde-worlde Vintage Inn in genuinely medieval creeper-covered building, several linked rooms with log fires in huge hearths, hop-hung beams, carvings and shiny ancient flagstones, decent food all day inc good lunchtime sandwiches, well kept ales and good choice of wines by the glass, friendly young well trained staff; lovely flagstoned heated terrace by a stream full of greedily plump perch, long restored footbridge

to island (owned by pub) with ducks and peacocks, abbey ruins opp *(01865) 302071*

295. ⌂ BURFORD
Burford House (0.4 miles off A40 via A361; High St)
£120, plus winter breaks; 8 cosy individually decorated rms. Attractive partly stone and partly timbered 14th-c building, with plenty of personal touches in the two comfortable lounges (one for residents only), log fires, super breakfasts, and lots of plants in pretty stone courtyard; may cl 2 wks Jan/Feb *(01993) 823151*

296. ✕ ⌂ BURFORD
Lamb (0.4 miles off A40, via A361; Sheep St, left off High St)
£150, plus special breaks; 15 rms. Very attractive 500-year-old Cotswold inn with lovely restful atmosphere, spacious beamed, flagstoned and elegantly furnished lounge, classic civilised public bar, bunches of flowers on good oak and elm tables, three winter log fires, antiques, modern British food in lovely restaurant, and pretty little walled garden; disabled access; dogs in bedrooms, bar and lounges *(01993) 823155*

297. ✕ ⌂ LITTLE BARRINGTON
Inn For All Seasons (on A40 W of Burford)
£97; handsome and civilised old inn with an attractive, mellow lounge bar, low beams, stripped stone and flagstones, a big log fire, old prints, country magazines to read, particularly good fresh fish (from Brixham) and other food, well kept real ales and wines, lots of malt whiskies, and a pleasant garden surrounded by lots of walks; cl 1 wk Jan; disabled access *(01451) 844324*

298. ✕ ⌂ NORTHLEACH
Wheatsheaf (0.8 miles off A40, via A429 from junction roundabout, then left into town; West End)
£60; handsome and civilised 16th-c stone-built dining pub on a quiet street of similarly attractive buildings, and with new licensees this year; three light and airy big-windowed rooms, flagstones, bare boards and carpet matting, modern horse-racing oil paintings, and log fires; appeal-

ing choice of imaginative food, good interesting wines, and well kept real ales; pretty back garden with picnic-sets on tiers of grass among flowering shrubs *(01451) 860244*

299. 🏛 GOODRICH
Goodrich Castle *(0.7 miles off A40 SW of Ross)*
Proper-looking 12th-c castle built using the same red sandstone rock it stands on, so that it seems almost to grow out of the ground. Still plenty to see, with towers, passageways, dungeon and marvellous views of the surrounding countryside. Snacks (summer only), shop; cl 1-2pm, Mon-Tues in Nov-Mar, 24-26 Dec, and 1 Jan; *(01600) 890538*; £3.70. These formidable ruins are a feasible objective for stout-hearted walkers from Symonds Yat, or could be a start point for Wye Valley gorge walks. Coming by road, beware the A4137, England's second most dangerous road. The partly Norman Spread Eagle at Walford, back to its original name now after a spell as the Mill Race, has good value food.

300. ⊨ MONMOUTH
Riverside Hotel *(1 mile off A40 via A466 and B4293, keeping left at Cinderhill St roundabout)*
£61.85, plus special breaks; 17 rms. Comfortable, warmly welcoming bustling hotel overlooking River Monnow and the 13th-c fortified gatehouse, with good value bar meals, enjoyable food in newly refurbished restaurant, a bustling lounge bar, and conservatory; disabled access; dogs in bedrooms and bar *(01600) 715577*

301. ✕ ⊨ CRICKHOWELL
Bear *(on A40)*
£95; 35 rms, the back ones are the best, and some have jacuzzis. Particularly friendly coaching inn with calmly civilised atmosphere, excellent food using local produce and home-grown herbs (some welsh specialities), fine wines and ports, well kept real ales, and prompt attentive service; lots of antiques, deeply comfortable seats, and a roaring log fire in the heavily beamed lounge, and a partly no smoking family room; children over 8 in restaurant; disabled access *(01873) 810408*

MOTORWAY BREAKS

302. ✕ CRICKHOWELL
***Nantyffin Cider Mill** (on A40 W, by A479)*
Handsome pink-washed dining pub with striking raftered restaurant, smart relaxed atmosphere, fresh and dried flowers, woodburner, comfortable tables and chairs, beautifully presented imaginative food (much organic produce), excellent service, well kept real ales, good wines and charming views; cl Mon; disabled access *(01873) 801775*

303. ※ NARBERTH
***Oakwood Park** (1 mile off A40 from Canaston Bridge; A4075 S)*
Wales's premier theme park, with rides from the world's No 1 wooden roller-coaster Megafobia to the sky-coaster, Vertigo: you're strapped in a harness and winched to a height of up to 165 ft, then free-fall at 70mph back towards the ground – just in time you'll start swinging like a frantic pendulum. A nightmare cross between bungee-jumping and a parachute drop, this obviously wouldn't suit everyone, so rather than bump up the entry price, there's an extra charge of £11 per person (3 flyers). There's a real mix of other things, with younger children having their own little roller-coaster (there's another medium-sized one aimed at families), carousels and the like. During the school holidays, the park stays open until 10pm and the evening ends with a spectacular firework and waterscreen light show. Meals, snacks, shop, disabled access; cl Oct-Apr (exc school hols); *(01834) 861889*; £13.75.

304. ⌂ SPITTAL
***Lower Haythog** (3 miles off A40 from Haverfordwest, via B4329 past Crundale)*
£55; 6 rms. Centuries-old farmhouse on working dairy farm in 250 acres of unspoilt countryside, with comfortable lounge, log fire, books and games, traditional breakfasts, good cooking in the dining room, and friendly owners; swing and slide in the garden, trout ponds in the woods; self-catering also *(01437) 731279*

305. ✕ LETTERSTON
***Something Cooking** (on A40 (Haverfordwest Rd just S of B4331))*
Enthusiastically run and very friendly fish restaurant with truly outstanding fresh fish, served by neat uniformed waitresses – very reasonable prices too; cl winter Sun, 2 wks Christmas; disabled access *(01348) 840621*

A41

306. ⌂ WIGGINTON
Rangers Cottage *(0.9 miles off A41; village signed from exit roundabout at E end of Tring bypass; Tring Park, Highfield Rd)*
£65; 3 individually decorated rms, each with mini fridge. Built in 1880 by the Rothschild family for their estate manager, this attractively extended, no smoking cottage has fine country views, a pretty garden with seats on a sunny terrace, helpful friendly owners, enjoyable breakfasts using eggs from their own hens and home-made marmalade, and nearby pubs and restaurants for evening meals; good bird-watching and walks *(01442) 890155*

307. ⌂ AYLESBURY
Hartwell House *(1.4 miles from A41, via A418 Oxford Rd)*
£260, plus special breaks; 46 rms, some large and well equipped, others with four-posters and fine panelling, inc 10 secluded suites in restored 18th-c stables with private garden and statues. Elegant Grade I listed building with Jacobean and Georgian façades, wonderful decorative plasterwork and panelling, fine paintings and antiques, a marvellous Gothic central staircase, splendid morning room, and library, exceptional service, fine wines, and excellent food; 90 acres of parkland with ruined church, lake and statues, and spa with indoor swimming pool, saunas, gym and beauty rooms, and informal buttery and bar; tennis, croquet, and fishing; children over 8; good disabled access; dogs in Hartwell Court *(01296) 747444*

308. ※ WADDESDON
Waddesdon Manor *(on A41)*
One of the spectacular mansions built for Baron Ferdinand de Rothschild at the end of the 19th c, and designed as a showcase for his french art collection rather than a home. Plenty of rooms to see, each as lavish as the last, and filled with a dazzling array of furnishings, porcelain, portraits and other objects, and there's an unrivalled display of Sèvres china. The fabled wine cellars have huge vintage bottles, and a collection of labels designed or painted by some of the century's greatest artists. Quite splendid late Victorian formal gardens surround the

MOTORWAY BREAKS

house, and they still use the rococo-style aviary. An extremely satisfying place to visit, but it does get busy; they operate a timed ticket system for the house (can be bought in advance, but £3 booking charge), and last recommended entry is 2.30pm. Good meals, snacks, shops, disabled access; house open Weds-Sun and bank hol Mon; best to phone for detailed opening times; *(01296) 653226*; £11 house and grounds, £4 grounds only; NT.

309. ✕ ⇌ WADDESDON
Five Arrows (on A41)
£85; rather grand small hotel – part of the Rothschild estate – with an informally pubby bar made up of several open-plan rooms, a relaxed but civilised atmosphere, Rothschild family portraits and old estate-worker photographs on the walls, sturdy furnishings on parquet flooring, newspapers and magazines, enjoyable food, a no smoking country house-style restaurant, a formidable wine list, well kept real ales, efficient service, and sheltered back garden *(01296) 651727*

310. ⇌ TILSTON
Tilston Lodge (2 miles from A41; turn off in Duckington)
£72; 3 thoughtfully equipped rms, 2 with four-posters. Warmly friendly and beautifully restored Victorian house in 16 acres of grounds that include award-winning gardens, ponds, and a collection of rare breed farm animals; comfortable and attractive public rooms with original features, open fire in dining room, and good breakfasts with home-made jams and marmalades; cl Christmas *(01829) 250223*

A44

311. ※ WOODSTOCK
Blenheim Palace (just off A44)
One of England's most impressive stately homes: given to the 1st Duke of Marlborough by Queen Anne as a reward for his victory over the forces of Louis XIV. The house and courtyards cover 14 acres, and the grounds stretch for well over 2,000. It's astonishingly grand: highlights include the sumptuous State Rooms, 183-ft Long Library, and elaborate ceiling in the Great Hall, along with luxurious furnishings and

sculpture. Churchill was born here in 1874, and there's a permanent exhibition on his life. You can walk around on your own, or guided tours leave regularly (although not guaranteed during peak season). Capability Brown landscaped the extensive parkland; you can picnic just about anywhere. Various monuments and statues are dotted around the grounds, and the formal gardens are magnificent, particularly the water terraces and italian garden. There's also a miniature railway, butterfly house, symbolic hedge maze (its design inspired by Grinling Gibbons's carvings in the palace), a model village, and play areas. Meals, snacks, shops and plant centre, some disabled access; house and gardens are open daily mid Feb-end Oct, and from Weds-Sun Nov-mid Dec; park is open all year round except 25 Dec; *(08700) 602080*; full ticket £13, park and gardens £8, park only (when palace and gardens are closed) £2.50 – prices are less off peak.

312. ✗ ⋈ WOOTTON
Kings Head (0.9 miles off A44; Chapel Hill, up High St)
£80; pretty beamed 17th-c Cotswold stone pub with civilised no smoking lounge, a nice mix of furniture, open log fire, very good imaginative food inc lovely puddings, well kept real ales, and decent wines; cl Sun evening and Mon; no children *(01993) 811340*

313. ✗ ⋈ LITTLE COMPTON
Red Lion (just off A44 NW of Chipping Norton)
£55; 3 rms, shared bthrm. Attractive 16th-c stone inn with low beams, log fires, separate dining area, extensive menu with tasty food, no smoking area, real ales, long wine list, and seats in the sizeable attractive garden; children over 8 *(01608) 674397*

314. ✗ ⋈ GREAT WOLFORD
Fox & Hounds (2 miles off A44 E of Moreton-in-Marsh)
£70; inviting 16th-c stone inn with a good mix of locals and visitors in the cosy low-beamed old-fashioned bar; candlelit tables, flagstones and a roaring log fire, really enjoyable imaginative daily specials, and a little tap room with several changing real ales; cl Mon; disabled access *(01608) 674220*

MOTORWAY BREAKS

315. ⏃ MORETON-IN-MARSH
White Hart Royal (A44, junction with A429)
£95; 19 good rms. Busy and comfortable, partly 15th-c inn with interesting Civil War history, oak beams and stripped stone, big inglenook fire in lounge area just off main bar, friendly helpful staff, well kept real ales, and decent food in bar and pleasant restaurant; attractive courtyard; disabled access *(01608) 650731*

316. ⏃ BROAD CAMPDEN
Malt House (3 miles off A44, via B4081)
£118.50; 7 rms with sloping floors and mullioned windows. 16th-c house in an unspoilt Cotswold village with ancient oak panelling, old beams, open fires, antiques and home-grown flowers, and a peaceful old-fashioned atmosphere; dinner party-type evening meals, super breakfasts, afternoon teas with home-made biscuits and cakes (served in the thatched summer house in warm weather), and friendly staff and owners; 3-acre garden with croquet; cl Christmas; dogs in bedrooms *(01386) 840295*

317. ✕ BROAD CAMPDEN
Bakers Arms (2.9 miles off A44, via B4081)
Atmospheric ex-granary in tranquil village with good value bar food (inc children's menu), a fine range of real ales, cosy beamed bar, log fires, friendly cats, pleasant service, and nice garden; open all day wknds and summer; cl 25 Dec, pm 26 Dec *(01386) 840515*

318. ⚘ BROADWAY
(1 mile off A44 from B4632 roundabout)
Exceptionally harmonious stone-built Cotswold village, with the golden stone and uneven stone-tiled roofs perfectly blending the grand houses and the humbler cottages together, in a long, grass-lined main st. It's decidedly on the coach-tour trail, and gets very busy indeed in summer. Fine things for sale in expensive antiques shops, and a very grand old inn, the Lygon Arms, with a useful side brasserie. The Broadway Hotel also does good bar lunches and the Crown & Trumpet in Church St is an archetypal Cotswold pub, and the Buckland Manor does good teas.

319. ⚬ BROADWAY
Broadway Hotel *(1 mile off A44 from B4632 roundabout; turn right on High St)*
£130; 20 well kept rms. Lovely 15th-c building, once a monastic guest house, with galleried and timbered lounge, cosy beamed bar, attractively presented food served by attentive staff in airy comfortable restaurant, and seats outside on terrace; dogs in some bedrooms *(01386) 852401*

320. ⚬ EVESHAM
Evesham Hotel *(off A44 via B4035 into centre; Coopers Lane, off Waterside)*
£124, plus special breaks; 40 spacious rms with games and jigsaws. Comfortably modernised and cheerful family-run hotel with a warmly friendly, relaxed and jokey atmosphere, popular restaurant with very good food (esp lunchtime buffet), huge wine and spirits list, and sitting room with games and toys; indoor swimming pool surrounded by table tennis and table football, and grounds with croquet, trampoline, swings and putting; particularly well organised for families (but they do not get overrun by children); cl 25-26 Dec; disabled access; dogs in bedrooms only *(01386) 765566*

321. ✕ WYRE PIDDLE
Anchor *(just off A44 NW of Pershore)*
Relaxing 17th-c pub with lovely views over lawn, river and on over the Vale of Evesham; friendly, neatly kept little lounge with log fire in attractively restored inglenook, comfortable bar, and generous reasonably priced popular food; cl 26 Dec; disabled access *(01386) 552799*

322. ⚭ LEOMINSTER
(on A44/A49)
An attractive centre, the medieval streets almost lined with black and white timbered houses; plenty of antiques and speciality food shops to browse around, and a Fri market. The red priory church still has many of its original Norman features; inside you can see a ducking stool. There's a little local folk museum in Etnam St (cl Sat pm, Sun, and Nov-Easter; *(01568) 615186*; free). The handsome old Talbot Hotel has decent food.

MOTORWAY BREAKS

323. ⋈ LEOMINSTER
Highfield (a mile off A44; on W edge turn into Newtown Lane, then left into Ivington Rd)
£56, plus special breaks; 3 no smoking rms. Edwardian house in large garden with open farmland views, two sitting rooms – one with television and french windows opening onto the terrace, the other with helpful books – and open fires; enjoyable home cooking using local produce in charming dining room, full english breakfast, and helpful, attentive owners; cl Dec-Feb; no children *(01568) 613216*

324. ⋈ PEMBRIDGE
(on A44)
One of Herefordshire's most striking black and white villages, full of fine timbered buildings inc a medieval market hall, the ancient New Inn (good bar food), a craft gallery in a former chapel (East St; cl 25-26 Dec; *(01544) 388842;* free), and a lovely church with an unusual detached belfry where you can watch the clock mechanism.

325. ✕ ⋈ TITLEY
Stagg (2.7 miles off A44; B4355 NE of Kington)
£70; attractive old pub with main emphasis on the two dining rooms, one quite big, the other intimate; well kept real ales, up to ten wines by the glass from a carefully chosen list, a fine collection of malt whiskies, and particularly good, imaginative food inc a formidable cheese range; helpful service; tables out in the garden, and lovely surrounding countryside; cl Sun pm, Mon (exc bank hols and then they close Tues), first 2 wks Nov, 1 wk Feb, 25-26 Dec, 1 Jan *(01544) 230221*

326. ⋈ KINGTON
Penrhos Court (on A44, just E)
£100, plus special breaks; 17 elegant rms. Beautifully restored 13th-c hall in six acres, with fine beams and flagstones, a magnificent hall for their organic dining, a huge wood fire, and very good carefully cooked food using seasonal organic home-grown herbs and vegetables; they run regular food and health courses; cl Jan; disabled access; dogs in self-catering unit *(01544) 230720*

327. 🐾 KINGTON
(just off A44)
Attractive border town by the River Arrow, well placed for walks. Antiques and bric-a-brac are noticeably cheaper here than – say – in Gloucestershire; there's a livestock market on Thurs (and a general market on Tues). On Mill St is a little local history museum (cl Sun, and Oct-Mar; *(01544) 231486*; free). The town is overlooked by St Mary's Church, which has a massive Norman tower; the nearby mound is all that's left of Kington Castle. Hergest Croft Gardens and the Small Breeds Farm Park and Owl Centre are both on the edge of town – phone the local tic for information *(01544) 230778*. The unassuming Queens Head (Bridge St) brews its own good beers and has good value snacks.

328. ✕ ⌂ OLD RADNOR
Harp (0.7 miles off A44 W of Kington)
£60; 5 pretty rms, most with own bthrm. 15th-c inn in superb tranquil hilltop position, with lovely views and good walks nearby; friendly attentive owners, traditional bars with good log fires, some slate flooring and antique settles, character dining room, good value home cooking inc good breakfasts, well kept ales; self-catering bungalow; seats outside with play area; cl wkdy lunchtimes and Mon *(01544) 350655*

A46

329. ✕ BARNOLDBY LE BECK
Ship (3 miles off A46 W of Grimsby; just off A18 S)
Carefully run home with charming Edwardian and Victorian bric-a-brac – stand-up telephones, violins, a horn gramophone, bowler and top hats, old rackets, crops and hockey sticks, stuffed birds and animals, and grandmotherly plants in ornate china bowls; a truly tempting choice of very reasonably priced fresh fish from Grimsby, plus meaty dishes and lovely puddings, too; well kept ales, an extensive wine list with plenty by the glass, tables outside; children in restaurant only *(01472) 822308*

MOTORWAY BREAKS

330. ⋈ BUSLINGTHORPE
East Farm House (2.4 miles off A46 S of Mkt Rasen)
£50, plus special breaks; 2 rms. 18th-c farmhouse surrounded by family farm, with beams, stripped pine, log fires, relaxed atmosphere, and good breakfasts (evening meals by arrangement); tennis and lots of walks; self-catering cottage; cl Christmas and New Year *(01673) 842283*

331. ✕ COLSTON BASSETT
Martins Arms (2.7 miles off A46 from Cotgrave; School Lane)
Civilised, rather smart pub with particularly good imaginative food in bar and no smoking restaurant (lovely puddings), a marvellous choice of up to eight well kept real ales, a fine choice of malt whiskies, quite a few wines by the glass, an open fire, and smart uniformed staff; disabled access *(01949) 81361*

332. ⋈ WILMCOTE
Pear Tree Cottage (2 miles off A46 NW of Stratford, via The Ridgeway N (first crossroads E of A46/A422 junction), then right at T)
£58; 5 rms. Charming half-timbered Elizabethan house owned by the same family for three generations, with beams, flagstones, country antiques, a cosy atmosphere, good breakfasts, and sizeable shady gaden; self-catering also; cl 24 Dec-31 Jan; children over 5 *(01789) 205889*

333. ⋈ WALCOTE
Walcote Farm (1.4 miles off A46 E of Alcester; minor rd N at crossroads 2.3 miles E of A46/A435 roundabout, then right at next crossroads)
£45; 3 rms with fine views, 1 with a late 16th-c window. Attractive 16th-c farmhouse in pretty hamlet with plenty of surrounding walks; a warm welcome from friendly owners, log fires in inglenook fireplaces, beams and flagstones, good breakfasts (several local pubs for evening meals), and pretty garden; no smoking; cl Christmas-New Year; children over 5 *(01789) 488264*

334. ⋒ ALCESTER
Ragley Hall (0.7 miles off A46/A435 via A435 and A422)
Privately owned family home of the Marquess and Marchioness of Hertford, this perfectly symmetrical Palladian house stands in nearly a

mile of parkland and formal gardens; excellent baroque plasterwork in Great Hall, fine paintings (inc some modern art) and a mural by Graham Rust; adventure playground, maze and woodland walks in the grounds, many special events inc good outdoor concerts. Meals, snacks, shop, disabled access; cl Mon-Weds, all Oct-Mar; *(01789) 762090* **£6**; grounds also open every day during main school hols. The nearby village of Arrow is attractive and interesting to stroll around, despite some development. Fruit farming around here is much rarer than it used to be, but you can still find delicious fresh dessert plums for sale in Sept. The county's best drive (partly in Worcs) circles this area, via Wixford (the Three Horseshoes has good food), Radford, Inkberrow, Holberrow Green, New End, Kings Coughton, Walcote, Aston Cantlow, Wilmcote and Temple Grafton.

A47

335. ⌂ SWAFFHAM
Strattons *(1.5 miles off A47; Ash Cl, off Lynn St nr centre)*
£100, plus special breaks; 8 interesting, pretty rms. No smoking and environment-friendly Palladian-style villa run by charming warmly friendly owners with comfortable individually decorated drawing rooms, family photographs, paintings, lots of china cats (and several live ones), antiques, patchwork throws, fresh and dried flowers, and open fires; delicious highly imaginative food using local (and home-grown) organic produce, a carefully chosen wine list illustrated with Mrs Scott's own watercolours, and super breakfasts; big cupboard full of toys and games for children; garden with croquet; cl 24-26 Dec; dogs in bedrooms *(01760) 723845*

336. ⚶ KING'S LYNN
(1 mile off A47/A17/A148 bypass)
Once England's fourth-largest town, it's quieter now, with pleasant corners, some attractive Georgian brick buildings, and a few much older places such as the 17th-c Custom House on the quay by the River Purfleet (now home to the Tourist Information Centre), the 15th-c church of St Nicholas (Chapel Lane; attractive for Festival concerts), the South Gates, Red Mount Chapel and the two medieval guildhalls.

MOTORWAY BREAKS

The first of these, the 15th-c St George's Guildhall (King St), is now the town's theatre, and home of the King's Lynn Festival (usually open 10-2pm Mon-Fri, cl bank hols and on concert days so best to ring *(01553) 764864)*. Tales of the Old Gaol House (Sat Market Pl) is a lively journey through the town's rich history, with spirited models, and spooky sights, sounds and smells; usually cl Weds and Thurs Nov-Easter, 25-26 Dec and 1 Jan, but phone to check *(01553) 774297*. There are interesting reconstructed room settings in the Town House Museum (Queen St) and Trues Yard (North St/St Anns St). At Caithness Crystal, you can watch them making glass. Tearoom, factory shop, disabled access; cl Easter Sun, 25-26 Dec, 1-2 Jan; *(01553) 765111/123*; free. Guided walks leave from the Old Gaol House; May-Sept, best to check for details of times and days *(01553) 763044*. On Tues the main market-place has some good crafts stalls; the Olde Maydens Heade there does popular lunches inc OAP bargains.

A49

337. ✕ SELLACK
Lough Pool *(0.9 miles off A49 just W of Ross)*
Attractive black and white timbered cottage in lovely countryside, with a log fire at each end of the beamed central room, flagstones and bunches of dried flowers, other individually decorated rooms leading off, lovely imaginative food, well kept real ales, several malt whiskies, local farm ciders, and a well chosen wine list; cl winter Sun pm, pm 26 Dec; well behaved children in snug or restaurant only *(01989) 730236*

338. ⌨ HOARWITHY
Old Mill *(2 miles off A49 (the incredibly ornate Italianate church is well worth a look))*
£50; 6 cottagey rms. Cream-painted 18th-c building with the mill-race flowing through the flower-filled garden; log fire and books in beamed sitting room, good breakfasts and enjoyable evening meals using local produce where possible, friendly helpful owners, and lots to do nearby; no smoking; disabled access *(01432) 840602*

339. ⌂ GRAFTON
Grafton Villa Farm *(just off A49 S of Hereford)*
£54; 3 pretty rms. Beautifully kept early 18th-c farmhouse with an acre of lawns and garden, panoramic views, and lots of animals; an open fire in lounge, enjoyable hearty breakfasts in large dining room using their own free-range eggs and home-made bread, and friendly owners; no smoking; nearby inn for evening meals; cl Christmas and New Year; self-catering; disabled access *(01432) 268689*

340. ॐ HOPE-UNDER-DINMORE
Hampton Court Gardens *(0.6 miles off A49 S of Leominster; A417)*
In the grounds of a romantic-looking castle (actually a grandly fortified medieval manor), these organic gardens mix old-fashioned formal planted walks interspersed with bridges to little follies, with carefully contrived wilder areas (woods, waterfalls in rocky grottoes), and a classic maze around a small tower. The surrounding parkland gives river walks. Meals and snacks (with produce from the new ornamental kitchen garden), shop, disabled access; cl Mon exc bank hols and Fri and Nov-25 Mar; *(01568) 797777*; £5. The interesting 16th-c Englands Gate over at Bodenham has enjoyable food.

341. ✕ STOCKTON CROSS
Stockton Cross Inn *(0.4 miles off A49 just N of Leominster, via A4112)*
Neatly kept black and white timbered pub with an old-fashioned atmosphere in its heavy-beamed long bar, a huge log fire and woodburner, solid furnishings, a wide choice of enjoyable food, well kept beer, and good welcoming service; seats in garden; cl Sun and Mon pms; children over 6 *(01568) 612509*

342. ॐ ASHTON
Berrington Hall *(0.6 miles off A49 N of Leominster)*
This elegant 18th-c house has a few activities that make it a reliable bet for families, inc quiz sheets and trails to follow going round the house (50p extra), as well as an I Spy sheet (10p) for the beautifully laid out grounds. The house itself has lots of interest; the finely painted ceilings and Regency furnishings are memorably elegant, and the main stairway is splendid. Many rooms are furnished in a way that lets you think they are still in use: there's a fully equipped Victorian nursery and a tiled

MOTORWAY BREAKS

dairy. Also a good adventure playground and a children's orienteering course, and plenty of walks and pathways. Capability Brown laid out the grounds (the house was built by his son-in-law); the most famous feature is the 14-acre lake with picturesque views, and there's also an attractive woodland garden, rows of yew trees, and a walled garden with some venerable apple trees. Meals, snacks, shop, some disabled access; open pm Sat-Weds in Apr-Dec; *(01568) 615721*; £5. The picturesque old Stockton Cross Inn (off A49 S) has good food.

343. ⌂ ✕ BRIMFIELD
Roebuck *(0.3 miles off A49, in village)*
£70; 3 rms. Smart country dining pub with an impressive inglenook fireplace in the quiet, old-fashioned locals' snug, two other civilised bars with small open fires, a cosy no smoking dining room, excellent food, well kept real ales, carefully chosen wines, and courteous staff *(01584) 711230*

344. ⌂ LUDLOW
Dinham Hall *(1.7 miles off A49; Dinham, which is rd to the Teme bridge below the Castle)*
£140; 4 individually decorated rms, 2 in cottage. Late 18th-c manor house in quiet walled gardens opposite the ruins of Ludlow Castle, with restful lounges, open fires, and period furnishings, friendly, helpful staff, and creative french cooking in the elegant no smoking restaurant; dogs in bedrooms *(01584) 876464*

345. ﷺ LUDLOW
(on A49)
Beautiful 12th-c town packed with lovely ancient buildings, especially down Broad St; the most famous is the lavishly carved and timbered Feathers Hotel on the Bull Ring. The Broadgate, the only one of the town's 13th-c gates to have survived, is interesting. Quite a few antiques shops, and they're proud of their food here, with a Sept food and wine festival (usually 2nd wk – check on *(01584) 861586*). Outstanding restaurants we can recommend are the Merchant House (62 Lower Corve St, *(01584) 875438*) and Olive Branch (2/4 Old St, *(01584) 874314*); the Unicorn (bottom of Corve St) and Church Inn (Buttercross) do nice pub lunches. If you've time for a break here, the Norman castle perched on its crag over the river is well worth a look

(01584) 873355. The pinnacled St Laurence church, with magnificent carvings, is an enclave of peace tucked behind the Buttermarket. The 13th-c/15th-c Castle Lodge (Castle Sq, *(01584) 878098*, usually open daily) is reputed to have more wood panelling than any other house in England (and has persian carpets for sale).

346. ✕ ⋈ BROMFIELD
Cookhouse Café Bar & Clive Restaurant With Rooms
(just off A49 NW of Ludlow)
£70; once the home of Clive of India, this handsome brick house looks from the outside like an immaculately maintained Georgian home, but inside is smartly contemporary and brightly modernised: fresh flowers on the sleek space-age bar counter, newspapers to read, and light wooden tables, and a cosier high-ceilinged back room with huge brick fireplace, exposed stonework, and soaring beams and rafters; very good well presented food in the café-bar style dining room, and a big open kitchen behind a stainless steel counter at one end; open all day, seats on secluded terrace outside, and now have 15 bedrooms; cl 25 Dec pm; disabled access *(01584) 856565*

347. ⋈ STREFFORD
Strefford Hall Farm (0.2 miles off A49; minor rd E, just under a mile N of A489 junction – farm is then on right)
£50; 3 rms. No smoking Victorian stone-built farmhouse surrounded by 360 acres of working farm; woodburner in sitting room, good breakfasts, and lots of walks; cl Christmas and New Year; disabled access; dogs welcome in bedrooms *(01588) 672383*

348. ✕ CHURCH STRETTON
Acorn Wholefood (0.2 miles off A49; Sandford Ave, on left)
Simple, unpretentious family-run restaurant with friendly service in several no smoking rooms, good filling food (mostly vegetarian) changing daily, delicious puddings and soups, and cream teas with a choice of around 30 teas; cl Weds-Thurs (but open Thurs during school hols), Nov-Feb; children must be well behaved *(01694) 722495*

MOTORWAY BREAKS

349. ⋈ ALL STRETTON
Jinlye (1.6 miles off A49; Castle Hill, off B4370 in village)
£60, plus special breaks; 7 spacious comfortable rms with lovely views. Charming 16th-c house in large grounds surrounded by National Trust land; log fires in the comfortable lounges (one has an inglenook fireplace, lots of heavy beams, and a mix of interesting furniture), good home cooking in big no smoking dining room, enjoyable breakfasts, and friendly owners; self-catering also; children over 12; disabled access *(01694) 723243*

350. ⋈ WESTON
Citadel (1.4 miles off A49, past Park entrance)
£90; 3 rms in twin turrets. Fine castellated house overlooking Hawkstone Park, with country-house atmosphere, baby grand piano and unusual strapwork ceiling in the elegant sitting room, full-sized table in snooker room, enjoyable food (bring your own wine) in no smoking dining room, and welcoming owners; cl Christmas and Easter; no children *(01630) 685204*

351. ☆ HAWKSTONE PARK
Hawkstone Park Follies (0.5 miles off A49 Shrewsbury—Whitchurch)
Delightful place, 100 acres of steeply wooded parkland, with various follies, the ruins of a medieval castle, intricate arches and passageways hewn out of the rock. The grottoes and gardens were constructed by the Hill family in the 18th c. There are spectacular views, not least from the top of the obelisk, which is said on clear days to offer views of 13 counties. There's a fantastic underground grotto with tales told by an eerily-convincing laser-powered animatron. You may need a torch for some of the caves and tunnels (some of these are closed in Jan). Dogs on leads are allowed. Meals, snacks, shop, limited disabled access (no charge for wheelchairs but you can't go much further than the picnic area); open wknds Jan-Mar, daily except Mon and Tues Apr/May/Sept/Oct, and every day June-Aug, plus some dates around Christmas; *(01939) 200611*; £5.75 adults. The Caspian Bar of the Hawkstone Park Hotel has good value food.

A51

352. ⌂ HOPWAS
Oak Tree Farm (just off A51 W of Tamworth; Hints Rd)
£85; 8 comfortable, spacious and pretty rms. Carefully restored no smoking farmhouse with elegant little lounge, fresh flowers, an attractive breakfast room, a friendly atmosphere, enjoyable breakfasts, gardens overlooking the River Tame, indoor swimming pool and steam room; cl Christmas-New Year; no children; dogs welcome in bedrooms *(01827) 56807*

353. ✕ SALT
Holly Bush (0.3 miles off A51, 1.3 miles NW of A518)
Thatched house dating in part from the 14th c, with pretty hanging baskets and a big back lawn, some ancient beams in several cosy spreading areas, a more modern back extension, coal fires, extremely good popular food (the daily specials are the thing to go for), Sun roasts, and well kept ales; children in eating area if eating; bar food all day Sat-Sun; disabled access *(01889) 508234*

354. ⌂ WORLESTON
Rookery Hall (1.5 miles off A51/A500 roundabout N of Nantwich, via B5074)
£110, plus special breaks; 46 individually decorated rms. Fine early 19th-c hotel in 38 acres of lovely parkland, with elegant lounges, log fires, intimate panelled restaurant with enjoyable food, and friendly service; disabled access; dogs in Coach House bedrooms *(01270) 610016*

355. ✕ BUNBURY
Dysart Arms (1.4 miles off A51 via Alpraham, S of A49 junction; Bowes Gate Rd)
By the village church, this neat former farmhouse has a civilised, old-fashioned atmosphere, log fires, lots of antique furniture, cosy alcoves, a no smoking library area, well kept ales and house wines, interesting food, friendly service, and tables in lovely elevated big garden; cl 25 Dec; children over 10 in evenings; disabled access *(01829) 260183*

MOTORWAY BREAKS

356. ✕ ⇌ WETTENHALL
Boot & Slipper *(2.4 miles off A51 Calveley-Alpraham, via Long Lane NE)*
£48; 4 attractive rms with showers. Pleasant 16th-c coaching inn on small country lane, with low beams and big log fire in quiet bars, a relaxed friendly atmosphere, and good breakfasts; children over 11 *(01270) 528238*

357. ✕ ⇌ COTEBROOK
Alvanley Arms *(1.9 miles off A51, via A49 N of Tarporley)*
£65; 7 rms. Handsome 400-year-old sandstone inn with pleasant beamed rooms (three areas are no smoking), big open fire, a chintzy little hall, shire horse décor (pictures, photographs, horseshoes, horse brasses, harness and bridles), generous helpings of good food, and a garden with lake and trout; shire horse centre and country park next door (free for residents) *(01829) 760200*

A52

358. ⋇ WAINFLEET
Batemans Brewery *(0.7 miles off A52 SW of Skegness; Mill Lane, just off B1195)*
Displays, models and an audio-guide take you through the brewing process, and there's a collection of thousands of beer bottles from all around the world. You can also go on a guided tour of this classic family-run traditional brewery (3pm daily, no disabled access). A games room has traditional pub games such as quoits, ring the bull and skittles, while outdoors you can have a go at croquet, giant draughts, and Connect Four. Meals, snacks, shop, disabled access to visitor centre; cl 25 Dec and 1 Jan; *(01754) 882009*; £2 (£4.95 with brewery tour, £8.95 in the evening).

A53

359. ✕ ⇌ LEEK
Number 64 *(just off A53; 64 St Edward St (A520))*
£85; grade II listed Georgian building renovated and restored with great

style and sympathy; at the front entrance to one side is Cottage Delight selling a range of pickles, preserves and so forth, and on the other side, a speciality food shop; upstairs coffee lounge, lovely ground-floor restaurant with fine doors to a landscaped garden, and wine bar in the original cellar (evening meals Tues-Fri); delicious modern cooking, carefully chosen wine list plus bottled beers and cocktails, and caring, knowledgeable staff; seats outside; cl Sun pm, Mon *(01538) 381900*

360. 🕸 MEERBROOK
Tittesworth reservoir (just off A53 (and A523) N of Leek)
Large reservoir with visitor centre and restaurant, nature trails and bird hides, adventure playground and a sensory garden for the partially sighted; restaurant, shop; cl 25 Dec; *(01538) 300400*. The Three Horseshoes on nearby Blackshaw Moor is a reliable food stop.

A55

361. 🛏 ROWTON
Rowton Hall (1.2 miles off A55; A41 S, then village signed right)
£150, plus wknd breaks; 38 attractive rms. 18th-c country house in eight acres of award-winning gardens with tennis courts and croquet lawn; conservatory lounge, comfortable bar, log fires, a relaxed atmosphere, and smart oak-panelled restaurant; swimming pool, gym, sauna and solarium; children must be over 6 to use health club; disabled access *(01244) 335262*

362. 🛏 LLANSANFFRAID GLAN CONWY
*Old Rectory Country House (1.7 miles off A55 **junction 19** via A470 S)*
£169 inc dinner, plus special breaks; 6 deeply comfortable rms. Georgian house in pleasant gardens with fine views over Conwy estuary, Conwy Castle and Snowdonia; delightful public rms with flowers, antiques and family photos, delicious food of the highest restaurant standards, and marvellous wines; good breakfasts, warmly friendly staff; cl 15 Dec-15 Jan; children under 9 months or over 5; dogs in coach house only *(01492) 580611*

MOTORWAY BREAKS

363. 🕉 CONWY
Conwy Castle *(1.5 miles off A55 **junction 17** via A547)*
One of the best known in Wales, and one of the most important examples of military architecture in the whole of Europe. Built for Edward I in 1283-9, it's very well preserved, still looking exactly as a medieval fortress should – despite the ravages of the Civil War and beyond. There's an exhibition on Edward and the other castles he built. The tops of the turrets offer fine panoramic views; the most dramatic views of the castle itself are from the other side of the estuary. Shop; cl 24-26 Dec, 1 Jan; *(01492) 592358*; £3.50, joint ticket with Plas Mawr £6.50; Cadw.

364. ⍰ CONWY
Sychnant Pass House *(2.5 miles off A55 **junction 16** via Sychnant Pass Rd towards Conwy through Dwygyfylchi and Capelulo)*
£80; 10 rms. Victorian house in two acres among the foothills of the Snowdonia National Park; big comfortable sitting rooms, log fires, a relaxing, friendly atmosphere, and enjoyable food (the restaurant is open to non-residents, too); dogs welcome away from restaurant *(01492) 596868*

365. ✕ COLWYN BAY
Pen-y-Bryn *(1.5 miles off A55 junction 20 via B5113 S; Wentworth Ave)*
Big modern bar with plenty of space, well spaced tables in varying sizes, oriental rugs on pale stripped boards, big pot plants and a profusion of pictures, shelves of books, two coal fires, and thoughtful friendly service; interesting modern food, well kept real ales, thoughtfully chosen wines, proper coffee, and freshly squeezed orange machine; big windows look down over the town to the sea (with a telescope), and there are tables out on terraces *(01492) 533360*

A57

366. ⍰ LINCOLN
Carline *(0.5 miles off A57, via B1273 Yarborough Rd, turn right into Carline Rd)*
£48, plus special breaks; 9 well equipped rms. Spotlessly kept and com-

fortable double-fronted no smoking Edwardian guesthouse 5 mins from the cathedral, with helpful and cheerful owners, quiet dining/sitting rooms, and fine breakfasts; cl Christmas and New Year; children over 3 *(01522) 530422*

A58

367. ⌂ BROMLEY CROSS
Last Drop Village Hotel (2.5 miles off A58, via A676 and B6472)
£88; 128 rms. Big well equipped hotel complex cleverly integrated into olde-worlde pastiche village complete with stone-and-cobbles street of gift and tea shops, bakery, etc, even a spacious creeper-covered pub with lots of beamery and timbering, popular buffet, and heavy tables out on attractive flagstoned terrace; disabled access; dogs in bedrooms *(01204) 591131*

A59

368. ⌂ KNARESBOROUGH
Newton House Hotel (A59 nr centre; York Pl)
£80, plus special breaks; 11 newly refurbished, very well equipped rms. Elegant family-run 18th-c house close to the river and market square, with a warm welcome for guests of all ages, comfortable sitting room with magazines, books, sweets and fresh fruit, and good generous english breakfasts in no smoking dining room; no evening meals but plenty of places a short walk away; cl 1 wk Christmas; dogs in bedrooms and public sitting room/bar; bowls and blankets available *(01423) 863539*

369. ☗ RUFFORD
Rufford Old Hall (on A59)
Lovely timber-framed Tudor house built by the Hesketh family in the 16th c, with an intricate hammer beam roof in the Great Hall, and impressive collections of 17th-c Lancashire oak furniture, and 16th-c arms, armour and tapestries. Some later rooms too; audio tour. Meals, snacks, shop, disabled access to ground floor and grounds; house cl am, Thurs-Fri, and Nov-mid Apr, garden and tearoom cl Thurs-Fri, and

MOTORWAY BREAKS

25 Dec-mid Apr; *(01704) 821254*; £4.70, £2.60 garden only; NT. The Red Lion over in Mawdesley has good food.

370. ⋈ LANGHO
Northcote Manor *(just off A59; Northcote Rd, just W of A666 roundabout)*
£130, plus special breaks; 14 attractive rms with antiques and board games, reached up a fine stairway. In pretty countryside, this neatly kept red brick Victorian house is more of a restaurant-with-rooms, with beams and oak panelling, big log fires, and two comfortable lounges, wonderful breakfasts, and delicious food in the civilised dining room; cl 25 Dec and 1 Jan; partial disabled access *(01254) 240555*

371. ✕ DOWNHAM
Assheton Arms *(0.7 miles off A59; village signed)*
Charmingly set dining pub in prettily preserved village, with rambling beamed bar, a massive stone fireplace, no smoking area, popular bar food (lots of good fresh fish dishes), well kept real ales, and decent wines; cl first wk Jan *(01200) 441227*

372. ✕ SAWLEY
Spread Eagle *(0.6 miles off A59; village signed)*
Proficiently run dining pub with light and airy continental-feeling main bar (partly no smoking), comfortable banquette seating, plenty of paintings and prints and lovely photographs of local views, a roaring winter coal fire, big picture windows overlooking a pretty stretch of the River Ribble, and well kept real ales and well chosen wines; highly thought of imaginative food, and attentive, smartly dressed staff; 12th-c Cistercian abbey ruins opposite, and pub is handy for Forest of Bowland; cl Sun pm, Mon *(01220) 441202*

373. ✕ ⋈ BOLTON ABBEY
Devonshire Arms *(just off A59/B6160 roundabout)*
£220, plus special breaks; 41 individually furnished rms with thoughtful extras. Close to the priory itself and in lovely countryside, this civilised former coaching inn owned by the Duke of Devonshire has been carefully furnished with fine antiques and paintings from Chatsworth; log fires, impeccable service, beautifully presented imaginative food in ele-

gant Burlington restaurant and more informal brasserie and bar, and super breakfasts; health centre; children over 12 in restaurant; disabled access; dogs in some bedrooms; not near restaurants *(01756) 710441*

374. 🕍 BOLTON ABBEY
***Bolton Abbey** (0.7 miles off A59 via B6160)*
Beautiful spot in lovely rolling wooded parkland on a knoll above the River Wharfe. Most of the priory buildings, dating from the 12th to the 16th c, are in ruins, but the central core of the main church is still used for Sunday services. 19th-c additions such as stained glass (some by Pugin) and murals oddly don't strike a false note. The car park gets rather full in summer. The Devonshire Arms on the way is very fine for lunch. Attractive walks lead off in most directions: the landscape has a lowland beauty, with the ruined abbey, the turf banks of the Wharfe and the oaks of the Strid Wood.

375. 🛏 KNARESBOROUGH
***Dower House** (on A59, just W of B6165; Bond End)*
£75, plus special breaks; 31 clean, comfortable rms. Creeper-clad 15th-c former dower house with attractively furnished public rooms of some character, good food in Terrace Restaurant, super breakfasts, helpful service, and leisure and health club; partial disabled access; dogs in annexe bedrooms only *(01423) 863302*

A60

376. 🕍 NEWSTEAD ABBEY
(0.8 miles off A60 at Ravenshead, via B6020 Blidworth Rd)
Splendid former home of Lord Byron, in gorgeously romantic grounds; many of his possessions can still be seen. Rooms are decorated in a variety of styles from medieval through to Victorian, and there are substantial remains of the original priory. Adventure playground, and dressing up for children. Meals, snacks, summer shop, limited disabled access; house cl am and Oct-Mar, grounds cl 25 Dec and last Fri in Nov only; *(01623) 455900*; house and gardens £6, gardens only £3. The Horse & Groom in the attractive nearby village of Linby is a useful stop, as is the Griffins Head at Papplewick (B683/B6011).

MOTORWAY BREAKS

377. ⌂ BLIDWORTH
Holly Lodge (0.2 miles off A60 via Rickett Lane towards Blidworth (first turning off A60 N of A6020))
£56; 4 neat, comfortable rms in converted stables. Victorian hunting lodge in 15 acres with fine country views, a woodland walk, and tennis; log fire in sitting room, a relaxed and friendly atmosphere, light suppers if ordered (local restaurants and pubs close by), good breakfasts, and helpful owners; no smoking; children at owners' discretion *(01623) 793853*

A61

378. ✕ WOOLLEY MOOR
White Horse (2 miles off A61 at Stretton; B6041 W, fork right into B6036; turn left into Badger Lane)
Popular old pub run by very friendly people – and much liked by locals; very good food (all Sun afternoon, not Sun evening) using best local produce, lots of daily specials, decent wines and beers, conservatory, lovely view from garden (pleasant Ashover Valley walks), good play area; disabled access *(01246) 590319*

379. ☸ HAREWOOD
Harewood House & Bird Garden (on A61)
The area's most magnificent stately home. The 18th-c exterior is splendidly palatial, and inside is some glorious restored Robert Adam plasterwork. Fine Chippendale furnishings, exquisite Sèvres and chinese porcelain, and paintings by Turner, El Greco, Bellini, Titian and Gainsborough. Capability Brown designed the grounds which stretch for well over a mile, with very pleasing lakeside and woodland walks, a spectacular formal cascade, an outstanding collection of rhododendron species and other more recently introduced Himalayan and chinese plants, and the famous landscaped bird garden (you could spend half a day in just this part). Charles Barry's Terrace has an excellent gallery with contemporary art and crafts. Try to visit the 15th-c church, with a splendid array of tombs, and a curious tunnel under the wall of the churchyard, so that servants could arrive unseen by sensitive souls. The adventure playground is first-class. Meals, snacks, shop, disabled access; cl Nov-Mar (exc wknds Nov-Dec); *(0113) 218 1010*; £9.50 everything, £6.75 bird garden and

grounds only (please quote reference 434 with discount voucher, which excludes Sun and bank hols). The Harewood Arms opposite has good food, and just N Wharfedale Grange has pick-your-own fruit.

380. 🕸 HARROGATE
Harlow Carr (1.5 miles off A61 via B6162 W, then right on Crag Lane)
Now one of the Royal Horticultural Society's gardens, nearly 60 acres of lawns, streams, pools, rockeries, rhododendrons, woodland, spring bulbs and many other interesting plants. *Gardens Through Time* consists of seven historical gardens created in styles typical from 1800 to 1970. Also a museum of gardening, model village and scented garden, and courses and workshops. The finest strolling ground near Harrogate and getting quite busy these days, though still a place of real peace and fresh moorland air out of season, when the excellent collection of heathers comes into its own. Good meals and snacks, plant centre, disabled access; (01423) 565418; £5.50. The New Inn on the B6162, and the adjacent Harrogate Arms, also have good value food.

381. 🕸 HARROGATE
(on A61/A59)
This elegant and self-confident inland resort has kept its Victorian spa-town atmosphere, despite now filling many of its handsome hotels with up-to-date conferences and so forth. The layout of the town is very gracious, and you couldn't ask for better shops (interesting antiques and some top-notch specialist shops). Almost every available space is filled with colourful plant displays, as if to shake off the gloom of the dark stone buildings. The first thing a visitor notices is the great sweep of The Stray, open parkland which runs right along and through the S side of the centre. The first sulphur well was discovered in the 16th c and named the Tewit Well, after the local word for the lapwings which led a local sporting gent to ride into what was then a smelly bog. It's up on The Stray, grandly encased in what looks like an Italianate mausoleum. The elegant buildings of the compact central area run down from here to the pleasantly laid-out Valley Gardens, very Victorian, with a curlicued central teahouse. The relaxed tempo of the place, and the clean bracing climate (it's quite high on the moors), have made it a popular retirement area. Besides the places detailed, the Drum & Monkey (fish restaurant/wine bar, Montpellier Gardens) and Hedleys

MOTORWAY BREAKS

(wine bar, Montpellier Parade) are good for lunch or a snack; the café of the Theatre Royal is also pleasant, as is the Lascelles Arms out in Follifoot.

382. ⌂ HARROGATE
Alexa House (on A61 N of centre; 29 Ripon Rd)
£70, plus winter breaks; 13 rms, some in former stable block. Attractive Georgian house with friendly staff, comfortable lounge, good home cooking in no smoking dining room, and marvellous breakfasts; good disabled access; dogs welcome in bedrooms *(01423) 501988*

383. 🐾 RIPLEY
Ripley Castle (just off A61 N of Harrogate)
Beautifully picturesque, in the same family for 26 generations. Most of the current building dates from the 16th c, inc the tower housing a collection of Royalist armour. For some the main attraction is the splendid gardens, the setting for a national collection of hyacinths and (under glass) a fine tropical plant collection; also lakeside walk. Very good meals and snacks, shops inc a superb delicatessen, some disabled access; cl Sept-May (exc Tues, Thurs and wknds), and 25-26 Dec and 1 Jan; *(01423) 770152*; £6, £4 gardens only. The attractive village was rebuilt around a french theme in the 1820s, and consequently has a rather continental feel; the Boars Head Hotel is a fine old place for lunch.

384. ⌂ RIPLEY
Boars Head (just off A61 N of Harrogate)
£120, plus special breaks; 25 charmingly decorated rms. In a delightful estate village, this fine old coaching inn has a relaxed, welcoming atmosphere, with comfortable sofas in attractively decorated lounges, long flagstoned bar, notable wines by the glass, fine food in bar and restful dining room, and unobtrusive service; games, videos and special menus for children; disabled access; dogs in some bedrooms (inc bed, bonio and bowls) and some public areas *(01423) 771888*

385. ✕ BREARTON
Malt Shovel (2.5 miles E off A61 just N of Ripley)
Popular village pub with friendly, helpful licensees, heavily beamed rooms with open fires and lively hunting prints, enjoyable bar food, well

kept real ales, and a fine choice of malt whiskies and wines; no food Sun pm, cl Mon *(01423) 862929*

386. ⋈ RIPON
Ripon Spa *(1 mile off A61, via B6265, turning right into High Skellgate (A6108) in centre, then next left; Park St)*
£105, plus special breaks; 40 individually furnished rms, many overlooking the grounds. Neatly kept friendly and comfortable Edwardian hotel with seven acres of charming gardens, yet only a short walk from the centre; attractive public rooms, winter log fires, and good food in bar and restaurant; disabled access; dogs in bedrooms *(01765) 602172*

387. ⋈ MARKINGTON
Hob Green *(2 miles off A61 S of Ripon; keep on through village)*
£115, plus winter breaks; 12 well equipped pretty rms. Lovely gardens and over 800 acres of rolling countryside surround this charming 18th-c stone hotel; comfortable and pretty lounge and garden room, log fires, antique furniture, fresh flowers, relaxed atmosphere, good interesting food, decent choice of wines, and friendly service; dogs in bedrooms and main hall *(01423) 770031*

388. 🐾 FOUNTAINS ABBEY
Fountains Abbey & Studley Royal Water Garden *(3.5 miles off A61 via B6265 through Ripon)*
The largest monastic ruin in the country, this romantic place was founded in 1132 by Cistercian monks, in a delightful riverside setting. Most of the remains are 12th c, but the proud main tower is 15th c. Opposite are the lovely landscaped gardens begun by John Aislabie in the 1760s, which include ornamental temples and follies, formal water gardens, lakes aflutter with waterfowl, and 400 acres of deer park. The most beautiful approach is through the extraordinarily ornate Victorian church at the far end (may be restoration in progress, best to phone for opening), and this 'back-door' entrance is the most tranquil too; you can also explore three floors of the 12th-c watermill that produced flour for the monks. A helpful modern visitor centre blends in and doesn't spoil the view. Meals, snacks, shop, good disabled access; cl Fri Nov-Jan, and 24-25 Dec; *(01765) 608888*; £5.50, deer park – an

MOTORWAY BREAKS

excellent strolling ground – free; NT. The very civilised Sawley Arms in Sawley just W does good food.

A63

389. 🏛 HULL
The Deep (just off A63 in centre on waterfront; Tower St, Sammy's Point)
This hi-tech exhibition on the sea offers far more than your average aquarium. It's an astonishing building; all the walls are at an angle, and the main bit juts out 100 ft above the Humber estuary. The focus is on the world's oceans: how they were formed, how marine life has developed, and how they're affected by outer space, the equator, and by man; lots of interactives, and the latest lighting and effects bring it all to life. The Polar Gallery has a pair of real ice walls, and they have around 500 species of fish from around the planet, some of which take their chances alongside the sharks in their gigantic showpiece aquarium. A futuristic centre has activities and experiments, inc the chance to pilot a submarine or work out a crew's diet. Meals, snacks, shop, disabled access; cl 24-25 Dec; (01482) 381000; £6.50 adults.

A64

390. 🛏 YORK
Middlethorpe Hall (just off A64 S bypass W of A19,
via Bishopthorpe Rd)
£194, plus special breaks; 29 elegant rms, most in the adjoining courtyard. Lovely, immaculately restored William III country house just S of the city, with fine gardens and parkland, antiques, paintings and fresh flowers in comfortable, quiet day rooms, and excellent food and service; indoor swimming pool and health and fitness spa; children over 8 (01904) 641241

391. 🛏 YORK
Curzon Lodge (1.7 miles off A64 S bypass, via A1036 towards centre;
23 Tadcaster Rd, Dringhouses)
£69, plus winter breaks; 10 rms, some in former old coach house and

116

stables. Charming early 17th-c house in marvellous spot just S of city centre overlooking Knavesmire racecourse, with an attractive and comfortable drawing room, a sunny farmhouse dining room (enjoyable breakfasts), and parking in grounds; no smoking throughout; cl Christmas; children over 7 *(01904) 703157*

392. 🎎 KIRKHAM ABBEY
Kirkham Priory (0.7 miles off A64 NE of York)
Remains of Augustinian priory in an attractive quiet spot by the River Derwent; finely sculpted lavatorium, graceful arcaded cloister, and handsome 13th-c gatehouse with some finely carved sculptures and shields. Snacks, shop, disabled access; cl wkdys Nov-Mar, 25-26 Dec and 1 Jan; *(01653) 618768*; £2.70. The Stone Trough overlooking the ruins has good food (not Mon exc bank hols), and a pleasant path meanders S by a placid stretch of the River Derwent, to Howsham Bridge and beyond.

393. 🎎 CASTLE HOWARD
Castle Howard (2.5 miles off A64 SW of Malton, via Welburn)
Magnificent 18th-c palace designed by Sir John Vanbrugh, who up to then had no architectural experience whatsoever, but went on to create Blenheim Palace. The striking 300-ft long façade is topped with a marvellous painted and gilded dome, an unforgettable sight beyond the lake as you approach from the N. Splendid apartments, sculpture gallery and long gallery (192 ft long to be exact), magnificent chapel with stained glass by Burne-Jones, and beautiful paintings inc a Holbein portrait of Henry VIII. The grounds are impressive but inviting, inc the domed Temple of the Four Winds by Vanbrugh, a beautiful rose garden with over 2,000 roses, a notable woodland garden, and the family mausoleum designed by Hawksmoor. There's a good unobtrusive adventure playground. Meals, snacks, shop, disabled access; cl Nov to mid-Feb; *(01653) 648333*; £9. A grand public road runs through the grounds, from Slingsby on the B1257; the vast estate is also threaded by a few public footpaths which gain glimpses of the great house and the landscaped parts of its grounds. The Bay Horse at nearby Terrington has good food.

MOTORWAY BREAKS

394. 🏠 MALTON
Eden Camp *(1 mile off A64; A169 N then first left on Edenhouse Rd)*
Created around a former prisoner of war camp, this popular place brings wartime Britain vividly to life. Each hut takes a different theme, from the rise of the Nazis, to the Blitz, and the role of women in wartime. One hut has all the front pages of the war, while six others take a chronological overview of its politics and events. A look at other wars includes a re-created trench from World War I, and displays on conflicts since 1945. Some displays attempt to create a tangible impression with sights, sounds and smells: there's a bombed-out street, reconstructed period shops, and Bomber Command ops rooms. Children enjoy the 20-minute puppet Music Hall show with most of the well known wartime songs. Outside are quite a few wartime and military vehicles, and an assault course includes a section for younger children. Dogs are welcome on a lead (except in café). Meals and snacks in NAAFI, picnic areas, shop, disabled access; cl 24 Dec to mid-Jan; *(01653) 697777*; £4.50.

A65

395. 🏠 SKIPTON
Skipton Castle *(1 mile off A65/A629 roundabout)*
12th-c, and properly romantic, with sturdy round towers, broad stone steps, and a lovely central flagstoned and cobbled courtyard with a seat around its 350-year-old focal yew tree. One of the best-preserved medieval castles in Europe, it really is remarkable how much is left, interior and all – very few other castles have kept their roofs and stayed habitable. The medieval arched gateway still stands – the word 'Desormais' meaning 'Henceforth' carved above it is the motto of the family who lived here 1310-1676. Meals, snacks, shop; cl Sun am, 25 Dec; *(01756) 792442*; £5.20. The Black Horse opposite is popular for lunch.

396. ✕ ⇌ LONG PRESTON
Maypole *(on A65 towards NW end of village)*
£49.50, plus winter breaks; 6 comfortable rms. Neatly kept 17th-c pub with generous helpings of enjoyable traditional food (and nice breakfasts) in spacious beamed dining room, open fire in lounge bar, real ales, and helpful service; dogs in bedrooms and bar *(01729) 840219*

397. ✗ ⋈ WIGGLESWORTH
Plough (2.1 miles off A65/A682 just SE of Long Preston, via B6478)
£88, plus special breaks; 12 well equipped rms. Friendly and well run early 18th-c country inn with popular food in conservatory restaurant, oak panelled dining room and bar, and lots of little rooms surrounding bar area – some smart and plush, others cosy and friendly; big breakfasts, packed lunches, and views of the Three Peaks; no smoking family room; seats in secluded garden; disabled access *(01729) 840243*

398. ⋔ SETTLE
(just off A65)
The town has wound down a bit in recent years, with many of the old shops gone, but market day (Tues) around the Shambles still makes for an invigorating break from the trunk rd; look out to the right of here for the Folly, an extraordinary 17th-c townhouse. Mary Milnthorpe & Daughter is a good antique jewellery and silver shop, Poppies tearoom provides welcome relief from shopping, and the Golden Lion has good food.

399. ⋈ FEIZOR
Scar Close Farm (a mile off A65 just NW of Settle)
£50, plus special breaks; 4 clean well appointed rms. Friendly converted barn on working farm with big guest lounge, books, magazines and TV, and big breakfasts and homely evening meals – packed lunches, too; lovely quiet countryside; disabled access *(01729) 823496*

A66

400. ✗ MIDDLESBROUGH
Purple Onion (0.2 miles off A66 from A172 roundabout; head towards Cleveland Centre but from Wilson St turn left not right into Corporation Rd)
Bustling Victorian building filled with bric-a-brac, ornate mirrors, and house plants, an informal atmosphere, downstairs cellar bar with live music, particularly good interesting food, friendly staff, and decent wine list; cl Sun, Mon; disabled access *(01642) 222250*

MOTORWAY BREAKS

401. ✕ ⋈ GRETA BRIDGE
Morritt Arms *(just off A66 on village loop)*
£87.50, plus special breaks; 23 rms. Smart, old-fashioned coaching inn where Dickens stayed in 1838 to research for *Nicholas Nickleby* – one of the interesting bars has a colourful Dickensian mural; comfortable lounges, fresh flowers, good open fires, and pleasant garden; coarse fishing; pets allowed; attractive garden with children's play area; disabled access; dogs in bedrooms, bar and lounge *(01833) 627232*

402. ⋔ APPLEBY
(well signed just off A66)
This riverside village is well worth a turn-off; the main street, rising from the harmonious 12th-c church to the castle, is still a grand sight despite the cars, with a good few handsome buildings inc a lovely courtyard of almshouses, and pleasant strolls by the River Eden. The Royal Oak is useful for a pub lunch. If you've time to spare, Appleby Castle is interesting, with one of the best-preserved Norman keeps in the country (the rest of the buildings are later additions); terrific views from the ramparts. The Clifford family lived here for nearly 700 years, though they moved later to the grander house next door; the Great Hall has recently been renovated. A Conservation Centre in the attractive grounds has a big collection of birds, waterfowl and farm animals, in a lovely setting above the river. Meals, snacks, shop, limited disabled access; usually open Easter-end Sept but best to check; *(017683) 53823*; £5. Appleby Manor (Roman Rd, parallel to A66 between the town access rds) is a very friendly family-run hotel with 31 well equipped rms in the original house (the nicest), coach house annexe or modern wing. Fine views, log fires in two of the three comfortable lounges, relaxed bar with wide range of whiskies, excellent service, good interesting food in panelled restaurant, and leisure centre; enjoyed by families; cl 24-26 Dec; disabled access; £128 *(01768) 351571*.

403. ⋔ BROUGHAM
Brougham Castle *(just off A66 S of Penrith, via B6262)*
A sturdy Norman ruin on steep lawns above riverside sheep pastures; climb to the top of the keep for the best view. Traces of Roman remains too, with a small exhibition of tombstones. Snacks, shop, disabled access; cl Nov-Mar; *(01768) 862488*; £2.20; EH. Under a mile

further on the B6262, Brougham Hall Craft Centre has lots of different craft workshops inc metal workers, furniture restoration, smoked foods and home-made chocolates, in the attractive stone courtyard of a 15th-c hall. Plenty to see around the house and grounds inc Cromwellian chapel and a collection of dolls and dolls' houses. Meals, snacks, disabled access; cl 25 Dec; *(01768) 868184*; £2 for Hall.

404. 🏌 DACRE

Dalemain Historic House & Gardens *(2 miles from A66 via A592; brown signs)*
A medieval, Tudor and Georgian house, so an appealing variety of periods and style. Some rooms are grand, others are charming, with splendid furnishings and paintings and some bits for children to enjoy too. Particularly interesting Chinese Room with hand-painted wallpaper. There are deer in the carefully landscaped park with mountain views. Atmospheric restaurant in a medieval hall, shop, plant centre, limited disabled access; open Sun-Thurs 20 Mar-Oct; *(017684) 86450*; £6, £4 grounds; discount voucher not valid for special events. The village church has pre-Norman sculpture, and quaint medieval stone bears in the graveyard. The Horse & Farrier has good value food.

405. 🏌 KESWICK

(a mile off A66, via A5271)
In this busy tourist centre, full of breeches, boots and backpacks in high season, the Dog & Gun (Lake Rd/Main St) is very popular, with straightforward bar food all day, a log fire and a welcome for children. Maysons (Lake Rd) is a busy restaurant with an interesting range of highly enjoyable food; cl Weds in Jan/Feb, cl evenings Nov-Easter; partial disabled access. The Lakeside Tea Gardens (Lake Rd) have home baking, lots for children, pleasant modern furniture and crockery inside, and in a garden with trees and chaffinches; cl wknds in Jan. George Fisher (Borrowdale Rd) is a good big outdoors shop. Among quite a lot of tourist places here, we like Cars of the Stars (Standish St), the surprisingly interesting Pencil Museum (Southey Works), Puzzling Place (Museum Sq) and the odd Teapottery (Central Car Park Rd – this one's free).

MOTORWAY BREAKS

406. ✕ ⋈ BASSENTHWAITE LAKE
Pheasant (just off A66 on loop rd just E of B5291)
A good stop for a bar lunch, a restaurant meal, or overnight stay (16 comfortable rms, **£140**, *(017687) 76234*). This civilised inn has a delightfully old-fashioned pubby bar, restful lounges with open fire, antiques, fresh flowers and comfortable armchairs, and interesting gardens merging into surrounding fellside woodlands; cl 25 Dec; children over 8; disabled access. Curiously, the lake is the only body of water in the Lake District to be called purely a lake (the others, even Lake Windermere, are all 'waters', 'meres' or 'tarns'). The surrounding scenery lacks the grandeur of the better-known lakes, but in recent springs and summers it's been the hunting ground for England's only ospreys. You can hire rowing boats on it. Off the B5291 (and just 1.4 miles from the A66, signed as Trotters and Friends) is 25-acre Trotters World of Animals, with lots of animals from rare breeds of pigs, cattle and goats, through birds of prey, lizards and snakes, to otters, llamas and gibbons. Throughout the day, at certain times, you might be able to bottle-feed a baby goat, cuddle the rabbits, or have a hawk fly down to your wrist, and helpful uniformed staff are on hand to answer questions. For an extra charge they usually have trailer, tractor and pony rides; there's an adventure playground, and plenty of space for a picnic. Quite a few things are under cover, and in winter they keep up a full range of indoor activities. Their birds of prey centre has the region's only breeding golden eagles and caracaras. Meals, snacks, shop, disabled access; cl wkdys Nov-Jan, and 25 Dec, 1 Jan; *(017687) 76239*; £5.25.

A68

407. ✕ ⋈ CARTERWAY HEADS
Manor House Inn (just off A68 just N of Co Durham border)
£60; popular slate-roofed stone house with fine southerly views over moorland pastures; enticing food from a wide changing menu (served all day now), a partly no smoking restaurant (with a huge collection of jugs), and a friendly atmosphere; comfortable bdrms, nice breakfasts; cl pm 25 Dec *(01207) 255268*

408. ✖ GREAT WHITTINGTON
***Queens Head** (2.9 miles off A68; first right turn heading N from B6318 roundabout, then bear right)*
Simple but civilised stone inn with two beamed, comfortable and neatly furnished rooms, a wide choice of good interesting food, a no smoking restaurant, log fires, well kept real ales, decent wines, and quite a few malt whiskies; cl Mon exc bank hols; children lunchtime only; disabled access *(01434) 672267*

409. ❦ JEDBURGH
***Jedburgh Abbey** (just off A68)*
The most complete of the ruined 12th-c Borders monasteries founded by David I, and an impressive sight despite its town setting. Imposing 86-ft tower, splendid W door, and audio-visual show in visitor centre. Snacks, shop, disabled access; *(01835) 863925*; £4; HS. The Pheasant has good food (and makes a point of having good value pheasant in season). Just off the A68 S of town are the mainly 16th-c ruins of Ferniehurst Castle.

A69

410. ✖ HAYDON BRIDGE
***General Havelock** (on A69)*
Very civilised old stone terraced house with smart stripped-stone back dining room overlooking the Tyne, good interesting bar lunches and stylish restaurant meals from a monthly changing menu, well kept real ales, good wines by the glass, pleasant service, and a friendly local atmosphere; cl Sun pm, Mon; disabled access *(01434) 684283*

411. ⌂ BRAMPTON
***Farlam Hall** (1.8 miles off A69, via A689)*
£265, inc dinner, plus special breaks; 12 comfortable rms. Charmingly Victorian (though parts are much older) and very civilised country house with log fires in spacious lounges, excellent attentive service, good 4-course dinner using fine china and silver, marvellous breakfasts, and peaceful spacious grounds with croquet lawn and small pretty lake; cl 25-30 Dec; children over 5; disabled access; dogs welcome but not to be left alone at any time *(016977) 46234*

MOTORWAY BREAKS

412. 🏃 ✕ ⊨ TALKIN TARN
(0.9 miles off A69 via B6413)
A calm respite from the main rd: country park around lovely partly wooded lake with peaceful mountain views, plenty of space for strolling; nature trail, orienteering and rowing boats; disabled access, teas. Just past here in the pretty village, the cosy Blacksmiths Arms has good bar food, a pretty restaurant, well kept local ales, a great choice of wines by the glass, open fires, and comfortable bedrooms; *(016977) 3452*. Or you can stay at Hullerbank, a nearby comfortable and very friendly no smoking Georgian farmhouse in unspoilt countryside, with a relaxed atmosphere and inglenook fireplace in homely lounge, enjoyable breakfasts, and packed lunch on request; cl Dec-Jan *(016977) 46668*

A74

413. ⊨ LOCKERBIE
Dryfesdale Hotel *(1 mile off A74 junction 17; B7076 N)*
£95, plus wknd breaks; 16 rms, 7 on ground floor. Relaxed and comfortable former manse in five acres, open fire in homely lounge, good food in pleasant restaurant, garden and lovely surrounding countryside, putting and croquet; cl Christmas; good disabled access; dogs in bedrooms *(01576) 202427*

414. ⊨ BEATTOCK
Auchen Castle *(2 miles off A74(M) junction 15; B7076 N)*
£110; 25 pleasantly decorated rms, some in Lodge. Smart but friendly country-house hotel in lovely quiet spot with a trout loch and spectacular hill views, good food, and peaceful comfortable bar *(01683) 300407*

A75

415. ⊨ CLARENCEFIELD
Comlongon Castle *(2.5 miles off A75, via B725 E of Dumfries)*
£150; 14 rms. Magnificent 15th-c castle keep with 18th-c mansion house adjoining – suits of armour and a huge fireplace in oak-panelled great hall, good food in Jacobean dining room, and a relaxing drawing

room; dungeons, battlements, archers' quarters and haunted long gallery; cl first 2 wks Jan *(01387) 870283*

416. ✖ CROSSMICHAEL
Plumed Horse *(3 miles off A75 via A713)*
In an unremarkable building, this simply but attractively decorated restaurant offers perfectly timed and presented modern cooking with quite an emphasis on absolutely fresh fish; especially good value set lunch, charming service, and a short wine list; cl Mon, Sat am, Sun pm; well behaved children welcome, disabled access *(01556) 670333*

417. ⚑ GATEHOUSE OF FLEET
Cally Palace *(2.5 miles off A75 via B727 or B796)*
£176, inc dinner, plus special breaks; 55 rms. 18th-c country mansion, a hotel since 1934, with marble fireplaces and ornate ceilings in the public rooms, relaxed cocktail bar, enjoyable food in elegant dining room (smart dress required), evening pianist and Sat evening dinner dance, helpful friendly staff, 18-hole golf course, croquet and tennis, indoor leisure complex with heated swimming pool, private fishing/boating loch; cl Jan, cl wkdys in Feb; disabled access; dogs welcome in bedrooms *(01557) 814341*

418. ❀ STRANRAER
Castle Kennedy Gardens *(on A75, 4 miles E)*
Prettily set between two lochs (with lots of good walks around), these gardens were first laid out in the early 18th c, then after years of neglect were restored and developed in the 19th. They're particularly admired for their walled garden, rhododendron collection and flowering shrubs. Snacks, shop, limited disabled access; cl Oct–Mar; *(01776) 702024*; £4.

A77

419. ❀ CULZEAN
Culzean Castle *(3 miles off A77, from Kirkoswald; A719)*
(pronounced 'Cullane') A day here is one of the most popular outings in the region. The 18th-c mansion is one of great presence and brilliance, and the grounds (nearly a square mile) are among the finest in

MOTORWAY BREAKS

Britain, lushly planted and richly ornamental, with woods, lake, an abundance of paths, bracing clifftop and shoreline walks, and an 18th-c walled garden. The house was splendidly refashioned by Robert Adam, and has been well restored to show off his work to full effect. Meals, snacks, shop, disabled access; house cl Nov-Apr, park open all year; *(01655) 884455*; £12; NTS. You can stay in rather smart self-contained apartments on the top floor.

A82

420. 🕺 LOCH LOMOND
(alongside A82)
Loch Lomond, and the Trossachs, have recently been designated a National Park. Straddling the Highland-Lowland divide, the park covers 580 square miles, and in spite of being so close to Glasgow and on every coach company's hit list, the loch (Britain's largest freshwater lake) does have a serene beauty that seems unspoilt by the visitors. Wee birdies sing and wild flowers spring – and the water is often calm enough to reflect the mountains. The best views are from the narrower N end. Surprisingly, there aren't many paths: the shoreline track, partly metalled, on the quieter E side, comes closest to the water; the Oak Tree at Balmaha round here serves enterprising food. Cruises round the lake leave from Balloch, as well as from the pretty village of Luss, a good place to hire a boat for pottering about on the water (there's a visitor centre here too).

421. 🛌 BALLACHULISH
Ballachulish House *(0.8 miles off A82 via A828)*
£125, plus special breaks; 8 rms with views. Remote 17th-c house with a friendly atmosphere, elegant rooms, log fires, honesty bar, hearty helpings of good food using local fish and beef, and walled garden, croquet lawn, adjacent golf course; children over 10 *(01855) 811266*

422. 🛌 ONICH
Allt-Nan-Ros *(off A82)*
£110, plus special breaks; 20 rms, many with views over the gardens to the water. Victorian shooting lodge with fine Scottish food, friendly atmosphere, bright airy rooms, and magnificent views across Loch

Linnhe and the gardens; cl Dec/Jan but open New Year; disabled access; dogs in bedrooms *(01855) 821210*

423. ⌂ FORT WILLIAM
Grange (just off A82; Lundavra Rd from SW roundabout, first right into Grange Rd)
£98, plus special breaks; 4 rms with loch views. Charming Victorian house in quiet landscaped gardens with log fire in comfortable lounge, fine breakfasts in dining room overlooking Loch Linnhe, and helpful hard-working owners; cl Nov-Mar; children over 12 *(01397) 705516*

424. ✕ ⌂ FORT WILLIAM
Alexandra (just off A82; The Parade)
Popular hotel in town square with meals and snacks in the Great Food Stop (open all day) and evening restaurant; disabled access *(01397) 702241*

425. ✕ ⌂ SPEAN BRIDGE
Letterfinlay Lodge (on A82 7 miles N of Spean Bridge/A86 junction)
£80, plus special breaks; 13 rms, most with own bthrm. Secluded and genteel family-run country house right on the edge of our East Scotland area and well placed for the west too, with picture window in extensive modern bar overlooking loch; elegantly panelled small cocktail bar, good popular food, friendly attentive service; grounds run down through rhododendrons to the jetty and Loch Lochy; fishing can be arranged; cl Nov-Easter; dogs welcome away from dining room *(01397) 712622*

426. ⌂ DRUMNADROCHIT
Polmaily House (2.5 miles off A82 via A831 W)
£126, plus special breaks; 11 light, elegant rms. Very relaxing and comfortable hotel in 18 acres, with drawing room and library, open fire and excellent food in the no smoking restaurant (wonderful packed lunches too); a happy place for families with well equipped indoor play area with lots of supervised activities, baby sitting and listening, hundreds of children's videos, plenty of ponies and pets, evening children's club, indoor heated swimming pool, tennis, croquet, fishing, boating, and riding; disabled access; dogs in bedrooms *(01456) 450343*

MOTORWAY BREAKS

427. ⌂ INVERNESS
Dunain Park (on A82 SW)
£158; 13 rms inc 6 suites with own lounge. 18th-c Italianate mansion in six acres of well tended gardens and woodland, a short walk from the River Ness and Caledonian Canal; charming owners, traditional homely décor with family photographs and china ornaments, log fires and fresh flowers, wonderful food using home-grown produce and local game, fish and aberdeen angus meat, generous breakfasts, and 200 whiskies; small warm swimming pool, sauna, lots of walks and golf courses nearby; cl 5-21 Jan; disabled access; dogs welcome in bedrooms *(01463) 230512*

428. ⌂ INVERNESS
Bunchrew House (3 miles off A82 via A862)
£140, plus special breaks; 14 individually decorated rms. Friendly 17th-c mansion W of town by Beauly Firth with fine views and landscaped gardens, log fire in the elegant panelled drawing room, and traditional cooking using local produce and local game and venison; cl Christmas; dogs in bedrooms *(01463) 234917*

A83

429. ✗ CAIRNDOW
Loch Fyne Oyster Bar (A83 NW, past loch head)
Relaxed restaurant in converted farm buildings by Loch Fyne, serving good seafood and smoked fish (they have their own smokehouse); reasonably priced wine list and a warm welcome; cl 25-26 Dec and 1-2 Jan; disabled access *(01499) 600236*

430. ⚜ INVERARAY
Inveraray Castle (just off A83 just N of village)
Built in 1745, and still the home of the Duke and Duchess of Argyll, it has particularly impressive state rooms, and a striking hall. Snacks, shop, ground-floor disabled access; cl Fri and 1-2pm in Apr-May and Oct, Sun am, and Nov-Mar; *(01499) 302203*; £5.90. Nearby woodland trails include a view over Loch Fyne from Dun na Cuaiche Tower.

A84

431. 🦌 MINARD
Crarae Gardens *(on A83 SW of Inveraray)*
Lovely gardens noted for their rare ornamental shrubs and rhododendrons, azaleas and conifers, in a beautiful gorge overlooking Loch Fyne. Snacks, shop, and interesting plant sales (summer only), limited disabled access; open all year; *(01546) 886614*; £5; NTS.

432. 🛏 TARBERT
Columba Hotel *(0.8 miles off A83 via A8015 (Harbour St); East Pier Rd)*
£74, plus special breaks; 10 rms. In a peaceful position on Loch Fyne with views of the surrounding hills, this family-run hotel has log fires in the friendly bar and lounge, an informal and relaxed atmosphere, very enjoyable food using fresh local produce, and quite a few malt whiskies; dogs welcome in bedrooms *(01880) 820808*

A84

433. 🦌 BLAIR DRUMMOND
Safari and Adventure Park *(just off A84 N of Stirling)*
Wild animals in natural surroundings, with plenty of other activities included in the price, from gentle rides for younger children to the exhilarating Flying Fox slide over the lake. You can explore part of the water in pedal-boats, and boat trips circle Chimpanzee Island leaving the chimps to enjoy their natural habitat undisturbed. Sea lion and falconry show times are posted in the park. Meals, snacks, shop, disabled access; cl Oct-mid-Mar; *(01786) 841456*; £9.50. The Lion & Unicorn at Thornhill does good family lunches.

434. 🛏 CALLANDER
Poppies *(on A84 (Leny Rd))*
£56, plus special breaks; 9 rms. Small private hotel with excellent food in popular and attractive candlelit dining room, comfortable lounge, helpful friendly owners, and seats in the garden; children over 12; cl Jan; dogs welcome in bedrooms *(01877) 330329*

MOTORWAY BREAKS

435. 🏃 CALLANDER
Kilmahog Woollen Mill (on A84 just N)
Restored flax mill with 250-year-old working wheel, selling cashmere, highland dress, tartans and other woollen gifts and whisky (daily tastings). Meals, snacks, shop; cl 25 Dec; *(01877) 330268*; free. The Lade Inn out here has good food.

A85

436. ✕ ⇌ ST FILLANS
Four Seasons (on A85)
£106; long white family-run hotel with wonderful Loch Earn views, generous helpings of very good scottish food inc super fish and game dishes; lunchtime snacks, too; can eat in Tarken Bar, on terrace or in smarter restaurant; comfortable bdrms and chalets; cl Jan-Feb *(01764) 685333*

A86

437. ✕ ⇌ KINGUSSIE
Cross (0.3 miles off A86; turn N off High St into Ardbroilach Rd then bear left into Tweed Mill Brae)
£130; converted 19th-c stone tweed mill by stream, now a no smoking restaurant-with-rooms, with a relaxed friendly atmosphere, extremely good eclectic scottish cooking (evenings only) using the best local produce, excellent wine list, marvellous cheeses, and super breakfasts; cl Sun-Mon pms and Christmas-Jan; disabled access *(01540) 661166*

A87

438. ⇌ SHIEL BRIDGE
Kintail Lodge (on A87)
£65, plus special breaks; 12 good value big rms. Pleasantly informal and fairly simple former shooting lodge on Loch Duich, with magnificent views, four acres of walled gardens, newly refurbished residents' lounge bar and comfortable sitting room, good well prepared food inc local

seafood in new conservatory restaurant, and fine collection of malt whiskies; cl Jan-mid-Feb; dogs in bedrooms *(01599) 511275*

439. 🚶 DORNIE
Eilean Donan Castle (0.5 miles off A87)
Connected to the mainland by a causeway, and unforgettably beautiful. First built in 1220, destroyed in 1719, and then restored at the beginning of the last century, it's perfectly positioned at the meeting point of Lochs Long, Duich and Alsh. Visitor centre with teas and shop, disabled access; The castle is cl late Nov-mid-Mar, but the shop stays open; *(01599) 555202*; £4.75. The Dornie Hotel has good reasonably priced food inc local seafood.

440. 🛏 PORTREE
Rosedale (0.4 miles off A87 via A855; on Bank St take sharp right down Quay Brae)
£70, plus special breaks; 18 rms, many with harbour views. Built from three fishermen's cottages with lots of passages and stairs, this family-run waterfront hotel has two traditional lounges, small first-floor restaurant with freshly cooked popular food, lots of whiskies in the cocktail bar, helpful staff, marvellous views; cl Nov-Mar; dogs in 3 bedrooms and in lounge *(01478) 613131*

441. 🛏 SKEABOST
Skeabost Country House (2 miles off A87 via A850 W)
£100, plus special breaks; 21 rms, some in annexe in Garden House. Smart and friendly, recently refurbished little hotel in 29 acres of landscaped grounds on the shores of Loch Snizort; 9-hole 18-tee golf course and 8 miles of salmon and trout fishing; log fires, comfortable day rooms, friendly, helpful staff, and good, enjoyable food; cl mid-Jan to Feb; disabled access *(01470) 532202*

A90

442. 🚶 SOUTH QUEENSFERRY
Dalmeny House (just off A90 by B924 junction)
Despite its Tudor Gothic appearance, this splendidly placed house

MOTORWAY BREAKS

dates only from the 19th c – it has a superb hammer beamed roof, as well as fine furnishings, porcelain and portraits. Good walks in the grounds and on the shore. Snacks; open Sun-Tues pms July-Aug; *(0131) 331 1888*; £5. In Dalmeny Norman St Cuthbert's church is well preserved and interesting.

443. 🏛 SOUTH QUEENSFERRY
(just off A90)
Notable for its views of the two great Forth bridges on either side, with piers to potter on; the Hawes Inn, famous from *Kidnapped*, is still going strong, and the Two Bridges has a pleasant conservatory restaurant looking up to the bridges.

444. 🏛 NORTH QUEENSFERRY
Deep-Sea World *(1.5 miles off A90 via B981 S from first exit N of Forth Bridge)*
This elaborate aquarium has a spectacular underwater safari, with moving walkways along a transparent viewing tunnel as long as a football pitch, surrounded by all kinds of underwater creatures in a million gallons of water; divers hand-feed the fish and even answer questions, using waterproof communication systems. The sea-horses are popular, and you can stroke some of the creatures kept in the big rock pools, pilot an underwater camera, and try their new tornado boats. Also one of Europe's largest collections of sand tiger sharks – you can watch spectacular diver feeds, and see piranha and other dangerous species in the Amazon Experience. The programme of talks, activities and feeding displays is good, and the free behind-the-scenes tours give a good insight into the demands of looking after so many creatures, and an introduction to their successful breeding and conservation programmes. They also have a good collection of amphibians, taking in the world's most poisonous frog, and some snakes. Meals, snacks, shop, disabled access; cl 25 Dec, 1 Jan; *(01383) 411880*; £7.50 (inc face-painting); they also offer 'shark dives' to over-16s for £100; *(01383) 411880*

445. 🏛 GLENCARSE
Glendoick Gardens *(0.5 miles off A90 just NE of Glencarse, about 8 miles NE of Perth; Glendoick Garden Centre clearly signed, go through car park and turn right on drive)*

World-famous woodland gardens and rhododendron nursery, full of rare and beautiful species; good value plant sales, restaurant; open mid-Apr to mid-June (cl wknds exc first and third Sun in May; garden centre open all year)

446. ✕ ⌂ ABERDEEN
Ferryhill House *(1.4 miles off A90 from A4093/A945 roundabout; A4093 into city, then at next roundabout right into Fonthill Rd; then left into Bon Accord St)*
£60; 9 rms. Well run small hotel with comfortable communicating spacious bar areas, well over 100 malt whiskies, real ales, friendly staff, a wide choice of food in bar and restaurant and lots of tables on neat well sheltered lawns *(01224) 590867*

A92

447. ⌂ GLENROTHES
Balbirnie House *(0.5 miles off A92 N of A911, via B9130)*
£190, plus special breaks; 30 rms. Fine Georgian country house in 400-acre park landscaped in Capability Brown style, with fresh flowers, open fires and antiques in gracious public rooms, extremely good inventive food, and a big wine list; disabled access; dogs in bedrooms *(01592) 610066*

448. ✕ FALKLAND
Kind Kyttock's Kitchen *(2.5 miles off A92 via A912 NW; Cross Wynd)*
Popular well known tearoom nr village centre, with enjoyable light home-made meals and super afternoon teas; friendly staff; cl Mon and 24 Dec-5 Jan *(01337) 857477*

A95

449. ⚜ BALLINDALLOCH
Ballindalloch Castle *(on A95 NE of Grantown)*
Romantic castle in a lovely spot in the heart of Speyside whisky country, grandly enlarged around 1845, and still lived in by the Macpherson-Grants whose ancestors settled here in the mid-16th c. Furnishings

inside are cheerfully light, and there's a fine collection of 17th-c spanish paintings. The Rivers Spey and Avon run through the grounds, which also include a large rock garden, and the oldest herd of aberdeen angus cattle in the world. Enjoyable afternoon teas, well stocked gift shop, disabled access to tearoom and ground floor of castle only; cl Sat, and Oct-Maundy Thurs exc by appointment; *(01807) 500206*; £6.

450. GRANTOWN ON SPEY
Culdearn House (just off A95; Woodlands Terr (off A939 at SW end of High St))
£110, plus special breaks; 7 rms. Carefully run Victorian granite stone house with homely décor, friendly atmosphere, and enjoyable scottish food; packed lunches on request; cl Dec/Jan; children over 10; partial disabled access *(01479) 872106*

A96

451. OYNE
Archaeolink (1.5 miles off A96 NW of Inverurie via B9002)
This lively centre is a fun exploration of the past. A remarkable turf-roofed building houses an audio-visual presentation, there's an exhibition on myths and legends, and you can try out ancient crafts such as weaving, grinding and arrow-making. Outside are the remains of an Iron Age hill fort, a reconstructed Iron Age farm, a Roman marching camp and a sandpit play area, where younger members of the family can dig for the past. Meals, snacks, shop, disabled access; *(01464) 851500*; £4.75.

452. DALCROSS
Easter Dalziel Farm (1.8 miles off A96 just E of Inverness, via B9039)
£48; 3 rms with shared bthrm. Early Victorian farmhouse on 210 acres of family-run mixed farm (beef cattle and grain) with friendly helpful owners, log fire in lounge, good scottish breakfasts in big dining room and – when farm commitments allow – evening meal using own beef, lamb and veg; self-catering cottages, too; cl Christmas and New Year; dogs welcome by arrangement away from restaurant *(01667) 462213*

A130

453. ⋈ ELGIN
Mansion House *(just off A96; heading E from High St/Hay St roundabout take first left into Blackfriars Rd then left on Haugh Rd)*
£135; 23 rms. Relaxed and friendly scottish baronial mansion in private woodland with extensive lawns, pretty public rooms, fresh flowers, lovely food inc fine breakfasts, and good wine list; leisure club facilities inc swimming pool *(01343) 548811*

A99

454. ⋈ LYBSTER
Portland Arms *(on A99, and handy too for A9)*
£80, plus special breaks; 22 comfortable rms. Big hotel with really friendly staff, log fire in small cosy lounge bar, bistro and informal locals' bar, generous helpings of good fresh food and fine breakfasts; shooting/fishing can be arranged; cl 31 Dec-2 Jan; disabled access to ground floor *(01593) 721721*

A120

455. ⋈ WIX
Dairy House Farm *(2 miles off A120; N towards Bradfield)*
£50; 2 comfortable bdrms. No smoking Victorian farmhouse on 700 acres of arable land and fruit farm with fine country views, many original features, a cosy sitting room, home-made cake on arrival, and enjoyable breakfasts with home-made preserves in elegant dining room (no evening meals); garden with croquet; children over 12 *(01255) 870322*

A130

456. 🚶 BATTLESBRIDGE
(0.6 miles off A130; village signed from A132 roundabout)
Attractive village, with popular antiques and crafts centre, walks to head of Crouch estuary; the Barge is useful for food all day

MOTORWAY BREAKS

457. ✕ PLESHEY
White Horse *(2.2 miles off A130; Pleshey Rd, just N of B1417 junction)*
Cheerful 15th-c pub with fascinating array of bric-a-brac in lots of nooks and crannies, sturdy good value traditional lunchtime food with more restauranty evening dishes and set Sun lunch, arts and crafts gallery; cl Sun-Tues evenings *(01245) 237281*

458. ⌹ PLESHEY
Yew Tree Farm *(1.8 miles off A130; just N of village, and most quickly reached via Hall Chase)*
£50; 2 attractive rms. Peacefully set farmhouse with a warm welcome from the charming owners, good english breakfasts, croquet lawn, and exercise paddock; no smoking; cl Christmas; dogs in bedrooms by prior arrangement *(01245) 231229*

A131

459. ✕ YOUNGS END
Green Dragon *(0.5 miles off new A131 Braintree bypass, just N of Essex Showground)*
Well run dining pub with attractive understated barn theme in no smoking restaurant area, extensive range of good interesting bar food inc lots of fish, well kept real ales, and plenty of seats in back garden; disabled access *(01245) 361030*

460. ✕ GOSFIELD
Green Man *(1.6 miles off A131; A1017)*
Smart dining pub with a relaxed chatty atmosphere, two little bars and no smoking dining room, good daily changing food (not Sun evening) inc marvellous lunchtime cold buffet and nice puddings, well kept real ales and decent wines, many by the glass; no food Sun pm; partial disabled access *(01787) 472746*

A134

461. 🚶 LONG MELFORD
Melford Hall (0.9 miles off A134; in village, just S of A1092)
Turreted Tudor house mostly unchanged externally since Elizabeth I with hundreds of servants and courtiers stayed here in 1578; it also still has the original panelled banqueting hall. Fine collection of chinese porcelain and Beatrix Potter memorabilia; the gardens have a Tudor banqueting house. Some disabled access; cl am, Nov-Mar, Mon-Tues May-Sept, wkdays April and Oct; *(01787) 379228*; £4.70; NT.

462. ✕ 🛏 LONG MELFORD
Black Lion (0.8 miles off A134; in village bear off W on A1092, hotel immediately on right)
£109.50; comfortable, well run and civilised hotel with a mellow bar, an oak serving counter, deeply cushioned sofas, leather wing armchairs and antique fireside settles, and an eating area with leather dining chairs around handsome tables set for the good, stylish, daily changing bar food; no smoking restaurant, large portraits, of racehorses and of people, and helpful efficient service by neatly uniformed staff; real ales, a fine range of wines by the glass (inc champagne), and good generous cafetière coffee; appealing Victorian walled garden *(01787) 312356*

463. 🚶 LONG MELFORD
Kentwell Hall (just off A134 N end of village)
Beautiful Tudor mansion with genuinely friendly lived-in feel, best during their enthusiastic re-creations of Tudor and 1940s life (several wknds Apr-Sept), when everything is done as closely as possible to the way it would have been done then – even the speech. It's surrounded by a broad carp-filled moat, and there's a rare breeds farm in the grounds. Meals, snacks and picnic area, shop, disabled access; house usually cl am, Sat (exc event wknds) plus Oct-mid-July (exc Sun and half term in Oct), best to check; *(01787) 310207*; most re-creations cost around £9.75, though the Great Annual one is £12.95. On non-event days entry is £7.15, or £5 garden and farm only.

MOTORWAY BREAKS

464. ✗ ⌂ MUNDFORD
Crown (0.2 miles off A134 roundabout; first fork left off A1065)
£65; 20 good rms. Friendly small village pub, originally a hunting inn and rebuilt in the 18th c, with an attractive choice of reasonably priced straightforward food, very welcoming staff, a happy atmosphere, and well kept real ales; dogs welcome; disabled access; dogs in some bedrooms if well behaved *(01842) 878233*

465. ※ OXBOROUGH
Oxburgh Hall (2.6 miles off A134)
Henry VII stayed in this attractive moated manor house in 1487, which shows hangings worked by Mary, Queen of Scots. Most of the house was thoroughly refurbished during Victorian times, but the gatehouse remains as an awe-inspiring example of 15th-c building work, 80 ft high. The garden has a colourfully restored french parterre, and there are pleasant woodland walks. Meals, snacks, shop, disabled access to ground floor only; house cl Thurs, Fri and Nov-late Mar, garden also open wknds all year; *(01366) 328258*; £6, £3 garden only; NT. The Bedingfeld Arms opp has decent food.

A140

466. ✗ ⌂ BROME
Cornwallis (0.3 miles off A140; Rectory Rd (first left off B1077))
£112; very civilised largely 19th-c country hotel grandly approached down a tree-lined drive through its 20-acre grounds, with imaginative choice of excellent food in elegant restaurant, nicely planted Victorian-style side conservatory, and beamed and timbered 16th-c bar – stylish and comfortable, with a good mix of old and antique tables, oak settles and cushioned library chairs, and a handsome woodburner; well kept real ales, an extensive, carefully chosen wine list with 20 by the glass, and warm friendly service from attentive young staff; comfortable bdrms *(01379) 870326*

467. ⌂ PULHAM MARKET
Old Bakery (1 mile off A140 via B1134)
£64; 3 large rms. No smoking 16th-c house with lots of beams and

timbers, an inglenook with a fine log fire in lounge, good breakfasts using local produce, and friendly atmosphere; cl Christmas and New Year; children over 12 *(01379) 676492*

468. 🛏 STOKE HOLY CROSS
Salamanca Farm (1.3 miles off A140; in village centre turn left on to old Norwich Rd)
£50; 4 rms. Mainly Victorian farmhouse (parts are much older) just a short stroll from the River Tas, with guest lounge, spacious dining room with separate tables, a flower arranger's garden, and farm shop; no smoking; cl 15 Dec-15 Jan; children over 6 *(01508) 492322*

469. 🚶 BLICKLING
Blickling Hall (2.3 miles off A140, via B1354 through Aylsham)
Magnificent house dating mainly from early 17th c, though the hedges that flank it may be older. Dramatic carved oak staircase and splendid paintings (inc a famous Canaletto), but best of all is the 125-ft Long Gallery with its ornate Jacobean plaster ceiling, and the chinese bedroom, still lined with 18th-c hand-painted wallpaper. The gardens and grounds are lovely, with several miles of footpaths. Meals, snacks, shop, plant centre, good disabled access (a lift in the house); house open Weds-Sun pm Apr-Oct, garden also open am, Tues-Sun in Aug and winter Thurs-Sun; *(01263) 738030*; £6.90, £3.90 garden only; NT. There's a pleasant walk from the Buckinghamshire Arms (useful for lunch), and free public access to the parkland on the W side of the pike-filled lake with its water birds, with large tracts of woodland and pasture, as well as a disused railway line, perhaps even kingfishers on the River Bure. There are circular walks within the park.

470. ✕ 🛏 ERPINGHAM
Saracens Head (2.3 miles off A140; keep straight on past Erpingham itself, then through Calthorpe to Wolterton)
£75; comfortably civilised inn with simple but stylish two-room bar, a nice mix of seats, log fires and fresh flowers, excellent inventive food, very well kept real ales, interesting wines, and a charming old-fashioned gravel stableyard; good bdrms; cl 25 Dec; limited disabled access *(01263) 768909*

MOTORWAY BREAKS

471. 🏛 ERPINGHAM
Alby Crafts & Gardens (on A140)
4½ acres of interesting shrubs, plants and bulbs, and eight working craftsmen inc sculpture, wood-turning, stained glass and jewellery. Crafts gallery, tearoom, shop, some disabled access; cl Mon (exc bank hols), and 23 Dec-mid Jan; *(01263) 761590*; free, gardens £2.50, bottle museum 30p. The Saracens Head out at Wolterton is very good for lunch.

472. 🛏 THORPE MARKET
Elderton Lodge (3 miles off A140 via A149)
£95, plus special breaks; 11 rms. 18th-c shooting lodge for adjacent Gunton Hall, with lots of original features, fine panelling, a relaxing lounge bar with log fire, an airy conservatory where breakfast and lunch are served, and Langtry Restaurant with good food using fresh fish and game; six acres of mature grounds overlooking herds of deer; children over 6; partial disabled access; dogs in bedrooms and lounge *(01263) 833547*

A143

473. ✕ IXWORTH
Theobalds (0.5 miles off A143 bypass; 68 High St)
Consistently good imaginative food in 17th-c restaurant with log fires, beams and standing timbers in cosy rooms, very good wine list, and kind service; cl Sat am, Sun pm, Mon, Tues and Thurs am, 10 days in summer; children in evening over 8 only *(01359) 231707*

474. ✕ ST OLAVES
Priory Farm (on A143 Beccles Rd)
Good interesting food inc fresh fish and children's menu; right by ruined 13th-c St Olaves Priory (the fine brick undercroft in its cloister is well worth a look); open all day June-Sept (normal hours the rest of the year), but cl 26-30 Dec; disabled access *(01493) 488432*

A148

475. 🕺 HOLT
(on A148)
Pleasant little town with some handsome Georgian buildings. The friendly Feathers Hotel (Market Pl) has good value food and decent bedrooms; the Owl Tea Rooms (White Lion St, cl Sun) has good home baking, home-made preserves, and local organic veg in a Georgian building. This is the terminus of the North Norfolk Steam Railway from Sheringham.

476. 🕺 HOUGHTON
Houghton Hall *(1.2 miles off A148)*
Built for Robert Walpole, Britain's first prime minister, and obviously designed to impress, this is a spectacularly grand Palladian mansion in charming parkland containing a herd of white fallow deer, 5-acre walled garden and model soldier museum with 20,000 model soldiers and other displays. The state rooms were decorated and furnished by William Kent. Meals, snacks, shop, disabled access; open 27 Mar-29 Sept, Weds, Thurs, Sun and bank hol Mon; *(01485) 528569*; £7, excluding house £4.50. Driving along the C road nr North Pole farm you may spot brown, white or red deer. The Rose & Crown in Harpley has good value home cooking.

477. 🛏 GRIMSTON
Congham Hall *(2 miles off A148 via B1153 from Hillington)*
£175, plus special breaks; 14 individually decorated rms. Warmly welcoming and handsome Georgian manor in 30 acres inc herb, vegetable and flower gardens (herbs for sale, and garden with around 500 different herbs in traditional layouts, open to public), tennis court, paddock and orchards – also, walks leaflets; lovely drawing room, a pretty orangery formal restaurant with excellent modern cooking (lighter lunches in bar), and exemplary service; children over 7 in restaurant *(01485) 600250*

A158

478. 🕸 SNIPE DALES
(off A158 in Hagworthingham, between there and B1195)
Country park and nature reserve, managed by the county council, covering 210 acres rich in bird and plant life; the country park is a 90-acre area of pine woods, while the adjacent nature reserve has a trail leading through two valleys and to a viewpoint over the Wolds. The George & Dragon in Hagworthingham has good value food.

479. ✕ HORNCASTLE
Magpies (on A158 (East St))
Popular well run restaurant with a relaxed atmosphere and good, enjoyable food using top-quality fresh local ingredients; cl Sun, Mon, bank hols; no children; disabled access *(01507) 527004*

480. ⇋ EAST BARKWITH
Bodkin Lodge (3 miles off A158, via A157 Louth Rd from Wragby; Torrington Lane left)
£58; 2 pretty ground-floor rms. Run by the same warmly friendly family as the farm, this carefully extended bungalow has a comfortable sitting room with books, fresh flowers, open fire and baby grand piano, good breakfasts in big dining room with home-made bread and jams (light suppers by arrangement), award-winning wildlife farmland trails from the door, and marvellous country views; cl mid-Dec-New Year; children over 10; disabled access *(01673) 858249*

481. ⇋ LINCOLN
D'Isney Place (0.2 miles off A158 via Greetwellgate into Eastgate)
£95, plus special breaks; 17 charming rms. Friendly 18th-c hotel with lovely gardens (one wall of the cathedral close forms its southern boundary), a relaxed and homely atmosphere, good breakfasts using free-range eggs served on bone china in your room (there are no public rooms), and friendly owners; partial disabled access; dogs welcome in bedrooms *(01522) 538881*

A164

482. ⇔ WILLERBY
Willerby Manor *(0.6 miles off A164 via B1232, second exit from next roundabout into Gt Gutter Lane E; right on Main St then left into Well Lane; handy too for A63 and Humber Bridge)*
£118; 51 individually decorated rms. Originally the home of an Edwardian shipping merchant, this carefully extended hotel is surrounded by three acres of gardens; airy and attractive conservatory, dining bar and more formal restaurant, good food, helpful service, and health club with swimming pool *(01482) 652616*

A165

483. ⋈ BRIDLINGTON
(on A165/A164)
Famous for its bracing image in the heyday of the traditional seaside resort, and the way the scenery rolls down to the long sands of the shore still gives that feeling. The centre is a quay and small harbour, with the usual summer attractions, but the original core of the town is half a mile in from the sea, with some charming old houses among the more modern ones around the heavily restored priory church. A 14th-c gateway (the Baylegate) gives some idea of how imposing the priory must have been before the Dissolution. The cheerfully nautical Hook & Parrot (Esplanade) has decent lunchtime food. The coast to the S is generally much flatter.

A167

484. ✕ DURHAM
Bistro 21 *(0.7 miles off A167 from A691 roundabout; take unclassified rd then right on to B6532 Shireburn Rd, then second exit from next roundabout, bearing right to Aykley Heads House)*
Light and airy mediterranean-style restaurant in former 17th-c farmhouse, with pine dining chairs on wooden or flagstoned floors, a good

MOTORWAY BREAKS

choice of very enjoyable interesting modern cooking, a thoughtful wine list, and professional but relaxed service; cl Sun pm, 25 Dec, 1 Jan *(0191) 384 4354*

A170

485. 🕅 SCARBOROUGH
(on A64/A170/A171/A165)
Obviously a destination rather than somewhere to pop into en route, with all the usual seaside attractions in a place of some style, its two great curves of firm sandy beach separated by the small harbour below a high narrow headland. Between castle and cliff are the remains of a Roman signal station, one of five such structures built in the 4th c to warn of approaching raiders. To the S is the older part of the resort, with antique tracked cliff lifts between prom and the pleasant streets of the upper town; a house associated with Richard III here is now a restaurant. The train station has one of the longest benches in the world – 456 ft long, it can seat 228 people; the Steven Joseph theatre opposite is run by Alan Ayckbourn. Interesting churches include medieval St Mary's, where Anne Brontë is buried, and 19th-c St Martin's with elaborate work by William Morris, Burne-Jones and other Pre-Raphaelites. One entertainingly quaint tradition is the summer staging of miniaturised sea battles with all sorts of special effects among the ducks on the lake of Peasholm Park in the less seasidey N part of town; phone the tourist information for dates and times; *(01723) 373333*. Good views of the bay from the top of Oliver's Mount (and harbour views from the Golden Ball on the front); good value food all day in the very grand Lord Rosebery (Westborough), and the stylish Raffels (Falsgrave Rd/Belgrave Cres), a former gentleman's club, has a plush restaurant.

486. 🕅 PICKERING
(just off A170)
Attractive small town, usually very quiet (busier Mon market day), with vividly restored medieval murals in the splendid tall-spired church. The White Swan restaurant-with-rooms has good food and is a very comfortable place to stay in; *(01751) 472288*. The 17th-c Beck Isle Museum

has a wonderful collection of local bygones and period shops; cl Nov-Mar; *(01751) 473653*.

487. ⋈ MIDDLETON
Cottage Leas Country Hotel *(1.5 miles N off A170 just W of Pickering, via Middleton Lane/Nova Lane)*
£68, plus special breaks; 12 comfortable rms. Delightful, peaceful 18th-c farmhouse with extensive gardens, comfortable informal rooms, beamed ceilings, open log fire in cosy lounge, a well stocked bar, and enjoyable creative food; partial disabled access; dogs in some bedrooms *(01751) 472129*

488. ✕ ⋈ HAROME
Star *(1.6 miles S off A170 E of Helmsley)*
£120; pretty thatched 14th-c inn, an outstanding place, with a charming interior, plenty of bric-a-brac and interesting furniture, two big log fires, daily papers and magazines, and a no smoking dining room; excellent inventive food using the best local produce (and a marvellous bakery/delicatessen), fantastic breakfasts, well kept real ales, freshly squeezed juices, and quite a few wines by the glass from a fairly extensive wine list; seats and tables on a sheltered front terrace with more in the garden behind; superb bedrooms in converted farm buildings; cl Mon, 3 wks winter/spring; disabled access *(01439) 770397*

489. ※ HELMSLEY
(on A170)
Lanes run straight up on to the moors from this attractive neatly kept small market town (the B1257 is one of the best moorland roads). There's a large cobbled square (busy Fri market), and enough antiques and craft shops (craft fair most wknds) to please a visitor without seeming too touristy. A lively and bustling place, with a lot of class. The Royal Oak (open all day) does substantial food.

490. ⋈ HELMSLEY
Black Swan *(on A170; Market Pl)*
£150, plus special breaks; 45 well equipped and comfortable rms. Striking Georgian house and adjoining Tudor rectory with beamed and panelled hotel bar, attractive carved oak settles and windsor armchairs,

MOTORWAY BREAKS

cosy and comfortable lounges with lots of character, and a charming sheltered garden; dogs in bedrooms and certain lounges *(01439) 770466*

491. 🕯 HELMSLEY
Duncombe Park *(just off A170; B1257 from W edge of town, then immediate first left)*
Beautifully restored early 18th-c house, rebuilt after a fire a hundred years ago. The landscaped gardens, with grand terracing, are magnificent, covering around a tenth of the 300 acres of memorable parkland. Meals, snacks, shop, some disabled access; cl Fri-Sat, and end Oct to May; *(01439) 770213*; £6, £3 gardens only. You can wander through the parkland, run as a nature reserve, for £2. The separately owned friendly 18th-c Walled Garden here (cl Nov-Mar; *(01439) 771427*) has a restored Victorian orchid house, beautiful clematis and roses, an excellent choice of plants for sale, and a good café.

492. 🕯 RIEVAULX
Rievaulx Terrace & Temples *(3 miles off A170 from Helmsley, via B1257 NW)*
This half-mile grass-covered 18th-c terrace overlooks the abbey, with dramatic views. Each end is adorned with a classical temple; one a small Tuscan rotunda built to while away the hours in peaceful contemplation, the other, an elaborate Ionic creation, for hunting parties. An ideal spot for a picnic, with good frescoes and an exhibition on landscape design. Snacks, shop; cl Nov to mid-Mar; *(01439) 798340*; £3.80; NT.

493. 🕯 SUTTON BANK
(on A170)
This steep escarpment gives an enthralling view, particularly from the very popular section of the Cleveland Way that runs S from the A170 along the level clifftop to the white horse cut into the hill. Immediately N of the A170 you can combine the path along the top of the slope with a venture down the nature trail into Garbutt Wood, a nature reserve abutting Gormire Lake, the only natural lake in the National Park. The Black Swan at Oldstead does decent meals.

A171

494. ✕ MARTON
Appletree *(1.7 miles S of A170, from Sinnington)*
Stylish and spotlessly kept dining pub with carefully co-ordinated colour schemes and lighting, a relaxed beamed lounge with comfortable settees and open fire, terracotta-walled dining room with well spaced farmhouse tables, fresh flowers, and masses of evening candles, delicious food using top-quality local produce (free bottle of mineral water and warmly fragrant savoury breads), a good choice of a dozen changing wines by the glass, well kept real ales, and friendly service; they sell their own chutneys, preserves and so forth; seats on a sheltered flagstoned terrace *(01751) 431457*

A171

495. ⛳ SCARBOROUGH
Wrea Head Hotel *(just off A171 N of town; heading N, take last left turn in Scalby, on to Barmoor Lane, then bear left after North St)*
£130, plus special breaks; 20 individually decorated rms inc 2 luxury four-poster rms. Victorian country house in 14 acres of parkland and gardens; friendly staff, minstrels' gallery in oak-panelled hall and lounge, open fires, a bow-windowed library, pretty flowers, and good food in airy restaurant *(01723) 378211*

496. ✕ ⛳ STAINTONDALE
Falcon *(just off A171 N of Cloughton)*
£55; big dependable open-plan bar, neatly kept and well divided, light and airy, with comfortable banquettes and other seats on turkey carpet, good value honest food in quantity (no booking, but worth the wait for a table), well kept ales, particularly good friendly family service, log fire in big stone fireplace, distant sea view from end windows; piped music; picnic-sets on walled lawn, good bdrms with own bathrooms *(01723) 870717*

497. 🚶 ROBIN HOOD'S BAY
(2.5 miles off A171 via B1447)
Picturesque fishing village, once popular with smugglers and still largely unspoilt (though there are quite a few shops and cafés for visitors

MOTORWAY BREAKS

now), its cottages clustered steeply above the rocky shore – a rich hunting-ground for fossil hunters at low tide, when a surprising expanse of sand is exposed beyond the fascinating rock pools. You can walk along a fine section of cliffs to Ravenscar, where a geological trail takes in old alum quarries; an abandoned railway provides an easy walkway back. The Laurel down in the village is a charming fishermen's pub; the Victoria Hotel up on the cliff has a good choice of food. The village car park is also up at the top – quite a climb.

498. 🐾 WHITBY
(just off A171)
Famous as the port at which Count Dracula came ashore; Bram Stoker got the idea for the book in the fishermen's graveyard of the partly Norman abbey church, 199 steps up from the harbour, an impressive set of ruins on its windswept clifftop and an evocative spot for a picnic. Away from the bright waterfront the town is steep and quite attractive, with picturesque old buildings (now often rather smart shops and cafés) and some quaint cobbled alleys in its original core E of the busy harbour, where excellent fresh fish is sold straight from the catch in the early morning. Fans of the TV series will enjoy visiting the *Heartbeat Story* in the Shambles (cl wkdys Nov-Mar; *(01947) 825067)*. Besides excellent fish and chips from the Magpie Café, the Duke of York (Church St, at the bottom of the 199 steps) does decent food all day. In the two wks around the summer solstice the sun both rises and sets above the sea. A replica of Captain Cook's ship will be visiting Whitby, provisionally 13 May-14 June, phone the tourist information centre to check; *(01947) 602674*.

A229

499. 🐾 SISSINGHURST
Sissinghurst Garden *(1.3 miles off A229 just N of Cranbrook; A262 E)*
Created by Vita Sackville-West and her husband Sir Harold Nicolson, these several charming gardens are themed according to season or colour, all offset by the lovely Elizabethan tower (not open). Meals, snacks, shop, disabled access; cl Weds, Thurs, and Nov-Mar, best to check; *(01580) 710700*; £7.50; NT. The Three Chimneys on the way to Biddenden is nice for lunch.

500. ✕ STAPLEHURST
Lord Raglan *(0.6 miles off A229, turning into Chart Hill Rd opposite Cross at Hand Garage)*
Unpretentious yet quite civilised country inn with hops along low beams, comfortably worn dark wood furniture on nice parquet flooring, a coal fire, a pleasantly relaxed atmosphere, and charming licensees; very generous attractively presented food (the imaginative daily specials are the thing to choose), well kept real ales, and a good wine list; small french windows lead to an enticing little sheltered terrace; wooden picnic-sets in side orchard; cl Sun; partial disabled access *(01622) 843747*

A259

501. 狄 RYE
(just off A259)
Enchanting, and still relatively unspoilt despite its many charms. Before the wind and sea currents did their work, the little town was virtually surrounded by sea, and as one of the Cinque Ports played an important part in providing men and ships for coastal defence. It's built on a hill crowned by the partly Norman St Mary's church (with a notable churchyard, and very early turret-clock, two quarter-jacks by it striking the quarter-hours); up here the largely cobbled streets still follow a 12th/13th-c narrow layout, with most of the houses lining them dating from the 16th c. The town is full of antiques shops, book shops, craft shops and a good kitchenware shop; Rye Art Gallery (107 High St) is a non-profit trust with several floors selling the best of local art and craft. The views are lovely, and steep Mermaid St with its handsome old Mermaid Inn is famously photogenic. Other places to stay that we can recommend are Jeakes House (Mermaid St, *(01797) 222828*), Little Orchard House (B&B, West St, *(01797) 223831*), and Old Vicarage (B&B, 66 Church Sq, *(01797) 222119*). Good food at the Flushing Inn (4 Market St, *(01797) 223292*), Landgate Bistro (evenings only, 5-6 Landgate, *(01797) 222829*), and for a pub meal the Ypres Castle (Gun Garden, steps down from Ypres Tower, *(01797) 223248*) or Inkerman Arms down by Rye Harbour (*(01797) 222464*).

MOTORWAY BREAKS

502. ⋈ FAIRLIGHT
Fairlight Cottage (1.9 miles off A259 via Fairlight Rd; in village, second right and on into Warren Rd)
£65, plus winter breaks; 3 rms, one with four-poster. Comfortable and very friendly no smoking house in fine countryside with views over Rye Bay and plenty of rural and clifftop walks; big comfortable lounge (nice views), good breakfasts in elegant dining room or on new balcony; children over 10; dogs in bedrooms *(01424) 812545*

A272

503. ✕ ⋈ FLETCHING
Griffin (1.1 miles off A272 (handy for A22 too))
£85; civilised and chatty old country inn with blazing log fires in quaintly panelled rooms, old photographs and hunting prints, very good innovative food, well kept beers, a good wine list with lots (inc champagne) by the glass, relaxed friendly atmosphere, and lovely two-acre garden; cl 25 Dec; disabled access *(01825) 722890*

504. ⋈ SHEFFIELD PARK
Sheffield Park Garden (2.1 miles off A272 via A275 N)
Wonderful 120-acre garden partly landscaped by Capability Brown, since then imaginatively planted with many varieties of tree unknown to him, especially chosen for their autumn colours. Also marvellous rhododendrons, azaleas and water-lilies on the lakes. Snacks, shop, disabled access; cl Mon (exc bank hols, and May and Oct), all wkdys Jan-mid-Feb; *(01825) 790231*; £5.50; NT. The Griffin at Fletching nearby is very good for lunch.

505. ⋈ CUCKFIELD
Ockenden Manor (0.6 miles off A272, from W roundabout via B2036)
£155, plus special breaks; 22 individually decorated, pretty rms. Dating from 1520, this carefully extended manor house has antiques, fresh flowers and an open fire in the comfortable sitting room, good modern cooking in fine panelled restaurant, cosy bar, and super views of the South Downs from the neatly kept garden (in nine acres); dogs in 4 ground-floor bedrooms *(01444) 416111*

506. ⛺ WISBOROUGH GREEN
Old Wharf (just off A272 E; Wharf Farm)
£75; 3 rms with views over farmland and canal. Carefully restored no smoking canal warehouse with fine old hoist wheel, comfortable sitting room with log fire, breakfasts using free-range eggs, walled canalside garden, and friendly atmosphere; cl Christmas and New Year; children over 12 *(01403) 784096*

507. 🏛 PETWORTH
Petworth House (on A272)
Splendid, its magnificent rooms filled with one of the most impressive art collections in the country, inc dutch Old Masters and 20 pictures by Turner. Other highlights include the 13th-c chapel, grand staircase with murals, and the carved room, elegantly decorated by Grinling Gibbons. You can see extra rooms Mon-Weds. Meals, snacks, shop, disabled access; cl Thurs, Fri and Dec-Feb; *(01798) 342207*; £7.50; NT. The deer park, with stately trees and prospects still recognisable as those glorified by Turner, is open all year; free. The town (cruelly carved up by busy traffic) is now an antiques honey-pot, with dozens of antiques shops in its narrow streets of attractive old houses. The Well Diggers (A283 E – almost a museum of the rural 1920s) and stylish Badgers (A285 S) have good food too.

508. ⛺ PETWORTH
Old Railway Station (1.5 miles off A272; A285 S)
£140, plus special breaks; 8 rms, some in Pullman railway cars. Petworth's former railway station, carefully restored, with large lounge and dining area (the former waiting room with original ticket office windows), fine breakfasts, friendly owners, and terrace (once the platform) and garden; disabled access *(01798) 342346*

509. ✕ ⛺ LODSWORTH
Halfway Bridge (on A272)
£75; civilised family-run pub with big helpings of inventive home cooking in no smoking restaurant or attractively decorated comfortable bar rooms, log fires, well kept real ales, ciders and wines; cl Sun pm in winter; children welcome over 10; disabled access *(01798) 861281*

MOTORWAY BREAKS

510. ✕ TROTTON
Keepers Arms *(just off A272, perched above S side)*
18th-c beamed and timbered pub, sofas by big log fire, some unusual pictures and artefacts, interesting medley of old or antique furniture, pretty candelabra, and bowls of fruit and chillies; particularly good interesting food inc yummy puddings, friendly service, relaxed atmosphere, well kept real ales and decent wines; country views from the latticed windows, and tables out on a terrace in front; cl Sun pm, Mon, 1 wk over Christmas; children must be well behaved; disabled access *(01730) 813724*

511. ⌂ ROGATE
Mizzards *(0.7 miles off A272, S through village)*
£70; 3 rms. 16th-c house in quiet country setting with a comfortable and elegant sitting room, enjoyable breakfasts in vaulted dining room, outside swimming pool, attractive landscaped gardens and lake, and fine farmland views; no evening meals; no smoking; cl Christmas and New Year; children over 9 *(01730) 821656*

512. ✕ ⌂ FROXFIELD
Trooper *(3 miles off A272, just W of A3 junction, towards Steep; at Cricketers crossroads turn left up old coach road NW)*
£89; interesting pub transformed by very jolly landlord, big windows looking across rolling countryside, airy feel, little persian knick-knacks, lit candles all around, fresh flowers, and log fire; attractive raftered restaurant, popular, enjoyable food from a sensibly short menu, well kept real ales, and decent house wines; lots of picnic-sets on lawn and partly covered sunken terrace; the horse rail in the car park ('horses only before 8pm') does get used; good bdrms; disabled access *(01730) 827293*

513. ✕ WEST MEON
Thomas Lord *(1.5 miles off A272; A32 S, pub signed off left in village)*
Thoughtful choice of interesting and enjoyable food from good sandwiches up in proper old-fashioned village pub atmosphere, well kept ales, good farm ciders and wines, good choice of coffees, sofa by log fire, cricket memorabilia inc club ties and odd stuffed-animal cricket match; tables in big garden *(01730) 829244*

A303

514. ✕ ⇌ CHERITON
Flower Pots (0.7 miles off A272; pub signed left off B3046 in village)
£60; 4 rms. Unspoilt and quietly comfortable village local run by very friendly family, with two pleasant little bars, log fire, decent bar food (not Sun evening), super own-brew beers, and old-fashioned seats on the pretty lawns; no credit cards; no accomm Christmas and New Year; no children; dogs in bedrooms and bars if well behaved *(01962) 771318*

A299

515. ✕ DARGATE
Dove (0.9 miles off A229; Plum Pudding Lane)
Tucked-away dining pub with charmingly unspoilt rambling rooms, plenty of seats on bar boards, a winter log fire, and exceptionally good restaurant-style food; well kept real ales, fine wines, and a pretty sheltered garden *(01227) 751360*

A303

516. ⚐ STONEHENGE
(just off A303/A344 junction, via A344)
One of the most famous prehistoric monuments in the world; everyone knows what it looks like, and how they got the stones here has been pretty much sorted out (the larger ones local, the smaller ones all the way from South Wales), but nobody's really sure exactly what Stonehenge (with its careful astronomical alignments) was for. In the interests of conservation, you can't normally go right up to the stones (see below), but you can get pretty close, and the fact that people are kept back means that your photos won't be cluttered by the crowds. The best views are very early in the morning from the track from Larkhill, and on the other side of the A344 and from byways 11 and 12 on the other side of the A303 towards Normanton Down burial mounds; or on a cold clear winter evening looking W past the monument towards the sunset; the ancient stones look very impressive silhouetted against the sky. Even in the crowded light of day the place never quite loses its power to inspire awe. The car park area and busy

MOTORWAY BREAKS

main roads nearby detract a little. Snacks inc home-made cakes, shop, disabled access (and a Braille guide); *(0870) 333 1181*; cl 24-26 Dec, 1 Jan; £5.50 (inc very good audio tour); EH. Stone circle access outside normal hours (not Oct-Nov) can be booked in advance, phone *(01980) 626267*; or Astral Travels *(0870) 902 0908* organise day trips from London. Good walks from here around associated ancient monuments.

517. ✕ ⌂ HINDON
Lamb (1.2 miles off A303, S from Chicklade (E of A350 junction))
£80; civilised inn with roomy long and traditional bar open all day, enjoyable food with some enterprising food alongside the familiar favourites, usually cream teas too, log fires, pleasant staff and good choice of wines by the glass; 13 comfortable bdrms *(01747) 820573*

518. ✕ CHISELBOROUGH
Cat Head (2 miles off A303 via A356 S; village signed off on left)
Relaxing country pub with neatly traditional flagstoned rooms, plenty of flowers and plants, woodburner, light wooden tables and chairs, some high-backed cushioned settles, and curtains around the small mullioned windows; a carpeted area to the right is no smoking; very good interesting bar food, real ales, nice wines, and friendly licensees; very attractive garden with seats, and views over the peaceful village *(01935) 881231*

519. ✕ ILMINSTER
George (1.4 miles off A303 via B3168, forking right into West St then next right into Silver St; North St, opp central butter market)
Good carefully made lunchtime food (not Sun exc first in month) and evening meals Tues and Fri, in quietly civilised pub with a difference, run by welcoming mother and daughter; neat gently lit up-to-date little bar and back dining area, interesting uncluttered decorations, good wines and west country ales, children and dogs welcome *(01460) 55515*

A338

520. ✗ ⇌ STUCKTON
Three Lions (0.8 miles off A338; village signed from A338/B3078 Fordingbridge roundabout)
Warmly welcoming restaurant with informal atmosphere, a neat airy bar, fresh flowers, very imaginative food inc local fungi and lovely puddings, a fine wine list, superb breakfasts, and charming owners; good atmosphere and friendly efficient service; cl Sun pm, Mon, 2 wks Feb; disabled access *(01425) 652489*

521. 🏃 BREAMORE
Breamore House (0.6 miles off A338, N of Fordingbridge)
Late Elizabethan manor house, with fine furnishings, tapestries and paintings (mainly 17th- and 18th-c Dutch School), and better than average countryside museum with displays of Roman artefacts found within the estate, and a rare 16th-c bavarian turret clock. Children aren't left out – there's a maze and adventure playground. Meals, snacks, shop, disabled access; cl am, all Mon and Fri, and all Sept-Easter (though open Tues and Sun in Apr); *(01725) 512468*; £6. The village has many thatched houses, and is within a pleasant walk of Breamore House – and the mysterious Mizmaze, cut in the turf. The Cartwheel at Whitsbury has enjoyable food.

522. ✗ ⇌ SALISBURY
Rose & Crown (0.3 miles off A338/A354 roundabout, via A3094; handy too for A36)
£130; 28 rms in the original building or smart modern extension. It's almost worth a visit just for the view – well nigh identical to that in the most famous Constable painting of Salisbury Cathedral; elegantly restored inn with friendly beamed and timbered bar, log fire, good bar and restaurant food, and charming Avonside garden; disabled access; dogs in bedrooms *(01722) 399955*

A346

523. 🚶 MARLBOROUGH
(on A346)
One of the area's most attractive towns; its very pleasing wide High St has a market each Weds and Sat. The annual autumn Mop Fair (as in most market towns, formerly for the hiring of servants) has been revived here as a general celebration. Even the more modern additions don't look obtrusively out of place among the harmonious mix of Georgian and Tudor buildings. You can see renovations in progress and sometimes craftsmen in action at the 17th-c Merchants House (High St) which has some completed and period furnished rooms; cl Mon-Thurs and all Oct-Easter; *(01672) 511491*. The Bear and Castle & Ball are useful for lunch. The Broad Hinton road N gives a good feel of the downs' great open spaces, as does the Manton—Alton Priors road to the SW, passing one of the area's several white horses cut into the chalk, and leading into a pleasant valley drive through Allington and Horton to Devizes. To the E, the quiet road along the Kennet Valley has some attractive views, with pleasant walks and a good food stop at the Red Lion in Axford; there are also walks through the surviving miles of Savernake Forest woodland.

A350

524. ✕ GREAT HINTON
Linnet *(0.9 miles off A350; first turning E about a mile S of A361 roundabout)*
Attractive old brick pub with pretty summer-flowering tubs and window-boxes; little right-hand bar with lots of interest on the green walls, comfortable wall banquettes, a biggish rather smart dining room with pink ragged walls, bric-a-brac, plenty of dining chairs and tables, reliably good food inc enjoyable bar snacks and imaginative daily specials and evening choices, real ales, quite a few malts, and nice summer Pimms *(01380) 870354*

A350

525. ✗ ⌂ WHITLEY
Pear Tree *(1.6 miles off A350 NW of Melksham; W on Westlands Lane from Beanacre, left on B3353 then first right into Top Lane)*
£90; attractive honey-coloured stone farmhouse with a civilised, friendly and chatty atmosphere, front bar with cushioned window seats, some stripped shutters, a mix of dining chairs around good solid tables, a variety of country pictures, and a little fireplace on the left, with a lovely old stripped stone one on the right; popular big back restaurant, enticing and delicious food beautifully presented and served by first-class staff, well kept real ales, a good wine list with ten by the glass, and seats on the terrace; good bdrms; cl 25-26 Dec; disabled access *(01225) 709131*

526. ⌂ GASTARD
Boyds Farm *(2.2 miles off A350 S of Lacock; Westlands Lane from Beanacre, then right on B3353)*
£53, plus special breaks; 3 rms. Friendly and handsome 16th-c house on family-run working farm with pedigree Herefords; homely lounge, patterned carpets, woodburner, traditional breakfasts; no evening meals (local pubs nearby); cl Christmas-New Year *(01249) 713146*

527. ※ LACOCK
Lacock Abbey *(0.5 miles off A350)*
Tranquil spread of mellow stone buildings around a central timber-gabled courtyard, based on the little-altered 13th-c abbey. Tudor additions include a romantic octagonal tower, and there was a successful 18th-c Gothicisation. Surrounded by meadows and trees, this was the setting for Fox Talbot's experiments which in 1835 led to the creation of the world's first photographic negative – a picture of part of the abbey itself. There's an interesting museum devoted to this in a 16th-c barn at the gates, and the gardens are evidence of Fox Talbot's skills in other fields. Limited disabled access (not to Abbey); Abbey cl Nov-mid-Mar,Tues and am. Grounds and Cloisters and Fox Talbot Museum cl Nov-late-Feb and Good Fri; *(01249) 730227*; £7.40; NT.

528. ※ LACOCK
(0.4 miles off A350)
A favourite village of both visitors and film-makers (see for instance the

157

MOTORWAY BREAKS

first Harry Potter film), its grid of quiet and narrow streets a delightful harmony of mellow brickwork, lichened stone and timber-and-plaster. The church is 15th c, and nothing in the village looks more recent than 18th c. It's remained so remarkably unspoilt because most of its buildings were owned for centuries by the Talbot family, until they left them to the NT in 1944. It gets very busy in summer, but the Trust has preserved it against a surfeit of antiques shops (you'll find all you want in the nearby old market town of Melksham). The village does on the other hand have a splendid collection of pubs – the George is the best.

529. ⋈ LACOCK
At the Sign of the Angel (0.5 miles off A350; Church St)
£99, plus special breaks; 10 charmingly old rooms with antiques This fine 15th-c house in a lovely NT village is full of character, with heavy oak furniture, beams and big fireplaces, a restful oak-panelled lounge, and good english cooking in three candlelit restaurants; cl Christmas period; dogs welcome in bedrooms (01249) 730230

A354

530. ✕ ⋈ FARNHAM
Museum Inn (1.5 miles off A354)
£75; 8 rms. Odd-looking thatched building with various effortlessly civilised areas – flagstoned bar with big inglenook fireplace, light beams and good comfortably cushioned furnishings, dining room with a cosy hunt-theme, and what feels rather like a contemporary version of a baronial hall, soaring up to a high glass ceiling, with dozens of antlers and a stag's head looking down on to a long wooden table and church-style pews; excellent food, three real ales, a fine choice of wines, and very good attentive service; dogs in bar and bedrooms (01725) 516261

531. ✕ ⋈ TARRANT MONKTON
Langton Arms (1.5 miles off A354)
£70; charmingly set and welcoming 17th-c thatched pub with beams and an inglenook fireplace, no smoking bistro restaurant in an attractively reworked barn, no smoking family room with play area in skittle alley, well kept interesting real ales, popular enjoyable bar food, and

garden with another play area; good nearby walks; bar open 7 days a week, best to phone for restaurant hours; disabled access *(01258) 830225*

A358

532. ⛨ HATCH BEAUCHAMP
Farthings *(0.5 miles off A358 SE of Taunton)*
£105, plus special breaks; 10 spacious rms (inc a cottage suite) with thoughtful extras. Charming little Georgian house in three acres of gardens with helpful and hard-working long-serving owners, open fires in quiet lounge and convivial bar, and good varied food using fresh local produce; can arrange golf and other activities; children must be well behaved; dogs in Maple Cottage suite only, by arrangement *(01823) 480664*

533. ⛨ BEERCROCOMBE
Frog Street Farm *(1.1 miles NE off A358, just NW of Ashill (and S of Hatch Beauchamp), bearing left into Stocks Lane)*
£60, plus special breaks; 3 rms. Peaceful 15th-c listed farmhouse deep in the countryside on a big working farm; beams, fine Jacobean panelling, inglenook fireplaces, a warmly friendly owner, delicious food (much produce from the farm, local game and fish; bring your own wine), and traditional breakfasts; no smoking; cl Nov-Mar; children by arrangement *(01823) 480430*

A361

534. ✕ TIVERTON
Four and Twenty Blackbirds *(1.3 miles off A361; B3391 into town, at second roundabout right into Station Rd; 43 Gold St (on central one-way system))*
Friendly teashop with beams, a mix of old tables and chairs, lots of interesting things to look at, and delicious food (all home-made); cl Sun *(01884) 257055*

MOTORWAY BREAKS

535. 🕺 TIVERTON
Tiverton Castle (0.6 miles off A361; first left off A396 S, into Park Hill)
The handsome castle was built in 1106 as a Royal fortress dominating the River Exe, and still has its Norman tower and gatehouse, as well as one of the best assemblages of Civil War armour and arms; pretty gardens too. You can stay in apartments in the building. Shop, disabled access to ground floor and garden; open pm Sun, Thurs and bank hol Mons Easter Sun-Oct; *(01884) 253200*; £4.

536. 🛏 WEST BUCKLAND
Huxtable Farm (2.3 miles off A361; in village turn right towards East Buckland)
£60, plus special breaks; 6 rms. 16th-c farmhouse surrounded by carefully converted listed stone buildings, open fields, fine views, sheep, chickens, and pigs; candlelit dinner with wholesome home-made food using home-grown produce, home-made wine and bread, a relaxing sitting room, and beams, open fireplaces with bread ovens, and uneven floors; sauna, fitness room, tennis court, games room, and play area with swings, sandpit and wendy house; good for families; cl Dec/Jan (but open New Year) *(01598) 760254*

A380

537. ✕ 🛏 MARLDON
Church House (0.5 miles off A380 northbound)
£60; well run bustling pub with several different attractive bar areas and restaurant, candles on tables, bare boards, hops and dried flowers, interesting bar food, well kept real ales, ten wines by the glass, and seats outside *(01803) 558279*

A384

538. ✕ 🛏 STAVERTON
Sea Trout (1.9 miles off A384; village signed from just W of Dartington)
£74; 10 cottagey rms. Comfortable pub in quiet hamlet nr River Dart with two relaxed beamed bars, log fires, popular food in bar and airy

dining conservatory, and terraced garden with fountains and waterfalls; cl Christmas; disabled access; dogs in bedrooms *(01803) 762274*

A385

539. ✕ TOTNES
Greys Dining Room *(0.5 miles off A385; High St)*
No smoking Georgian house with pretty china on a handsome dresser and partly panelled walls, lots of teas plus herb and fruit ones, sandwiches, salads and omelettes as well as lots of cakes and set teas; cl Weds and Sun; no pushchairs and children must be well behaved; partial disabled access. If you've time for a longer break, there's quite a lot to see in the partly Elizabethan town, including a working harbour and highly recommended river trips to Dartmouth *(01803) 866369*

540. ☸ DARTINGTON
Dartington Cider Press Centre *(just off A385 by A384 junction; Shinners Bridge)*
Cluster of 16th- and 17th-c buildings with craft shops, Dartington Crystal, farm foods, herbs and such, exhibitions and restaurants, inc a good vegetarian one. Street entertainers from jugglers to clog dancers, and a streamside nature trail. Disabled access; open all year, Mon-Sat plus Sun from Easter to Christmas; *(01803) 847500*; free. The Cott Inn is useful for lunch.

A386

541. ✕ ⌂ GULWORTHY
Horn of Plenty *(3 miles off A386, via A390 from Tavistock)*
£120; on the edge of Dartmoor in quiet flower-filled gardens, this relaxed, refurbished Georgian no smoking restaurant-with-rooms has excellent carefully cooked food using top-quality local produce inc lovely puddings and cheeses (wonderful breakfasts, too), a good wine list, and vine-covered terrace for aperitifs; comfortable bdrms; cl Mon am, 24-26 Dec; disabled access *(01822) 832528*

MOTORWAY BREAKS

542. 🏃 LYDFORD
Lydford Gorge (1.5 miles off A386, just past village)
Spectacular gorge formed by the River Lyd cutting into the rock, causing boulders to scoop out potholes in the bed of the river. Walks along the ravine take you to dramatic sights such as the 90-ft White Lady Waterfall and the Devil's Cauldron whirlpool (summer crowds around this bit). Children like it but need to be watched carefully as paths can be narrow and slippery. Meals, snacks (in ingeniously designed tearoom), shop, special path for the disabled; open late Mar-Oct (and perhaps Fri-Sun, when there's a Christmas shop, in Dec); *(01822) 820320*; £4.50; NT. The forbidding ruined castle has a daunting 12th-c stone keep, its upper floor once used as a court, and the lower as a prison; free. The adjacent Tudor Castle Inn *(01822) 820242* has masses of character in its low-beamed and flagstoned bar, log fires, lovely food in both bar and restaurant, and good wines and ales; open all day, bdrms.

543. ✕ LYDFORD
Dartmoor Inn (on A386)
The overall feel in the small bar here is of civilised but relaxed elegance: matt pastel paintwork in soft greens and blues, naïve farm and country pictures, little side lamps supplemented by candles in black wrought-iron holders, basketwork, dried flowers, fruits and gourds, and perhaps an elaborate bouquet of fresh flowers; limited choice of lunchtime bar snacks plus creatively cooked and beautifully presented restaurant food using top-notch local produce; well kept real ales, an interesting and helpfully short wine list, and polite young staff; tables on terrace, with a track straight up on to the moors *(01822) 820221*

A390

544. ✕ ⌂ LOSTWITHIEL
Royal Oak (Duke St; pub just visible from A390 in centre – best to look out for Royal Talbot Hotel)
£75; bustling and welcoming old town-centre pub open all day, with six particularly well kept ales, lots of bottled beers from around the world, and well liked home-made bar food; comfortable lounge, beamed and flagstoned bar, restaurant; bedrooms. The town was Cornwall's capital

in the 13th c, and its Norman castle (cl Nov-Mar) is well preserved, with a notable round keep, fine views over the Fowey Valley, and lots of flowers in spring *(01208) 872552*

545. ⋈ ST BLAZEY
Nanscawen Manor House (0.6 miles off A390; Prideaux Rd – first turn right if coming into village from E)
£99, plus winter breaks; 3 spacious, pretty rms overlooking the garden. Extended 16th-c house in five acres of lovely grounds and gardens with an outdoor heated swimming pool and whirlpool spa, and a sunny terrace; big sitting room with honesty bar, friendly helpful owners, enjoyable breakfasts in light conservatory (plenty of places nearby for evening meals), and a relaxed atmosphere; no smoking; the Eden Project is close by; children over 12 *(01726) 814488*

546. ✕ ⋈ CHARLESTOWN
Harbour Inn (0.8 miles off A390; Charlestown well signed from A391 roundabout)
£82; small well managed bar attached to comfortable Pier House Hotel in first-class spot looking over the little working china clay port; good choice of enjoyable traditional food and plenty of fresh seafood, good value cream teas, more tables in back area (no view), well kept ales, good wines, quick service, helpful charming staff; 27 rms, *(01726) 67955*. The harbour is picturesque, usually with great square-rigged sailing ships moored as well as modern cargo boats, and is much used as a film/TV setting. The Shipwreck & Heritage Centre (Quay Rd; cl Nov-Feb) has an exhibition about the *Titanic* and is good for local history.

A417

547. ✕ ⋈ NORTH CERNEY
Bathurst Arms (2.6 miles off A417, exit at NW end of Cirencester bypass heading N of main rd and across to turn left on to A435)
£65; 5 pleasant rms. Civilised and handsome old inn with lots of atmosphere, a nice mix of polished old furniture and a fireplace at each end of the beamed and panelled bar, small no smoking dining room, imaginative food, quite a few well chosen wines by the glass, well kept real ales,

MOTORWAY BREAKS

and an attractive garden running down to the River Churn; lots of surrounding walks; dogs welcome in bedrooms *(01285) 831281*

548. ✕ DUNTISBOURNE ABBOTS
Five Mile House *(1.5 miles off A417 at Duntisbourne Abbots exit sign; then, coming from Gloucester, pass filling station and keep on parallel to main rd; coming from Cirencester, pass under main rd then turn right at T junction)*
Welcoming 17th-c pub with charmingly old-fashioned bar and snug, daily papers, and steps down to back restaurant; really well prepared homely food, friendly staff, well kept ales and interesting wine choice *(01285) 821432*

549. ⊨ ASHLEWORTH
Ashleworth Court *(2 miles off A417, from Hartpury; keep on towards Ashleworth Quay)*
£50; 3 rms, shared bthrms. By a small elegant church and NT tithe barn, this striking ancient house is part of a working farm and has a homely kitchen with an Aga, a comfortable sitting room, enjoyable breakfasts served in what was originally part of the Great Hall, and chickens in the back garden; trampoline and wooden climbing frame for children; two good pubs in the village; cl Christmas *(01452) 700241*

550. ✕ ASHLEWORTH
Queens Arms *(1 mile off A417 in Hartpury)*
Immaculately kept low-beamed country dining pub, entirely no smoking, with interesting south african dishes alongside other good food from lunchtime snacks to restauranty dishes and delicious steaks; nice furnishings, civilised atmosphere *(01452) 700395*

551. ✕ ULLINGSWICK
Three Crowns *(1.1 miles off A417, N of A465)*
As well as a place for local farmers to enjoy their well kept ales, this bustling pub is very popular for its good imaginative food from an extensive seasonally changing menu (the choice is smaller at lunchtime); charming, cosy traditional rooms with hops on low beams, open fires, some no smoking areas, and carefully chosen wines; tables outside; cl Mon, 2 wks from 24 Dec; children must be well behaved; disabled access *(01432) 820279*

552. ⌂ STOKE LACY
Dovecote Barn *(2.3 miles off A417, via A465 towards Bromyard)*
£55; 2 rms. Carefully converted 17th-c barn on edge of peaceful village with lovely country views; beams and latched doors, comfortable sitting room, super breakfasts with home-made bread, jams and marmalade, enjoyable meals (by arrangement; dining pubs nearby also), and friendly owners; no smoking; lovely walks *(01432) 820968*

A419

553. ✕ FRAMPTON MANSELL
White Horse *(on A419, S of village)*
Excellent modern english cooking in this smart, friendly dining place with attractive furnishings in the main part, a cosy bar area with large sofa and comfortable chairs for those who want to pop in just for a relaxing drink; a well chosen wine list and well kept real ales; cl Sun pm, 24-25 Dec; disabled access *(01285) 760960*

554. ✕ WOODCHESTER
Ram *(1.9 miles off A419 S of Stroud, via A46)*
Bustling cheerful pub with spectacular valley views from terrace, attractive beamed bar, very enjoyable bar food inc interesting daily specials, prompt friendly service, and lots of real ales; children must be well behaved; partial disabled access *(01453) 873329*

555. ✕ SAPPERTON
Bell *(1 mile off A419, following village signs)*
Carefully renovated 250-year-old pub with a nice mix of wooden furniture in three separate cosy rooms, country prints on stripped stone walls, log fires and woodburners, fresh flowers, newspapers and guidebooks, imaginative bar food using local produce when possible, well kept real ales, up to ten wines (and champagne) by the glass, tables out on small front lawn and partly covered back courtyard; good surrounding walks, tether for horses; cl 25 and 31 Dec; children lunchtime only; disabled access *(01285) 760298*

A420

556. ⌘ KINGSTON BAGPUIZE
Fallowfields (0.9 miles off A420; A415 S, then first right on to Faringdon Rd; Southmoor)
£145, plus special breaks; 10 rms. Delightful Gothic-style manor house with elegant, relaxing sitting rooms, open fires, imaginative food using home-grown produce in attractive conservatory dining room, courteous helpful service, and 12 acres of pretty gardens and paddocks; no smoking; lots to see nearby and plenty for children; cl 24-27 Dec; dogs in bedrooms, *(01865) 820416*

557. ✕ ⌘ BUCKLAND
Lamb (0.3 miles off A420)
£95; rather smart 18th-c stone dining pub in a tiny village, with a civilised little bar, sheep and lamb pictures on the cream-painted walls, newspapers to read, and examples of their own chutneys and jams; delicious imaginative food, no smoking restaurant, a dozen wines by the glass, real ales, and smart helpful service; comfortable bdrms; pleasant, tree-shaded garden, and good walks nearby *(01367) 870484*

A421

558. ✕ WOBURN SANDS
Spooners (2 miles from A421, via A5130 from roundabout)
Smart, pretty restaurant with good value, highly enjoyable french and english cooking, and a welcoming atmosphere; good value snacks downstairs; cl Sun, Mon, 2 wks Christmas; disabled access *(01908) 584385*

A423

559. ✕ WHARF
Wharf Inn (just off A423 N of Banbury)
Open-plan pub by Bridge 136 of the South Oxford Canal with a smart tall-windowed dining area: plain solid tables and high-backed chairs on

mainly wood strip or tiled floors, a big oriental rug, walls in canary yellow, eau de nil or purple, modern artwork, and end windows so close to the water that you feel right by it; enjoyable food (inc full english breakfast), real ales, good coffee, and efficient, friendly service; canal shop, playhouse on stilts, and waterside garden *(01295) 770332*

A429

560. ✕ ⇔ MALMESBURY
Old Bell *(0.7 miles off A429; Abbey Row, just off B4014 through town)*
£150, plus special breaks; 31 attractive rms. With some claim to being one of England's oldest hotels and standing in the shadow of the Norman abbey, this fine wisteria-clad building has traditionally furnished rooms with Edwardian pictures, an early 13th-c hooded stone fireplace, two good fires and plenty of comfortable sofas, magazines and newspapers; cheerful helpful service, very good food, and attractively old-fashioned garden; particularly well organised with facilities and entertainments for children; disabled access; dogs in bedrooms, *(01666) 822344*

561. ⇔ CRUDWELL
Old Rectory Country House Hotel *(just off A429 in village)*
£98, plus special breaks; 12 big homely rms. Elegant, welcoming country-house hotel, formerly the rectory to the Saxon church next door; three acres of lovely landscaped Victorian gardens, an airy drawing room, interesting and enjoyable food in panelled no smoking restaurant, a relaxed atmosphere, and unpretentious service; dogs welcome in bedrooms *(01666) 577194*

562. ⇔ CLAPTON
Clapton Manor *(2.9 miles off A429 (first turn-off S of A436 junction on edge of Bourton), then bear left; easy reach too of A40 just E of Northleach)*
£80; 2 charming rms. Fine 16th-c Cotswold stone house in lovely interestingly planted gardens with marvellous views across the Windrush Valley; large inglenook fireplaces, heavy beams, mullioned windows, antiques, and a relaxed, informal family atmosphere; log fire and TV in residents' sitting room, and good breakfasts with home-made jams and their own eggs served in the dining room or on the terrace; no

MOTORWAY BREAKS

smoking; several restaurants and pubs nearby for dinner; cl Christmas and New Year's Eve *(01451) 810202*

563. ⌂ LITTLE RISSINGTON
Touchstone *(2.4 miles off A429; turn off at Bourton-on-the-Water and keep on Rissington Rd)*
£40; 3 rms with thoughtful extras. Attractive traditional Cotswold stone house with very friendly owners, good breakfasts in dining room with doors on to terrace, and lots of nearby walks; cl Jan; no children *(01451) 822481*

564. ⚘ LOWER SLAUGHTER
(0.7 miles off A429 S of Stow)
With its sister village Upper Slaughter, this is one strong candidate for the title of prettiest village in Britain – a perfect harmony of stone, water, grass and trees. It's not as overwhelmed by summer visitors as its nearby rival Bourton-on-the-Water, though it certainly gets its fair share. The riverside stroll from Lower to Upper Slaughter is a leisurely mile or so.

565. ⌂ LOWER SLAUGHTER
Lower Slaughter Manor *(0.4 miles off A429)*
£220; 16 luxurious rms. Grand 17th-c manor house in four neatly kept acres with a 15th-c dovecote, all-weather tennis court, and croquet; lovely flower arrangements, log fires, fine plaster ceilings, antiques and paintings, excellent modern cooking and most enjoyable wines, and attentive welcoming staff; children over 12; partial disabled access *(01451) 820456*

566. ⌂ UPPER SLAUGHTER
Lords of the Manor *(1.5 miles off A429, past Lower Slaughter)*
£200, plus special breaks; 27 rms carefully furnished with antiques, Victorian sketches and paintings. Warmly friendly hotel with mid 17th-c heart (though it's been carefully extended many times), lovely views over eight acres of grounds from very comfortable library and drawing room, log fires, and fresh flowers; fine modern english cooking in attractive candlelit restaurant overlooking the original rectory gardens, good breakfasts, and kind service; children over 7 in restaurant (high tea available); partial disabled access *(01451) 820243*

567. ⛉ STOW-ON-THE-WOLD
Grapevine (0.2 miles off A429; Sheep St (A436))
£130, plus special breaks; 22 individually decorated, attractive, no smoking rms. Warm, friendly and very well run hotel with antiques, comfortable chairs and a relaxed atmosphere in the lounge, a beamed bar, and imaginative food in the attractive, sunny restaurant with its 70-year-old trailing vine; partial disabled access; dogs in bedrooms, bar and lounge if small and well behaved (01451) 830344

568. ✕ STOW-ON-THE-WOLD
Queens Head (0.1 mile off A429; Market Sq, best entered from N end of town)
Friendly traditional local with bags of character, beams, flagstones, stripped stone, ancient settles and big log fire, good value pub food, well kept local Donnington beers, decent house wines, good friendly service; dogs and children positively welcome, tables in attractive garden (01451) 830563

569. ⛉ STOW-ON-THE-WOLD
Old Stocks (0.1 mile off A429; Market Sq, best entered from N end of town)
£90, plus special breaks; 18 rms. Well run 16th/17th-c Cotswold stone hotel with cosy welcoming small bar, beams and open fire, comfortable residents' lounge, good food, friendly staff, and sheltered garden; cl 18-28 Dec; disabled access; dogs welcome away from restaurant, (01451) 830666

570. ✕ ⛉ PAXFORD
Churchill (2.6 miles off A429, just S of Stretton-on-Fosse)
£70; bustling and friendly dining pub with restaurant extension off simply furnished flagstoned bar – low ceilings, assorted old tables and chairs, and a snug warmed by a good log fire in its big fireplace; well kept real ales, eight good wines by the glass, and constantly changing interesting food; in the best pub tradition, they don't take bookings, but your name goes on a chalked waiting list if all the tables are full; seats outside; disabled access (01386) 594000

MOTORWAY BREAKS

571. ⋈ BLACKWELL
Blackwell Grange (0.7 miles W off A429, S of A3400 junction)
£68; 3 pretty rms. 17th-c Cotswold farmhouse with log fire in comfortable beamed sitting room, large inglenook fireplace in flagstoned dining room, good home cooking using own free-range eggs (evening meal by arrangement; bring your own wine), pretty garden, and nice country views; cl 24-25 Dec; children over 12, but parents with younger children stay in annexe; good disabled access *(01608) 682357*

572. ✗ ⋈ ARMSCOTE
Fox & Goose (0.8 miles W off A429, by first turn off S of A3400 roundabout)
£90; attractive pub with contemporary décor, bright velvet cushions on wooden pews and stools, warm red and cream walls, big mirrors, lots of stylish black and white animal pictures, polished floorboards, flagstones and log fire; friendly service, imaginative enjoyable food, well kept real ales, good wines, and lots of soft drinks; tables on elegant deck overlooking big lawn with fruit trees; cl 25-26 Dec, 1 Jan *(01608) 682293*

573. ✗ ALDERMINSTER
Bell (2.5 miles off A429; first right heading S from A422 Ettington roundabout, then right on A3400)
£70; popular and rather civilised dining pub nr Stratford, with excellent imaginative food using fresh local produce (and they hold regular food and music evenings), several neatly kept communicating areas with flagstones and wooden floors, fresh flowers, good wines, real ales, obliging service, and no smoking restaurant; conservatory and terrace overlooking garden; disabled access *(01789) 450414*

574. ⋈ LOXLEY
Loxley Farm (1.2 miles off A429; first rd W S of Wellesbourne, then in village bear left on Stratford Rd)
£70; 2 suites with their own sitting rooms in attractive barn conversion. Not far from Stratford, this tucked-away, thatched and half-timbered partly 14th-c house has low beams, wonky walls and floors, antiques and dried flowers, open fire, helpful friendly owners, and good Aga-cooked breakfasts; peaceful garden, and fine old village church; cl Christmas and New Year; dogs welcome in bedrooms *(01789) 840265*

A433

575. ✕ TETBURY
Trouble House *(on A433 2 miles NW)*
Popular dining pub in attractively reworked ancient building, lots of hops in three relaxed rooms, chesterfield by a good fire in one big stone fireplace, a mix of stripped pine or oak furniture, imaginative food, a nice choice of wines by the glass, well kept real ales, friendly service; smaller helpings for children, and they sell quite a few of their own preserves; one room is no smoking; picnic-sets on the gravel behind or in a back paddock; cl Sun pm, Mon, 2 wks Jan, bank hols; no children in bar; disabled access *(01666) 502206*

576. ❀ WESTONBIRT
Westonbirt Arboretum *(just off A433 SW of Tetbury)*
Over 18,000 numbered trees and shrubs fill the 17 miles of pathways at this magnificent national collection, begun in 1829. Outstanding in spring and autumn, but interesting any time, with lots of wildlife hidden away among the trees; youll need more than one visit to see it all; June-Sept they host the international festival of contemporary garden design (£1.50 extra). Restaurant, picnic areas, shop, disabled access; open all year, though visitor centre cl winter bank hols; *(01666) 880220*; £6. The Hare & Hounds is handy for food.

A435

577. ❀ COUGHTON
Coughton Court *(on A435 S of Redditch)*
Several priests' holes are hidden in this mainly Elizabethan house, renowned for its imposing gatehouse and beautiful courtyard; the Throckmortons have lived here since 1409. Notable furniture and porcelain, and an exhibition on the Gunpowder Plot; the grounds have a lake, two churches, pleasant walks, formal gardens, and a play area. Meals, snacks, shop, plant sales, disabled access to ground floor; usually cl Mon (exc bank hols), and Tues Sept-June, and all Oct-Mar (exc wknds Oct and late Mar); *(01789) 400777*; £8.60 house and gardens,

MOTORWAY BREAKS

£5.90 grounds only, £2.50 walled garden only; NT. The Green Dragon on the fine old green at Sambourne and interesting Old Washford Mill at Studley are good for lunch.

A438

578. 🏃 SWAINSHILL
Weir Gardens (A438 W of Hereford)
Delightful riverside gardens at their best in spring, with displays of bulbs along woodland walks, and fine views from clifftop walks. Paths can be steep in places. Cl Nov-15 Jan, wkdys Jan, Mon-Tues Feb and April-Oct; *(01981) 590509; £3.60; NT.*

579. ✕ ⇌ HAY-ON-WYE
Old Black Lion (1.6 miles off A438 from Clyro via B4351; in town turn right on Broad St (B4350), then left up Lion St)
£80, plus special breaks; 10 individually designed rms, some in modern coach house. Smartly civilised hotel with low beams and panelling, convivial bar, wide choice of carefully prepared food in bar and no smoking beamed restaurant, and an extensive wine list; close to fishing and riding; cl 25-26 Dec; children over 5 *(01497) 820841*

580. ✕ LLOWES
Radnor Arms (on A438 NE of Glasbury)
Small, modest and very old place with log fire in the bar, neat little cottagey dining room, enjoyable food (nice puddings), friendly staff, and tables in imaginatively planted garden; cl Sun pm, Mon (exc bank hols), 2 wks Nov, 2 wks June; well behaved children welcome; partial disabled access *(01497) 847460*

A442

581. ✕ ⇌ NORTON
Hundred House (on A442 S of Telford)
£99, plus special breaks; 10 cottagey rms with swing and lavender-scented sheets. Carefully refurbished mainly Georgian inn with quite a sophisti-

cated feel, neatly kept bar with old quarry-tiled floors, beamed ceilings, oak panelling and handsome fireplaces, elaborate evening meals using inn's own herbs, friendly service, good bar food, and excellent breakfasts; delightful garden; dogs in bedrooms if well behaved *(01952) 730353*

582. ⚑ WORFIELD
Old Vicarage *(1.5 miles off A442, from Lower Alscot)*
£135, plus special breaks; 14 pretty rms. Restful and carefully restored Edwardian rectory in two acres; two airy conservatory-style lounges, very good interesting food in no smoking restaurant, a fine wine list, a cosseting atmosphere, and warmly friendly, helpful service; good disabled access; dogs in bedrooms *(01746) 716497*

A448

583. ⚑ CHADDESLEY CORBETT
Brockencote Hall *(just off A448)*
£145, plus special breaks; 17 individually decorated rms. Grand country-house hotel in 70 acres with half-timbered dovecote and lake, and plenty of wildlife; large, airy and attractively furnished rooms, conservatory lounge with garden views, elegantly refurbished restaurant with enjoyable modern french and english cooking, and very good service; disabled access *(01562) 777876*

A449

584. ✕ LLANDENNY
Raglan Arms *(just off A449 S of Raglan)*
Dining pub with extensive series of sturdily furnished linked rooms inc a conservatory, as well as a terracotta-walled flagstoned bar with leather sofas, daily papers and *Country Living* to read, and a big log fire in the handsome stone fireplace; good fresh food (plenty of fish and seafood cooked to order), well kept real ales, a well chosen wine list, and pleasant efficient service; best to book at wknds; garden tables *(01291) 690800*

MOTORWAY BREAKS

585. 🏰 LEDBURY
Eastnor Castle (1.5 miles off A449, via A438 just E)
Just what you want a castle to look like, with stirring battlements, exaggerated towers, and some breathtakingly extravagant rooms. Built 1810-24 by Robert Smirke (architect of the British Museum), it's a wonderful marriage of mock medievalism (Norman revival) and creature comforts (it's still very much a family home), with a huge warren of rooms. The entrance hall, originally austerely medieval, was converted to a cosy if still high-ceilinged sitting room, giving a much gentler impression as soon as you walk in; this part was redecorated in italian style in 1860. Pugin was responsible for the highly ornate Gothic drawing room, evidently the inspiration for Lord Irvine`s recent use of those notoriously pricey Pugin wallpapers in his official apartment. The attractive grounds have an arboretum, 300-acre deer park, and plenty of space for a picnic, but what younger visitors enjoy most is the growing yew maze, which has three trails to make it more fun. Adventure playground and assault course. You can stay in the house for the full castle experience. The outside looks especially dramatic in autumn, when the virginia creeper that all but envelopes the walls turns a fiery red. Dogs are welcome on a lead in the castle and grounds. Tearoom; open Sun and bank hols Easter-early Oct, daily (exc Sat) July and Aug; *(01531) 633160*; £7 adults, £5 garden only.

586. ✕ ⇌ LEDBURY
Feathers (just off A449; High St)
£99, plus special breaks; 19 carefully decorated rms making the most of the old beams and timbers. Very striking, mainly 16th-c, black and white hotel with a relaxed atmosphere, log fires, comfortable lounge hall with country antiques, beams and timbers, particularly enjoyable food and friendly service in hop-decked Fuggles bar, a good wine list, and a fine mix of locals and visitors; health and leisure spa with indoor swimming pool; dogs welcome in bedrooms *(01531) 635266*

587. ✕ ⇌ WELLAND
Anchor (2.7 miles off A449 S of Malvern, via A4104)
£60; pretty, fairy-lit Tudor cottage with a welcoming L-shaped bar, a spreading comfortably furnished dining area nicely set with candles and

pink tablecloths and napkins, attentive staff, an extensive choice of enjoyable, changing bar food, and well kept real ales; picnic-sets on lawn, and field for camping with tents or caravans; handy for the Three Counties Showground; cl Sun pm exc bank hols; children in restaurant if booked *(01684) 592317*

588. ⇔ MALVERN WELLS
Cottage in the Wood *(just off A449; Holy Well Rd, which is off W, just N of B4209)*
£99, plus special breaks; 31 compact but pretty rms, some in separate nearby cottages. Family-run Georgian dower house with quite splendid views across the Severn Valley and marvellous walks from the grounds; antiques, log fires, comfortable seats and magazines in public rooms, and modern english cooking and an extensive wine list in attractive no smoking restaurant; dogs in ground-floor bedrooms *(01684) 575859*

589. 🚶 GREAT MALVERN
Malvern Hills *(on A449)*
Forming a grand backdrop to the Vale of Evesham, these offer good walking. From a distance they look a formidable mountain range, but seem to get milder and more welcoming as you approach. The gentle up-and-down path along their spine makes one of England's great ridge walks, with the Cotswolds and Midlands plain on one side and wilder Wales on the other. The Herefordshire Beacon, capped by ramparts of an Iron Age hill fort, is easily reached from the car park on the A449 near Little Malvern. Great Malvern is well placed for the Worcestershire Beacon, the highest point of the range (1,395 ft), and for long circular walks. The Chase Inn at Upper Colwall, Malvern Hills Hotel by the British Camp car park on Wynds Point, and Brewers Arms at West Malvern are also useful start or finish points. On their Herefordshire side, Ledbury and Eastnor are good bases for rambles into the attractive western slopes.

590. ⇔ GREAT MALVERN
Cowleigh Park Farm *(0.8 miles off A449; A4219 NW)*
£62; 3 rms. Carefully restored and furnished black and white timbered 17th-c farmhouse in own grounds, surrounded by lovely countryside, with good breakfasts and light suppers or full evening meals (prior

MOTORWAY BREAKS

booking); self-catering also; cl Christmas; children over 7; dogs welcome in bedrooms *(01684) 566750*

591. 🕸 HARTLEBURY
Hartlebury Castle (0.7 miles off A449 via B4193)
Mainly 18th c, this is the official residence of the Bishop of Worcester, and (Tues-Thurs only) you can visit some of the elegant state rooms. It also houses the County Museum, inc Victorian folk life and costumes, room displays, and gypsy caravans. Snacks, shop; cl Mon, Good Fri, and all Dec-Jan; *(01299) 250416*; £3. The White Hart has good value food.

A456

592. 🕸 HAGLEY
Hagley Hall (0.5 miles off A456/A491 roundabout, via Park Rd and Hall Lane)
Completed in 1760, this was the last of the great Palladian houses; guided tours take in the fine rococo plasterwork, 18th-c furniture and family portraits inc works by Reynolds and Van Dyck, and then you can stroll around the picturesque deer park. Snacks; open pm wkdys Jan and Feb, plus some bank hol Sats, best to phone; *(01562) 882408*; £5. The Fountain over at Clent is a good dining pub.

593. 🕸 BEWDLEY
West Midlands Safari Park (off A456 towards Kidderminster; Spring Grove)
Visit a land that has animals from all corners of the globe and where you can see the largest family group of rare white tigers in the UK; all weather, four mile self-drive safari around the continents is home to a superb collection of rare and exotic species such as elephants, white lions, giraffe, rhino, african wild dogs, wolves, wallabies, zebra and many more. Discovery Trail has a variety of attractions such as Twilight Cave, Seal Island, Creepy Crawlies, seaquarium, Animal and Reptile encounters, Sealion Theatre and famous Reptile House, plus Hippo Lake and the friendly goat and deer park; interactive touch screen technology, amusement area with good choice of rides and games. Picnic area, meals, snacks, shop, mostly disabled access; open Mar-end Oct;

(01299) 402114; £7.99 inc a free return visit any time during the rest of the season (exc bank hols). Children under 4 are free; rides charged extra and buying multi-ride wristbands is the best option; under 1.2m £7.25, over 1.2m £8.75 or two ride tickets from machines for £3.

594. 🕌 BRIDGNORTH
Severn Valley Railway (0.4 miles off A456 via B4363 Oldbury Rd, then fork left into B4373; handy too for A442)
The leading standard-gauge steam railway, with a great collection of locomotives, carriages from the 1930s to 1960s. Lots of period details in the stations, and varied scenery along the route; trains run every wknd, plus daily May-Sept and school holidays. The Railwaymans Arms in the station fits in perfectly, good for a snack. At the Kidderminster end (where the station is a convincing modern replica of a Victorian station), you can join regular mainline trains. An unusual outing here is to combine a trip on the railway to Hampton Loade station with a connecting ferry across the Severn; return ferry fare £1, wknds and bank hol Mon, plus daily in school hols, Apr-end Sept.

595. 🕌 BURFORD
Burford House Gardens (just off A456 W of Tenbury Wells)
Delightfully set by the River Teme, these tranquil gardens are the home of a national collection of clematis. Lots of other colourful plants too and a wild flower meadow. Meals, snacks, plant sales, disabled access; *(01584) 810777*; £3.95. The Ship in Tenbury has good imaginative food.

A458

596. 🕌 MUCH WENLOCK
(just off A458)
Lovely little medieval market town, with lots of timbered and jettied buildings. The Talbot, George & Dragon, Gaskell Arms and Wheatland Fox all have enjoyable food. The remains of the 11th-c priory are well worth a look; *(01952) 727466.*

MOTORWAY BREAKS

597. ✕ ⋈ MUCH WENLOCK
Talbot (just off A458; High St)
£75, plus special breaks; 6 rms. Dating in part from 1360 and once part of Wenlock Abbey, this converted 18th-c malthouse is very civilised, with pretty flowers, log fires, prints, pleasant staff, good food in no smoking restaurant and bar (open all day wknds), and well kept real ales; cl 25 Dec *(01952) 727077*

A465

598. ⋈ GILWERN
Wenallt Farm (0.6 miles off A465; turn off S just W of A4077 junction, then bear left)
£56; 7 rms. Friendly and relaxing 16th-c Welsh longhouse on 40 acres of farmland in the Brecon Beacons National Park, with oak beams and inglenook fireplace in big drawing room, a TV room, good food in dining room, packed lunches on request, and lots to do nearby; cl Christmas; dogs welcome in bedrooms *(01873) 830694*

A470

599. ⋈ CAERPHILLY
Caerphilly Castle (3 miles off A470 via A468 and B4600)
One of the largest medieval fortresses in Britain, begun in 1268, with extensive land and water defences. Rising sheer from its broad outer moat, it's a proper picture-book castle, pleasing for this reason to the most casual visitor. It also enthrals serious students of castle architecture with its remarkably complex design of concentric defences. Look out for the incredible leaning tower, which appears ready to topple any second; audio-visual display and replica medieval siege engines; new visitor centre. Shop, disabled access to ground floor; cl 24-26 Dec, 1 Jan; *(029) 2088 3143*; £3; Cadw. In the oddly strung-out small town, the ancient Courthouse overlooking the castle has reasonably priced food.

A470

600. ✗ ⋈ FELINFACH
Griffin (just off A470 NE of Brecon)
£92.50; brightly painted opened-up roadside restaurant with good imaginative modern cooking using only local ingredients in two formally set out bare-boards or flagstoned no smoking front dining rooms with big modern prints; back bar area with stripped furniture and floors, mustard walls and bright blue dado, and leather sofas by the log fire; six good house wines in three glass sizes, polite service, and no smoking area; comfortable bdrms; cl Mon am, 25 Dec; disabled access *(01874) 620111*

601. ⋈ LLYSWEN
Llangoed Hall (on A470 N)
£180, plus special breaks; 23 very pretty rms with luxurious touches. Fine Edwardian mansion beautifully converted into a first-class hotel with lovely house-party atmosphere, handsome hall, elegant and spacious public rooms with antiques, pictures, fresh flowers and views over the grounds, imaginative modern cooking in charming restaurant (non-residents most welcome), an excellent wine list, and very good welsh breakfasts; marvellous surrounding countryside; children over 8 *(01874) 754525*

602. ⋈ RHAYADER
Beili Neuadd (2 miles off A470, via B4518 NE)
£52; 3 rms with log fires, and newly converted stone barn with 3 bunkhouse rms. Charming partly 16th-c stone-built farmhouse in quiet countryside (they have their own trout pools and woodland), with beams, polished oak floorboards, and nice breakfasts in new garden room; self-catering also; cl Christmas; children over 8; dogs by arrangement *(01597) 810211*

603. ⋈ DOLGELLAU
Tyddynmawr Farmhouse (2.7 miles off A470; turn off on A493 just W, then next left turn, then first right)
£56; 3 lovely spacious rms. Award-winning 18th-c farmhouse at the foot of Cadair Idris, with wonderful scenery, oak beams, log fires, and welsh oak furniture, marvellous breakfasts with home-made bread, preserves and muesli, and warmly welcoming owners; cl Dec-Jan; no children *(01341) 422331*

MOTORWAY BREAKS

604. ⋈ GELLILYDAN
Tyddyn Du Farm (just off A470 by A487 junction)
£70, plus special breaks; 4 ground-floor, private stable and long barn suites with jacuzzi baths, fridges and microwaves, one with airbath. 400-year-old farmhouse on working farm in the heart of Snowdonia, with beams and exposed stonework, and big inglenook fireplaces in lounge; children can help bottle-feed the lambs, and look at goats, ducks, sheep and shetland ponies; fine walks, inc short one to their own Roman site; partial disabled access; dogs welcome away from dining room *(01766) 590281*

605. ✗ ⋈ BLAENAU FFESTINIOG
Queen's Hotel (on A470 (High St))
£70, plus special breaks; 12 individually decorated rms named after locomotives. By the famous narrow-gauge railway and surrounded by Snowdonia National Park, this most attractively refurbished Victorian hotel has real ales in convivial lounge bar, good all-day food in bistro (converts to more formal evening restaurant with imaginative dishes), and swift friendly service; lots to do nearby; cl 25 Dec *(01766) 830055*

606. ⋈ BLAENAU FFESTINIOG
Llechwedd Slate Caverns (on A470 just N)
The same company has been mining and quarrying slate here for over 150 years, and their well organised tours of the huge caverns bring the history of the site vividly to life; it's well worth doing both the underground rides. In Deep Mine, Britain's steepest passenger railway takes you 450 ft below the summit of the mountain. Next is a hard-hat walk through ten stunning subterranean chambers, each with a sound and light show illustrating the world of a Victorian miner. You need to be relatively agile (61 steps going down, but 10 more on the way up if we counted right), and bring warm clothing even in summer. The highlight is an eerie underground lake, nicely lit to create atmospheric shadows on the water and the steep, craggy walls. The other tour (the Miners Tramway) explains more about the mining process: battery-powered trains take you around the Victorian workings, through splendid man-made caverns, some of which have tableaux or demonstrations of ancient mining skills. You get off at various points along the way, and the guides give useful talks. Outside you can explore the old buildings of Llechwedd village; the last residents left in the 1970s, but there's a

A470

Victorian pub (wholesome inexpensive food), and several shops stocking Victorian-themed goods which you can buy using period money; you can exchange your coins at the former bank, now a museum. Meals, snacks, shops, some disabled access with prior warning; cl 25-26 Dec, 1 Jan; *(01766) 830306*. The surface attractions are free.

607. 🕸 LLANRWST
Gwydir Castle (0.7 miles off A470; B5106)
Splendid Tudor courtyard house with later additions, partly built of Maenan Abbey stone after the Dissolution. The former ancestral home of the Wynn family, it is set in Grade I listed gardens in the Conwy Valley. Cl Nov-Feb, and some Sats for weddings – best to phone; *(01492) 641687*.

608. ✕ LLANRWST
Ty-Hwnt-i'r-Bont (just off A470 via B5106)
Charming little 500-year-old cottage by bridge with nice old country furniture under the beams and joists, interesting knick-knacks, light lunches, home-made cakes, shortbread and scones for enjoyable afternoon teas, and quite a choice of teas, coffees and milk shakes; homemade mustards to take away, and old books and bric-a-brac upstairs; cl Mon (exc bank hols), cl end Oct-mid Mar *(01492) 640138*

609. 🕸 TAL-Y-CAFN
Bodnant Garden (0.5 miles off A470 just N)
Started in 1875, this garden is among Britain's greatest. Part of the (80-acre) grounds has a beautiful woodland garden in a sheltered valley, notable for its rhododendrons and azaleas, while below the private house are five terraces in the italian style, with a canal pool, reconstructed pin mill and an open-air stage on the lowest. Many fine rare plants inc unusual trees and shrubs. Meals, snacks, shop, disabled access (but it is steep in places); cl Nov to mid-Mar; *(01492) 650460*; £5.50; NT. The Tal-y-Cafn Hotel on the main rd is good for lunch.

MOTORWAY BREAKS

A477

610. ⌂ CAREW
Old Stable Cottage (0.4 miles off A477 via A4075)
£60; 3 charming rms. Originally a stable and carthouse for the castle, this attractive place has an inglenook fireplace and original bread oven, a lovely sitting room with teak beams (probably from former shipyards), games room, conservatory overlooking the garden, and good Aga-cooked food; cl Dec-Jan inc; children over 3 *(01646) 651889*

611. ☗ PEMBROKE
Pembroke Castle (1.4 miles off A477 via A4139)
The birthplace of Henry VII and thus the Tudor dynasty, this mighty fortress is largely intact, and its endless passages, tunnels and stairways are great fun to explore; super exhibitions which tell the tale of medieval life. The 75-ft tower is one of the finest in Britain; there's also a brass rubbing centre. Summer events, snacks, disabled access to ground floor; cl 24-26 Dec, 1 Jan; *(01646) 681510*; £3 (guided tours Jun-Aug exc Sat).

612. ✗ PEMBROKE FERRY
Ferry Inn (just off A477; get down to pub from last roundabout S of bridge)
Former sailors' haunt by the water below Cleddau Bridge (not by the new ferry), open all day, with wide choice of very fresh fish dishes – non-fishy things too – nautical décor, good views, a relaxed pubby atmosphere, well kept real ales, decent malt whiskies, and efficient service; restaurant cl 25-26 Dec; disabled access *(01646) 682947*

A483

613. ✗ MONTGOMERY
Brickys (3 miles off A483 via B4385; in town turn left on B4386 Chirbury Rd, pub on left)
Plain-looking pub hiding really special food, from a short and interesting choice using unusually carefully chosen ingredients cooked with real

imagination, and served attractively on big plates; the bar (shiny red flooring tiles throughout) has an area on the left for eating, with seven or eight pub tables, a few modern prints, a big woodburner, real ales, organic cider, and a short but interesting choice of wines inc good ones by the glass; linen-set restaurant, and friendly and quietly helpful service; cl Sun evening, Mon/Tues, and winter wkdy lunchtimes *(01686) 668177*

614. ⌂ LLANWRTYD WELLS
Carlton House (just off A483, on Dolycoed Rd)
£65, plus special breaks; 6 well equipped rms. Warmly friendly owners run this comfortable Edwardian restaurant-with-rooms, and there's a relaxing little sitting room with plants and antiques, an attractive dining room with original panelling and log fire, exceptionally good modern british cooking using top-quality local produce (delicious puddings and home-made canapés and petits fours), super breakfasts with home-made bread and marmalade, and a thoughtful wine list; cl 10-29 Dec; dogs welcome in bedrooms *(01591) 610248*

615. ⌂ LLANGAMMARCH WELLS
Lake (2 miles off A483 via B4519, then first right)
£140, plus special breaks; 19 charming, pretty rms with fruit and decanter of sherry. Particularly well run 1860 half-timbered hotel in 50 acres with plenty of wildlife, well stocked trout lake, clay pigeon shoots, tennis and riding or walk their two friendly labradors; deeply comfortable tranquil drawing room with antiques, paintings and log fire, wonderful afternoon teas (in summer under the chestnut tree overlooking the river), courteous discreet service, fine wines and very good modern british cooking in elegant candlelit dining room, and liberal breakfasts; children over 7 in evening dining room; disabled access; dogs in some bedrooms *(01591) 620202*

616. ✕ ⌂ MONTGOMERY
Dragon (3 miles off A483 via B4385; Market Sq)
£79.50, plus special breaks; 20 rms. Attractive black and white timbered small hotel with a pleasant grey-stone tiled hall, comfortable residents' lounge, beamed bar, restaurant using local produce; indoor swimming pool, sauna; dogs welcome in bedrooms *(01686) 668359*

MOTORWAY BREAKS

617. 🎎 WELSHPOOL
Powis Castle (0.5 miles off A458/A483, 1m S)
In magnificent gardens with splendid 18th-c terraces, this dramatic-looking castle was built in the 13th c, but far from falling into decay like so many others, has developed into a grand house. It's been constantly occupied since its construction, once by the son of Clive of India – there are displays about his father's life. You can now also see the opulent 19th-c state coach used by the 3rd Earl of Powis, and mannequins show off the sumptuous garb of his coachman and footmen. Meals, snacks, shop; cl Tues and Weds (castle and museum cl am); *(01938) 551944 information line, (01938) 551920 property office;* £8.80, garden only £6.20; NT.

618. ✕ GRESFORD
Pant-yr-Ochain (0.7 miles off A483, via A534 (A5156) bypass E, then left on Old Wrexham Rd at next roundabout)
Stylishly decorated spacious pub in attractive grounds, with a gently upmarket atmosphere in the light and airy main room, a wide range of interesting prints and bric-a-brac, and a good mix of individually chosen country furnishings; open fires, a big dining area set out as a library, excellent food from a daily changing menu, a good range of decent wines, well kept real ales, lots of malt whiskies, and polite efficient service; one room is no smoking; children until 6pm *(01978) 853525*

A487

619. ⛵ FISHGUARD
Gilfach Goch (just off A487 a mile E)
£64; 5 rms. Traditional carefully modernised 18th-c stone-built farmhouse on 18-acre smallholding near Pembrokeshire coastal path, with sheep, donkeys, cats and fowl; lovely views, log fires, homely lounge, good country cooking, and a safe garden for children; no smoking; cl Oct-Easter; partial disabled access *(01348) 873871*

620. ⛵ FISHGUARD
Manor Town House (on A487 (Main St))
£65; 6 comfortable rms, most with sea views. Georgian house with fine

views of harbour from sheltered garden, a guests' lounge with books, an attractive, well planned basement restaurant with delicious home-made food using fresh local produce, and enjoyable breakfasts (and pre-dinner drinks), out on the terrace overlooking the sea in good weather; cl Christmas/November/January; dogs in bedrooms by arrangement *(01348) 873260*

621. ⋈ GLYNARTHEN
Penbontbren Farm (0.5 miles off A487 (third turn off S heading W from B4334; or third S, heading E from B4333))
£96, plus special breaks; 10 rms in converted stone farm outbuildings. Victorian farmhouse in lovely countryside with a little farm museum, and nearby beaches; period pine furnishings in bar, lounge and well liked restaurant, good honest country cooking and hearty breakfasts; cl 24-28 Dec; disabled access *(01239) 810248*

622. ⋈ EGLWYSFACH
Ynyshir Hall (just off A487 SW of Machynlleth)
£125, plus special breaks; 9 individually decorated, no smoking rms, two with four-posters. Carefully run Georgian manor house in 14 acres of landscaped gardens adjoining the Ynyshir coastal bird reserve, with particularly good service, antiques, log fires and paintings in the light and airy public rooms, extremely good food using home-grown vegetables, and delicious breakfasts; lots to do nearby; may cl 3 wks Jan; children over 9; disabled access to ground-floor rms; dogs in two bedrooms *(01654) 781209*

623. ⋈ MACHYNLLETH
Centre for Alternative Technology (just off A487 2.5 miles N)
Reached by a water-balanced cliff railway with lovely views, the 7-acre display gardens are crammed with exhibitions, displays and information. The Centre is concerned with presenting solutions to environmental problems in an interesting and informative way, and shows sustainable ways of living through environmental technologies – and how to save energy and money in your home. Wholesome vegetarian restaurant, good bookshop, partial disabled access; cl 25-26 Dec and 2 wks mid-Jan; *(01654) 705950/702400*; £8 summer, £5.35 winter. They do good value family tickets, and you can save 10% if you arrive by bus, bike or

MOTORWAY BREAKS

foot; you can also halve the cost of hiring a bike from Greenstiles (Heol Maengwyn); *(01654) 703543*.

624. 🏰 CAERNARFON
Caernarfon Castle (0.4 miles off A487, well signed)
With its nine polygonal towers and walls of colour-banded stone, this was planned by Edward I as a Royal residence and seat of government for North Wales. Edward's son was born here and presented to the people, setting the precedent for future Princes of Wales. Exhibitions include the regimental museum of the Royal Welch Fusiliers, and an impressive audio-visual display. Shop; usually cl 24-26 Dec, 1 Jan; *(01286) 677617*; £4.50; Cadw. The square outside, around the statue of former PM David Lloyd George, has a busy Sat market.

625. ⌂ CAERNARFON
Seiont Manor (2.7 miles off A487 via A4086 E)
£180, plus special breaks; 28 luxurious rms. Fine hotel built from the original farmstead of a Georgian manor house, in 156 acres of mature parkland; open fires and comfortable sofas in lounge, restful atmosphere in library and drawing room, imaginative food in restaurant's four interconnecting areas, and leisure suite with swimming pool, gym, and sauna; dogs welcome in bedrooms *(01286) 673366*

A494

626. ⌂ LLANFAIR D C
Eyarth Station (0.6 miles off A494 S of Ruthin)
£54, plus special breaks; 6 pretty rms. Carefully converted old railway station with quiet gardens and wonderful views, a friendly relaxed atmosphere, log fire in airy and comfortable beamed lounge, good breakfasts and enjoyable suppers in dining room (more lovely views), sun terrace and heated swimming pool, and lots of walks; cl Feb; disabled access; dogs in bedrooms by arrangement *(01824) 703643*

A505

627. ✗ FOWLMERE
Chequers (2 miles off A505 via B1368)
Civilised old coaching inn with professionally attentive staff, an imaginative menu in galleried restaurant, and thoughtful wine list; two comfortably furnished communicating rooms downstairs with an open log fire, while upstairs there are beams, wall timbering and some interesting moulded plasterwork; airy no smoking conservatory overlooking the neat garden; cl 25 Dec; children in family room; disabled access (01763) 208369

A508

628. ☖ LAMPORT
Lamport Hall (just off A508)
Mainly 17th- and 18th-c house in spacious park, with tranquil gardens containing a remarkable alpine rockery – the home of the first garden gnomes, only one of which now survives. Frequent antiques fairs, concerts and other events. Snacks, shop, disabled access to ground floor and gardens; open pm Sun Easter-Oct; guided tours 2.30 and 3.30 pm (also 2.30 pm Mon-Fri Aug); *(01604) 686272*; £4.50. The refurbished Swan has great views and bistro-style food.

629. ☖ KELMARSH
Kelmarsh Hall (A508, just N of A14 intersection)
James Gibbs designed this splendid Palladian-style house in the early 18th c; the most interesting features are the chinese room and double storey entrance hall. In the charming grounds the lake and triangular kitchen garden walls date from the 18th c, with other formal features added in the 20th, inc an 18th-c orangery that was moved here in the 1950s. A former owner bred the famous british white cattle whose descendants still graze the parkland. Tearoom, disabled access; house and gardens open pm Sun Easter-Sept, Thurs in July-Aug and bank hol Mon, £4.50; gardens open Tues-Thurs pm Easter-Sept, £3.50. The Stags Head at Maidwell (A508 S) is a pleasant food stop.

MOTORWAY BREAKS

630. ✗ GREAT OXENDON
George (A508, N of A14)
£62.50; though rather gaunt-looking on its bank high over the main road, inside this carefully decorated dining pub is really cosy and convivial; two opened-together rooms of the main beamed bar have attractive prints and engravings, and there's a no smoking conservatory overlooking the shrub-sheltered garden; very good popular food (well liked by older lunchers especially), well kept real ales, decent wines, and daily papers; cl Sun pm; disabled access *(01858) 465205*

A509

631. ⋒ OLNEY
(on A509)
Pleasant stone-built small town with a nice riverside stroll to the Robin Hood at Clifton Reynes, and a Thurs market. The Bull is HQ for the town's famous Shrove Tuesday pancake race, first run in 1445; the civilised old Swan (no under-10s) does good lunches.

A511

632. ⋒ COALVILLE
Snibston Discovery Park (0.7 miles off A511, from A447 junction; Ashby Rd)
Busy 100-acre site based around a former colliery (the first shaft was sunk by George and Robert Stephenson), with a huge outdoor science play area, a nature reserve, and historic mine buildings. At its centre an exhibition hall houses six (mostly interactive) galleries – children like the Science Alive gallery best, with plenty of experiments and hands-on activities, even the illusion of cycling with a skeleton. Similarly organised galleries look at transport, mining and fashion, and they've recently added a new gallery divided into Toy Town (for children under 5) and Toy Box (for the under-8s); there's also space for temporary exhibitions. Evocative tours of the old colliery are taken by former pitmen. Snacks, shop, disabled access; cl 25-26 Dec, 1 and 12-16 Jan;

(01530) 278444; £5.70. The charming old New Inn over at Peggs Green (off A512 Ashby—Shepshed) has lots of interesting old local photographs, inc colliery ones.

A515

633. ASHBOURNE
Callow Hall (0.5 miles off A515; Mappleton Rd, off B5035 (Union St))
£130, plus special breaks; 16 lovely well furnished rms, excellent bthrms. Quietly smart and friendly Victorian mansion up a long drive through grounds with fine trees and surrounded by marvellous countryside; comfortable drawing room with open fire, fresh flowers and plants, and period furniture, very good traditional food using home-grown produce in warmly decorated dining room, excellent breakfasts, and kind hosts; good private fishing; cl 25-26 Dec; disabled access; dogs welcome in bedrooms *(01335) 300900*

634. ILAM
(3 miles off A515, W from Tissington)
Attractive estate village in the Manifold Valley (nr its junction with Dove Dale), surrounded by a NT-owned country park which runs on both banks of the River Manifold and was formerly the parkland for 19th-c gothic Ilam Hall; free access to the park but pay and display parking; NT tearoom, shop and information centre.

635. TISSINGTON
(just off A515)
The Peak District's most beautiful village, its broad main street wonderfully harmonious, with wide grass verges, handsome stone houses inc a Jacobean hall (open pm Tues-Thurs late June to late Aug; *(01335) 352200*) and interesting church. The grey stone gardener's cottage is familiar from many calendars; garden centre, decent homely café.

636. BIGGIN-BY-HARTINGTON
Biggin Hall (0.8 miles off A515, just S of Hartington)
£76, plus special breaks; 20 spacious rms with antiques, some in converted 18th-c stone building and in bothy. Cheerfully run 17th-c house

MOTORWAY BREAKS

in quiet grounds with a very relaxed atmosphere, two comfortable sitting rooms, log fires, freshly cooked straightforward food with an emphasis on free-range wholefoods served at 7pm in the attractive dining room, and packed lunches if wanted; children 12 and over; limited disabled access; dogs in annexe only, by arrangement *(01298) 84451*

637. ✕ BUXTON
Coffee Bean Café (just off A515; Spring Gdns (first turn left coming S from A53))
Small bustling café, long and narrow, with old tea and coffee advertisements, 15 types of coffee, all-day breakfasts, savouries and light lunches, and delicious cakes; cl evenings; partial disabled access *(01298) 27345*

A523

638. 🕺 RUDYARD LAKE
(on A523 NW of Leek)
Though man-made it's perhaps one of Staffordshire's prettiest sights (Kipling owed his given name to his father's delight in it); you can hire a boat, and the muddy marshland provides a haven for wading birds. The meadows and forested slopes above are pleasant for walks and picnics; alternatively, the Knott Inn up the road at Rushton Spencer has good food, and is on the Staffordshire Way long-distance path.

639. ⋈ POTT SHRIGLEY
Shrigley Hall (2.5 miles off A523, in Adlington just N of Macclesfield)
£130, plus special breaks; 150 smart well equipped rms, some with country views. In over 260 acres of parkland, this impressive country house has a splendid entrance hall with several elegant rooms leading off, enjoyable food in the orangery and restaurant, and good service from friendly staff; championship golf course, fishing, tennis, and leisure centre in former church building; plenty to do nearby; disabled access; dogs welcome in bedrooms *(01625) 575757*

640. 🕺 ✕ ⋈ MACCLESFIELD
(on A523)
Away from the modern shopping streets are plenty of fine old buildings

A523

associated with the early industrial revolution and the silk industry; the weavers' cottages on Paradise St with their wide garret windows are of special note. Paradise Mill (Park Lane) has enthusiastic guides, often former silk workers, who demonstrate silk production on the mill's restored handlooms – room settings give a good idea of 1930s working conditions. Good disabled access; tours are 11.30, 1.00, 2.30 and 3.30; cl am Sun, 25-26 Dec and 1 Jan; *(01625) 612045*; £3.10. The nearby Park Green Silk Museum is in what used to be the art school, where silk designers were trained; displays on the properties of silk and design, and lots of historic machinery; cl am Sun, 25-26 Dec and 1 Jan; £3.10. In Roe St a former Sunday school for children who worked in the silk mills is now a heritage centre with a good silk museum – audio-visual displays, exhibitions and some fine examples of the end product. Meals, snacks, shop, some disabled access (and audio guides); cl 25-26 Dec, 1 Jan; *(01625) 613210*; £3.10. The West Park Museum (B5087) has a decent range of decorative arts (inc works by local bird artist Charles Tunnicliffe), and some interesting egyptian antiquities. Adjacent West Park is pleasant and has one of the largest bowling greens in the country. Shop, disabled access; cl am, all day Mon (exc bank hols), 24-26 Dec, 1 Jan; *(01625) 619831*; free. Behind St Michael's church is a more ancient core with quaint little cobbled alleys, the famous 108 steps, and fine views across the town to the Pennines. The tea shop at Arighi Bianchi furniture shop (Silk Rd) is highly recommended. **£94.95**; The Sutton Hall Hotel (Bullock Lane, Sutton, just S, *((01260) 253211*) has 9 marvellous rms; a welcoming and secluded historic baronial hall, full of character and style, with high black beams, stone fireplaces, suits of armour and so forth, friendly service, and good food; can arrange clay shooting/golf/fishing; partial disabled access. Finally, if you are heading east, you might like to work out a detour: the A537 from here to Buxton is England's most dangerous road.

641. 🍴 ⌂ PRESTBURY
(under a mile off A523, via A538)
Very prosperous-feeling now, with leafy surroundings, good shops, and pleasant riverside walks to the S, along the Bollin. The civilised 16th-c Legh Arms is appealingly furnished with several distinctive areas, giving a relaxing meal break: a good coal fire, well kept real ales, good coffee and wine list, daily papers, and interesting daily specials plus excellent

MOTORWAY BREAKS

bread; more elaborate choice in attractive restaurant, and pleasant service by uniformed staff; open all day, they have new bedrooms (**£80**; *(01625) 829130)*. Another place to stay here is the White House (**£123**, plus wknd breaks; *(01625) 829376)*; 11 individual, stylish and well equipped rms with antiques, in separate manor just a short walk from the restaurant. Carefully restored Georgian house with an exceptionally friendly and pretty restaurant, imaginative modern british cooking, thoughtful wine list and a spacious bar; breakfast in small conservatory lounge or in room; cl 25-26 Dec; children over 10.

A534

642. 🕸 HASLINGTON
Lakemore Country Park (under a mile off A534; Lane End Farm, Clay Lane – N of the village itself which is on the other side of the main rd)
Readers enjoy this 36-acre country park (now with full zoo status), and animals range from miniature donkeys, llamas, rare breed pigs and ornamental ducks; outdoor and indoor play areas – extra charge for donkey rides and craft sessions. Open Weds-Sun Easter-Oct and daily during school hols; *(01270) 253556*; £3.

643. ⊭ FULLERS MOOR
Frogg Manor (A534 just E of A41 junction)
£100, plus special breaks; 7 lavishly decorated rms with thoughtful extras. Enjoyably eccentric Georgian manor house full of ornamental frogs and antique furniture, open fires and ornate dried-flower arrangements, a restful upstairs sitting room, cosy little bar, a large collection of 30s/40s records, and good english cooking in elegant dining room which leads to conservatory overlooking the gardens; disabled access; dogs welcome in bedrooms *(01829) 782629*

A537

644. 🕸 KNUTSFORD
(A537 (and only 3 miles from M6 junction 19, via A556 and A5033))
Despite obvious present-day prosperity and some rather heavy traffic,

A556

this has a pleasantly old-world feel, with lots of striking Georgian and other period buildings. It might seem strangely familiar to you if you've read Mrs Gaskell's *Cranford* – its alias. Two good places to stay here: Longview (51-55 Manchester Rd, *(01565) 632119*), a good-sized friendly Victorian hotel with attractive period and reproduction furnishings, open fires in original fireplaces, pleasant cellar bar, ornate restaurant, and good well presented food (cl Christmas); and up the B5085 towards Mobberley, Laburnum Cottage (Knutford Rd, *(01565) 872464*), a neatly kept and friendly no smoking country guesthouse in an acre of landscaped garden; relaxed atmosphere in comfortable lounge with books, a sunny conservatory, and very good food. The Belle Epoque Brasserie (King St) is a popular restaurant-with-rooms decorated in art nouveau style with lavish drapes, marbled pillared alcoves, and smartly set tables, enthusiastic friendly staff and lovely modern cooking; cl Sun pm; children over 12. On Knutsford's northern edge, Tatton Park is a splendid place for a picnic; there's a per-car charge for the lovely grounds (cl winter Mon and 25 Dec), with an Edwardian rose garden, italian and japanese gardens, orangery and fern house, good adventure playgrounds, and big country park with mature trees, lakes, signposted walks, and deer and waterfowl. There are additional charges for further estate features, open Tues-Sun (and bank hols) Apr-Sept. The Home Farm (also open pm winter wknds) works as it did 80 years ago, with vintage machinery and rare breeds of animals. The magnificently opulent neo-classical mansion has a splendid collection of furnishings, porcelain and paintings (inc two Canalettos) in its state rooms, and tours of the restored kitchens and servants' quarters. Open only on summer wknds (and some in Dec), the Tudor Old Hall hints at the long history of the site. Among several appealing shops one specialises in produce from the estate. Meals, snacks, disabled access; *(01625) 534400*.

A556

645. 🕸 DELAMERE FOREST
(just off A556)
A good fresh-air break – several square miles of mainly coniferous plantation, with some older oak and other woodland, inc plenty of open stretches and picnic places, and some small stretches of reedy water. A

MOTORWAY BREAKS

section of the 30-mile Sandstone Trail long-distance path takes in much of the best bits, with good access from several places inc Delamere and Hatchmere, and decent prettily placed pubs in both villages.

A590

646. ⌂ LINDALE
Greenacres Country Guest House *(0.6 miles off A590, via B5271)* **£54**; 4 appealing rms. Charming 19th-c village house with friendly atmosphere, pretty sitting room, conservatory, log fire, big breakfasts in cosy dining room, and packed lunch on request; kind to families and will set aside the whole house for family parties; cl Christmas and New Year *(015395) 34578*

647. ※ × ⌂ ULVERSTON
(just off A590)
The Farmers Arms (Market Pl) is a friendly 16th-c pub with unusual mix of wicker chairs and sofas with beams and open fire, enjoyable fairly priced food, good new world wines by the glass and interesting real ales; open all day; *(01229) 584469*. For a good more restaurant meal or a very comfortable overnight stay, head right out past the Glaxo factory to the civilised and nicely placed Bay Horse (Canal Foot) overlooking Morecambe Bay, with attractively presented interesting food, well kept real ales and good wine list; comfortable rms **£160**; *(01229) 583972*; children in bar lounge only; cl Mon am; children over 12; disabled access; dogs welcome in bedrooms

A591

648. ※ SIZERGH
Sizergh Castle *(just off A591)*
Lovely country house surrounded by two lakes, over the centuries harmoniously extended from its original sturdy 14th-c tower by the family who have lived here for generations. Fine Tudor and Elizabethan carving, panelling and furniture, Jacobite relics, and terraced gardens surrounding a grand flight of steps down to the water. Lots to interest a gardener, inc

an enormous rock garden, japanese maples, water garden, wild flowers, and daffodils in the apple orchard; the autumn colours are lovely. Snacks, shop, disabled access to garden and ground floor of house; open pm Sun-Thurs Apr-Oct; *(015395) 60951*; £5.80, £3.50 garden only; NT.

649. ☼ ✕ SIZERGH
Low Sizergh Barn (brown sign off A591)
Highly recommended by readers for its fresh farm foods, and other local produce inc damson beer and Morecambe Bay shrimps. A nature trail around the organic dairy farm highlights its conservation work. The tearoom, upstairs in a 17th-c barn, is well worth visiting for its glorious array of local and organic produce; in a separate place there are crafts (inc a potter) and clothes that overlook the milking parlour. Meals, snacks, shop, cl 25-26 Dec and 1 Jan; *(015395) 60426*; free.

650. ☼ WINDERMERE
Holehird Gardens (off A591, 1.4 miles N up A591)
Lakeland Horticultural Society's hillside garden – ten acres of well grown plants, with three National Collections inc one of hydrangeas, extensive rock gardens, herbaceous borders and alpine houses; lovely lakeland views. Open all year, limited disabled access; *(015394) 46008*; £2 suggested donation (grounds and society are manned entirely by volunteers).

651. ⇌ WINDERMERE
Langdale Chase Hotel (on A591 N towards Ambleside)
£130, plus special breaks; 27 rms, many with marvellous lake view. Welcoming family-run hotel in lovely position on the edge of Lake Windermere with bathing from the hotel jetty; croquet, putting and rowing, afternoon tea on the terraces, gracious oak-panelled rooms with antiques, paintings, fresh flowers, open fires, very good food (huge breakfasts, too), and friendly service; disabled access; dogs in bedrooms, and in bar and lounges at management discretion *(015394) 32201*

652. ✕ ⇌ AMBLESIDE
Wateredge Inn (just off A591, via A5095 at Waterhead)
£90, plus special breaks; 21 good comfortable rms. Beautifully placed, warmly welcoming inn with neat gardens running down to Lake

MOTORWAY BREAKS

Windermere (embarkation point for cruising the lake); light airy bar (with fine views) and lounge, good meals in no smoking dining area (more lovely views), and excellent service; cl 4 days over Christmas; disabled access; dogs in bedrooms and part of bar *(015394) 32332*

653. ✕ ⇌ TROUTBECK
***Queens Head** (3 miles off A391, N up A591)*
£105; popular, warm-hearted and interesting gabled 17th-c coaching inn with several rambling bar rooms, some fine antique carving, a log fire and woodburner, efficient staff, popular bar food plus 3-course menu, and well kept real ales; cl 25 Dec; disabled access *(015394) 32174*

654. ⚭ ⇌ GRASMERE
(just off A591, via B5287 village loop)
The well run Wordsworth Hotel (**£140**; 37 pretty rms; *(015394) 35592*) is a comfortable stop, next to the churchyard where Wordsworth is buried; stylish lounges and airy restaurant overlooking landscaped gardens, a relaxed conservatory and popular pubby bar, friendly service, enjoyable food inc super buffet lunch, and heated indoor pool, mini-gym, and sauna; good disabled access. The pretty village swarms with visitors in summer, most of them here to see Dove Cottage – still much as Wordsworth had it in his most creative years, with his extensive cottage garden, but also an adjoining museum and new £3 million display centre, including a reconstructed Lakeland kitchen and contemporary art gallery. Informative guided tours cope well with the bustle, but in early morning (opens 9.30) out of season you may get some space to yourself. The place always was crowded; barely big enough for two, with the poet's children and friends it often had a dozen or more people living here. Meals, snacks, shop, limited disabled access; cl mid-Jan to mid-Feb, 24-26 Dec; *(015394) 35544*; £5.80 museum and house, £3 museum only. Sarah Nelson's gingerbread shop by the church is wonderfully old-fashioned.

A605

655. ✕ ⇌ OUNDLE
***Talbot** (0.9 miles off A605, via A427)*
£95, plus special breaks; 35 most attractive rms. Mary, Queen of Scots

walked to her execution down a staircase that's now in this carefully refurbished 17th-c hotel; attractive cosy lounge, big log fire, good food in timbered restaurant, and garden *(01832) 273621*

656. ✕ FOTHERINGHAY
Falcon *(2 miles off A605 NE of Oundle)*
Stylish but relaxed old country dining pub with a good mix of customers, comfortable lounge with fresh flowers and fireplaces at each end, no smoking conservatory and dining room, and little tap bar for locals; excellent food from a varied interesting menu, well kept real ales, and a fine wine list; neat garden; disabled access. The village is lovely, with interesting historical displays in the charming if slightly out-of-proportion 14th-c church across a watermeadow from the River Nene. It was part of a small pre-Reformation college and doubles as a memorial to the House of York, with some interesting heraldry. There's only a fragment left of the castle where Richard III was born, and 135 years later Mary, Queen of Scots was executed *(01832) 226254*

A606

657. ✕ ⌂ EMPINGHAM
White Horse *(0.3 miles off A606; Main St)*
£65, plus special breaks; 13 pretty rms, some in a delightfully converted stable block. Attractive, bustling old inn, handy for Rutland Water; a relaxed and comfortable atmosphere, a big log fire and fresh flowers in open-plan lounge, big helpings of very enjoyable food inc fine breakfasts, coffee and croissants from 8am, and cream teas all year; attractive no smoking restaurant, well kept real ales, and efficient friendly service; cots/high chairs; cl 25 Dec; good disabled access; dogs in bedrooms *(01780) 460221*

658. ✕ ⌂ UPPER HAMBLETON
Finches Arms *(1.8 miles off A606 just E of Oakham)*
£75; delightfully placed pub looking over Rutland Water, with stylish cane furniture in both the bar and more modern no smoking restaurant, super imaginative upmarket food, and real ales; no children *(01572) 756575*

MOTORWAY BREAKS

659. 🎣 RUTLAND WATER
(on A606)
Europe's biggest man-made lake, oddly shaped, with a number of attractions. On the N side are nature trails, an unusual drought garden created by the late Geoff Hamilton, places to hire bikes *(01780) 460705 or 720888*, and pm hourly boat trips; Apr-Sept; *(01572) 787630*; £5. You can fish in various parts of the water, and a visitor centre down at Normanton has a small museum in a church modelled on London's St John's, Smith Sq; open Easter-Sept, and wknds Oct. The refreshingly informal Normanton Park Hotel in waterside grounds here has good food, as do the White Horse at Empingham and — looking down on the water — the Finches Arms at Upper Hambleton (what was Lower Hambleton is now under water).

660. ⌨ MELTON MOWBRAY
Sysonby Knoll (0.6 miles off A606/A607 junction; A6006 Asfordby Rd)
£73; 30 rms, most facing a central courtyard, and 6 in annexe. Family-run Edwardian brick house on the edge of a bustling market town, home of pork pies and stilton cheese (you can still buy both traditionally made, locally); reception and lounge areas furnished in period style, winter open fire, friendly owners and excellent service, generous helpings of imaginative food inc lots of puddings in newly refurbished airy restaurant, and five acres of gardens leading down to the River Eye where guests may fish; no smoking exc in bar; cl 24 Dec-2 Jan; dogs welcome away from restaurant; plenty of nearby walks *(01664) 563563*

A617

661. ⌨ SOUTHWELL
Old Forge (1.7 miles off A617 from Hockerton via Hockerton Rd, keeping straight on through Normanton into Burgage Lane)
£76, plus special breaks; 4 rms. 200-year-old former blacksmith's house with welcoming owner, interesting furnishings, super breakfasts in conservatory overlooking the Minster, and pretty terrace; limited disabled access; dogs in bedrooms *(01636) 812809*

A623

662. ⋈ BASLOW
Fischer's Baslow Hall *(on A623 Calver Rd)*
£150, plus special breaks; 11 comfortable, pretty rms. Handsome Edwardian manor house with individually chosen furnishings and pictures, open fires, fresh flowers and plants, beautifully presented fine food using the best ingredients (some home-grown and lots of game and fish) in airy, no smoking dining room, and courteous attentive service; cl 25-26 Dec; no children in evening dining room *(01246) 583259*

663. ✕ ⋈ EYAM
Miners Arms *(0.5 miles off A623, via B6521)*
£60; cosy pub with restful atmosphere in its three little plush beamed rooms, good interesting food (not Sun evening) served by attentive staff, well kept ales, and decent nearby walks; disabled access. If you've time to look round the attractive secluded village, you find mementoes of a dark past: in the Great Plague sick villagers confined themselves here for fear of infecting people outside – plaques record who died where, and stones on the village edge mark where money was disinfected. Eyam Hall, the 17th-c manor house, is still very much a family home, with furniture, portraits and tapestries, fine Jacobean staircase and impressive flagstoned hall; there's a small craft centre in the stables. Meals, snacks, shop, some disabled access; house open Weds-Thurs, Sun and bank hol Mon June-Aug, craft centre open daily exc Mon, and over Christmas and New Year; *(01433) 631976*; £4.50 – timed ticket system. *(01433) 630853*

664. ✕ LITTON
Red Lion *(0.9 miles off A623; signed left off B6049 Tideswell rd, or directly down Mires Lane, just W of Three Stags Heads pub)*
Good value tasty food (not Sun evening) in prettily set 17th-c village pub, low beams, panelling, blazing log fires and cheerfully welcoming atmosphere, with well kept ales and decent wines; no children under 6; open all day Fri-Sun; rms £55 *(01298) 871458*

A629

665. ✕ ⇌ ROYDHOUSE
Three Acres *(2.4 miles off A629 S of Huddersfield, via B6116 through Kirkburton, then left on Cross Lane and Wool Row Lane)*
£80; 20 pretty rms. In lovely countryside, this civilised former coaching inn has a welcoming atmosphere in its traditional bars, an exceptional choice of wines, well kept real ales, marvellous imaginative food in two restaurants, and particularly good breakfasts; specialist delicatessen next door; cl 25 Dec, 31 Dec-1 Jan *(01484) 602606*

666. ✕ ⇌ HALIFAX
Shibden Mill *(2.3 miles off A629 via A58 NW, then after a mile and a bit turn left into Kell Lane at Stump Cross Inn, near A6036 junction; keep on, pub signed from Kell Lane on left)*
£80; great trunk-rd escape, quietly tucked-away restored mill with cosily enticing bar areas, big log fires, good imaginative bar food and upstairs restaurant, nice wines and real ales, relaxed atmosphere; children welcome, attractive heated terrace, comfortable bdrms, open all day wknds *(01422) 365840*

667. ⇌ HALIFAX
Holdsworth House *(1.2 miles off A629; heading N out of centre, fork right up Shay Lane)*
£120, plus wknd breaks; 40 traditional, individually decorated, quiet rms. Lovely, immaculately kept 17th-c house a few miles outside Halifax, with antiques, fresh flowers and fires in comfortable lounges, lots of sitting areas in the two bar rooms, friendly, particularly helpful staff, three carefully furnished dining rooms (one oak panelled) with enjoyable food and very good wine list, and garden; disabled access; dogs in bedrooms, bar, lounge and reception *(01422) 240024*

668. ✕ ⇌ HAWORTH
Old White Lion *(1.4 miles off A629 via A6033; fork right on B6142, then left into Main St; West Lane)*
£66.50, plus special breaks; 14 rms, many with lovely views. Friendly, warm and comfortable 300-year-old inn with three bars, cosy restaurant

A660

with enjoyable food, and oak-panelled residents' lounge; nr Brontë museum and church, and Keighley & Worth Valley steam railway; disabled access *(01535) 642313*

669. 🐾 HAWORTH
(1 mile off A629 via A6033; fork right on B6142, car park signed off on left)
A touristy village with plenty of craft shops, antiques shops and teashops catering for all the people drawn here by the Brontës (spelt Brunty before father Patrick went posh). A visit out of season catches it at its best, though at any time the steep cobbled main street has quieter more appealing side alleys. Most of the family are buried in the churchyard, except Anne, interred in Scarborough. For the most evocative views and atmosphere go up to the moors above town, very grand and not much different from when the Brontës knew them – despite the japanese footpath signs. The Old White Lion (West Lane) and the 17th-c Old Hall (Sun St) are good value for lunch.

A631

670. ✗ WALKERINGHAM
Three Horse Shoes *(1.6 miles off A631 via A161 N; High St)*
Warmly welcoming distinctive pub, rather like a french logis, with quite amazing flowers and hanging baskets (using 9,000 plants); a wide choice of often inventive food, and well kept real ales; disabled access *(01427) 890959*

A660

671. ⌂ OTLEY
Chevin Country Park Hotel *(1.8 miles off A660; up East Chevin Rd then first right on York Gate)*
£122, plus special breaks; 49 rms, some in log lodges deep in the woods. Built of finnish logs with walks through 50 acres of birchwood (lots of wildlife), this comfortable, newly refurbished hotel has its own leisure club, good food in lakeside restaurant, and friendly service; tennis and fishing; disabled access; dogs in bedrooms by prior arrangement only *(01943) 467818*

A683

672. ✘ TUNSTALL
Lunesdale Arms (on A683)
Civilised and brightly opened-up dining pub with enjoyable interesting food using home-baked bread, meat from local farms, and a lot of local organic produce; big unframed oil paintings (some for sale and often of bluebells) on yellow walls, cheerful bustling atmosphere, a couple of woodburners; well kept real ales, sensibly priced wines by the glass (in a choice of sizes), and good cafetière coffee; pretty Lune Valley village; cl Mon (exc bank hols), 25-26 Dec; disabled access *(01524) 274203*

A688

673. ✘ BARNARD CASTLE
Market Place Teashop (in centre, opp A67)
Long-standing tearoom in 17th-c building with flagstones and an open fire, smart uniformed waitresses, home-made cakes, light lunches, a good choice of teas, and a friendly relaxed atmosphere; cl Sun am, all day winter Sun, Christmas-New Year; disabled access *(01833) 690110*

674. ※ BARNARD CASTLE
Bowes Museum (0.2 miles off A67/A688 via Newgate)
Built over 100 years ago to house a private collection, this beautiful french-style chateau in 23 acres of parkland with a parterre garden is as lovely in the frosts of winter as it is in summer. The 40 rooms are filled with sumptuous fine arts and an outstanding display of paintings of national importance; also local history section, and a display of 1950s toys; a new interactive exhibition opens this year telling the romantic story of how the museum was founded. They hold temporary exhibitions, concerts and events throughout the year. Relatively few people find their way to this knock-out treasure-house, though it's one of the most worthwhile places to visit in the entire country. Meals, snacks, shop, disabled access; cl 25-26 Dec, 1 Jan; *(01833) 690606*; £6.

A696

675. 🎭 STAINDROP
Raby Castle (on A688)
Dramatic medieval castle built by the mighty Nevills and home to Lord Barnard`s family since 1626; well preserved halls and chambers that bring history to life and, throughout the castle, the rooms display fine furniture, impressive artworks and elaborate architecture. From the outside, where there are walled gardens, a deer park, and a carriage collection, it looks just as a castle ought to; woodland adventure playground and picnic area. Meals, snacks, shop (selling oven-ready game and venison from the estate), disabled access to grounds only; open Easter-end Sept; June-Aug daily except Sat; May and Sept open Weds and Suns, bank hols inc; open Easter Sat-following Weds. Park and gardens 11-5.30, castle 1-5pm; *(01833) 660202*; £9, £4 park and gardens only. The village is pretty. Up at Butterknowle the Malt Shovel has good value food, evenings and wknd lunchtimes.

676. ✖ NEWFIELD
Fox & Hounds (2.7 miles off A688; heading N take first left after A689 roundabout into Long Lane at 'Willington, Newfield' signpost; then left at Newfield signpost, and left again at Queens Head into Stonebank Terrace)
Comfortable and gently lit, mainly no smoking, with candles and flowers, big brass platters on dark pink timbered walls, and big windows looking over steeply rolling countryside; good winter fires, appealing attractively priced food (more elaborate in the evening), good house wines, and friendly, thoughtful service; Sat night fully booked well ahead; cl Sun pm, Mon; no children; disabled access *(01388) 662787*

A696

677. ⌨ CAMBO
Shieldhall (just off A696 via B6342)
£60; 4 well equipped suites, each with its own entrance. 18th-c stone house and carefully converted farm buildings around a courtyard, with antiques and other interesting furnishings (the Robinson-Gay family are all fine cabinet-makers), a library, bar, and cosy lounge with french windows opening on to the neatly kept big garden; enjoyable freshly

MOTORWAY BREAKS

produced food in candlelit beamed dining room; cl Christmas and New Year; children over 12 *(01830) 540387*

678. ⋈ KIRKWHELPINGTON
Cornhills (1.5 miles off A696; heading N out of village, turn left at Knowesgate crossroads)
£60; 3 rms. Big no smoking Victorian farmhouse on large stock-rearing farm, with marvellous views towards the coast and Tyne Valley; lots of original features, a comfortable lounge, good breakfasts (local pubs for evening meals), and indoor and outdoor games for children; cl Apr *(01830) 540232*

A697

679. ⋈ LONGHORSLEY
Linden Hall (just off A697 N of Morpeth)
£121, plus special breaks; 50 individually decorated rms. Georgian hotel in 450 acres of landscaped park with clay pigeon shooting, mountain biking (bike hire available), 18-hole golf course, pitch and putt, croquet, lots of leisure facilities inc a swimming pool, and health and beauty treatments; pubby bar, elegant drawing room, and good food in attractive restaurant; children in main restaurant early evening only; disabled access; dogs in two bedrooms only *(01670) 516611*

680. ✕ ⋈ WELDON BRIDGE
Anglers Arms (just off A697 S of Longframlington, via B6344)
£55; comfortable riverside hotel popular for good very generous bar food in its cosy and appealingly traditional two-room panelled bar, also a restaurant in a former dining car; good beers and wines, friendly staff, tables in attractive garden with good play area; nice bedrooms *(01665) 570271*

681. ⋈ LONGFRAMLINGTON
Embleton Hall (on A697)
£95; 13 comfortable, pretty and individually decorated rms. Charming hotel in lovely grounds surrounded by fine countryside, with a particularly friendly relaxed atmosphere and courteous staff; neat little bar, elegant lounge, log fires, excellent value bar meals, and very good food

in the attractive dining room; disabled access; dogs welcome in bedrooms *(01665) 570249*

682. ◻ ROTHBURY
Tosson Tower Farm (3.5 miles off A697 via B6341)
£55; 3 pretty rms. Traditional farmhouse on 170 acres of sheep pasture set in the Northumberland National Park, with friendly owners, log fire, TV, and plenty of books in comfortable and relaxing lounge, good farmhouse breakfasts in spacious dining room (plenty of eating places in Rothbury), lots of walks from the door, free fishing (salmon, sea trout and brown trout), and cycling; self-catering, too *(01669) 620228*

683. ◻ CROOKHAM
Coach House (A697 S of Cornhill)
£45; 10 individual rms with fresh flowers and nice views, 8 with own bthrm. 17th-c farm buildings around a sunny courtyard, with helpful and friendly staff, an airy beamed lounge with comfortable sofas and big arched windows, good breakfasts with home-made preserves (which you can also take home), afternoon tea, and enjoyable dinners using local vegetables; lots to do nearby; good disabled access; dogs in bdrms *(01890) 820293*

A828

684. ✕ KENTALLEN
Holly Tree (just off A828)
Super food in carefully converted railway station, cosy public rooms, lovely shoreside setting (best to book in winter); cl ams and Nov-Jan; disabled access *(01631) 740292*

685. ◻ ERISKA
Isle of Eriska Hotel (2 miles off A828 N of Connel)
£250; 19 rms. In a wonderful position on small island linked by bridge to mainland, impressive baronial hotel with very relaxed country house atmosphere, log fires and pretty drawing room, excellent food, exemplary service, and comprehensive wine list; leisure complex with indoor swimming pool, sauna, gym and so forth, lovely surrounding walks, and 9-hole golf course, clay pigeon shooting and golf – and plenty of wildlife

MOTORWAY BREAKS

inc tame badgers who come nightly to the library door for their bread and milk; cl Jan; children over 5 in pool and evening restaurant (high tea provided); disabled access; dogs welcome in bedrooms *(01631) 720371*

A832

686. ✕ ⇌ **MUIR OF ORD**
Dower House *(0.8 miles off A832 from station, via A862 N)*
£115; Very good modern cooking in attractive hotel restaurant, with fine wines, and friendly service; lovely gardens; cl Christmas and 2 wks in Nov *(01463) 870090*

A835

687. ☸ **FALLS OF MEASACH**
(just off A835 via A832)
With a mighty drop of 200 ft, these are the highlight of the mile-long, sheer-sided Corrieshalloch Gorge, owned by the National Trust for Scotland and equipped with a little viewing platform. The swaying suspension bridge high over the gorge is not for the faint-hearted, but gives spectacular views.

A4103

688. ✕ **BRANSFORD**
Bear & Ragged Staff *(just off A4103 SW of Worcester)*
Stylish dining pub with proper tablecloths, linen napkins, and fresh flowers, very good imaginative food inc super fresh fish dishes, fine views over rolling country from the relaxed and cheerful interconnecting rooms, open fire, no smoking restaurant, well kept beers, a fine choice of wines, lots of malt whiskies, and willing helpful service; children until 9pm; disabled access *(01886) 833399*

A6003

689. ✕ ⌧ LYDDINGTON
Old White Hart (1 mile off A6003; village signed S of Uppingham)
£80; warmly welcoming 17th-c village inn with just three tables in front of the log fire, heavy bowed beams, and dried flowers in the cosy softly lit bar; an attractive no smoking restaurant with corn dollies and a big oak dresser, and a tiled-floor room with some stripped stone, cushioned wall seats and mate's chairs, and woodburner; very popular imaginative bar food, well kept ales, and picnic-sets and boules in the pretty walled garden; good nearby walks, and handy for the Bede House; cl Sun pm, 25 Dec *(01572) 821703*

690. ⚘ UPPINGHAM
(on A6003)
Charming small town with an interesting square (Fri market) and curving 18th/19th-c High St. The Falcon Hotel does nice light lunches and teas. On most Weds lunchtimes in term-time, musicians from the famous local school (tours by arrangement *(01572) 821264*) give free concerts in the parish church; the Vaults next to it does decent food.

691. ⌧ UPPINGHAM
Lake Isle (just off A6003; High St E)
£75, plus special breaks; 12 rms with home-made biscuits, sherry and fresh fruit, and three cottage suites. In a charming market town, this 18th-c restaurant-with-rooms has an open fire in the attractive lounge, a redecorated bar (once a barber's where the schoolboys had their hair cut), good, imaginative food in refurbished restaurant (enjoyable breakfasts, too), a carefully chosen wine list, and a small and pretty garden; dogs in cottage suites *(01572) 822951*

KEY MAP

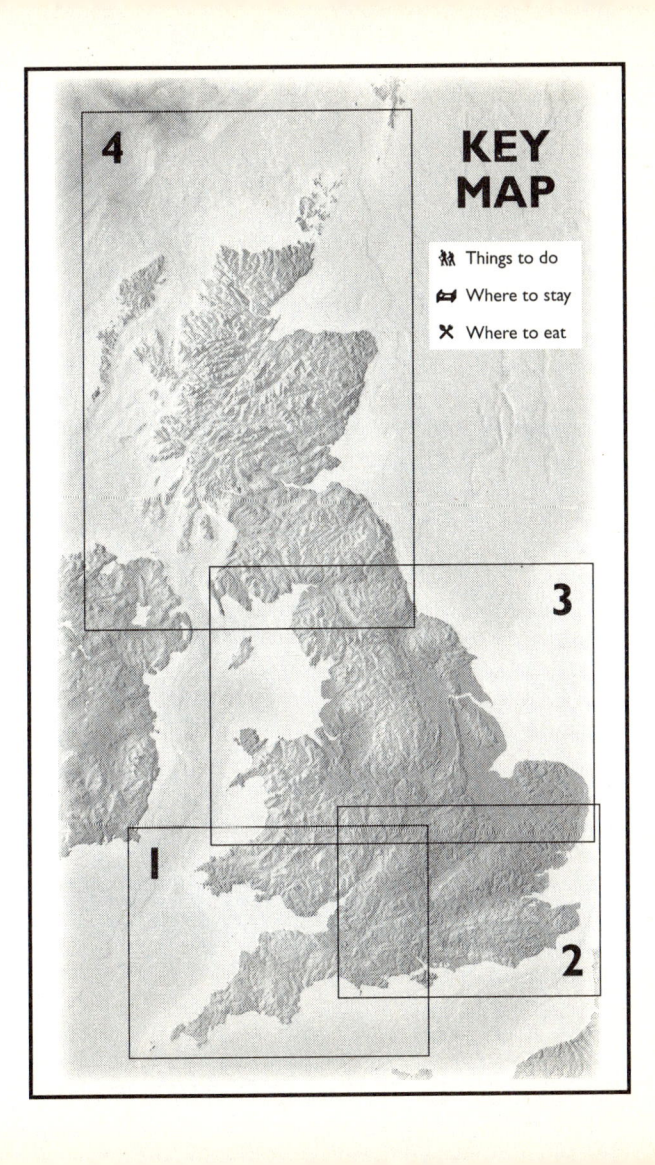

🚶 Things to do
🛏 Where to stay
✗ Where to eat

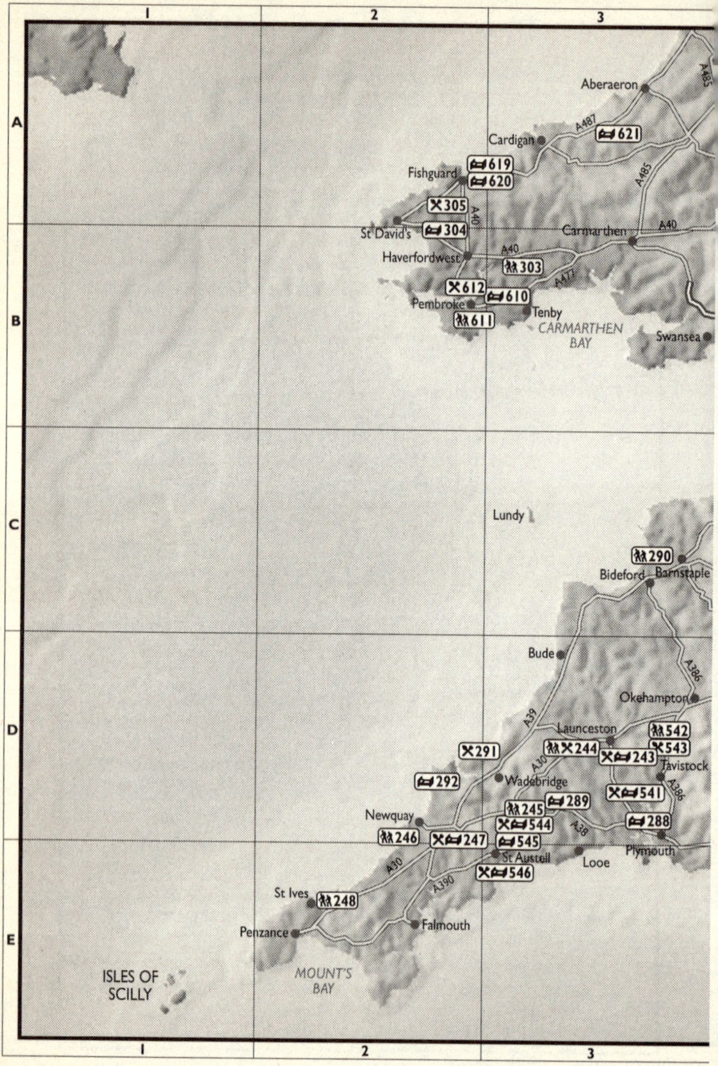
1
2
3
A
B
C
D
E
Aberaeron
A485
A487
621
Cardigan
619
620
Fishguard
305
A40
St David's
304
Carmarthen
A40
Haverfordwest
303
A477
612
610
Pembroke
611
Tenby
CARMARTHEN BAY
Swansea
Lundy
290
Bideford
Barnstaple
Bude
A386
Okehampton
A39
Launceston
542
543
244
243
291
A30
Tavistock
292
Wadebridge
541
A386
289
245
288
Newquay
544
A38
246
247
545
St Austell
Looe
Plymouth
A30
546
A390
St Ives
248
Penzance
Falmouth
MOUNT'S BAY
ISLES OF SCILLY
1
2
3

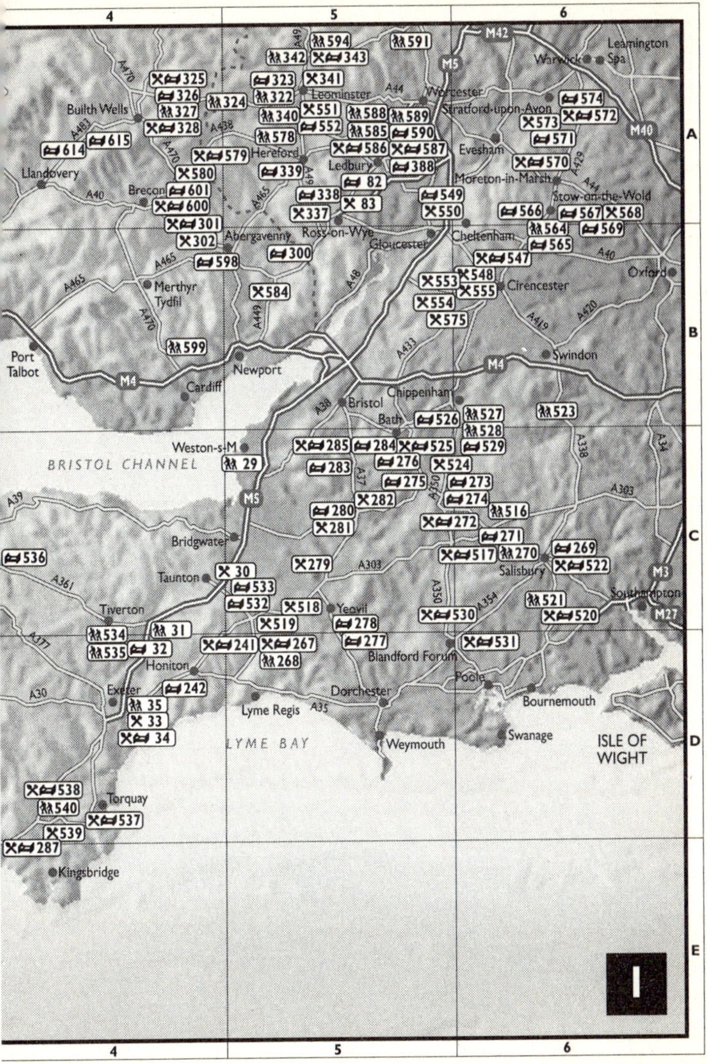
4
5
6
A
B
C
D
E
M42
Leamington Spa
Warwick
M5
M40
M4
M3
M27
A470
A49
A44
A438
A483
A40
A465
A429
A48
A449
A433
A419
A420
A38
A37
A350
A338
A34
A303
A39
A361
A377
A30
A35
A354
Builth Wells
Llandovery
Brecon
Hereford
Leominster
Worcester
Stratford-upon-Avon
Evesham
Ledbury
Moreton-in-Marsh
Stow-on-the-Wold
Abergavenny
Ross-on-Wye
Gloucester
Cheltenham
Merthyr Tydfil
Cirencester
Oxford
Swindon
Port Talbot
Newport
Cardiff
Bristol
Chippenham
Bath
Weston-s-M
BRISTOL CHANNEL
Bridgwater
Taunton
Salisbury
Southampton
Tiverton
Yeovil
Honiton
Blandford Forum
Exeter
Lyme Regis
Dorchester
Poole
Bournemouth
Swanage
LYME BAY
Weymouth
ISLE OF WIGHT
Torquay
Kingsbridge
594
591
342
343
325
323
341
326
324
322
327
340
551
588
589
574
572
328
552
585
590
573
571
615
614
578
579
586
587
570
580
339
388
601
82
600
338
83
549
301
337
550
566
567
568
302
564
569
565
300
547
598
548
553
555
584
554
575
599
526
527
523
528
285
284
525
529
29
283
276
524
275
273
282
274
280
516
281
272
271
536
279
517
270
269
522
30
533
532
518
521
530
520
519
278
534
31
535
32
241
267
277
531
268
242
35
33
34
538
540
537
539
287
I

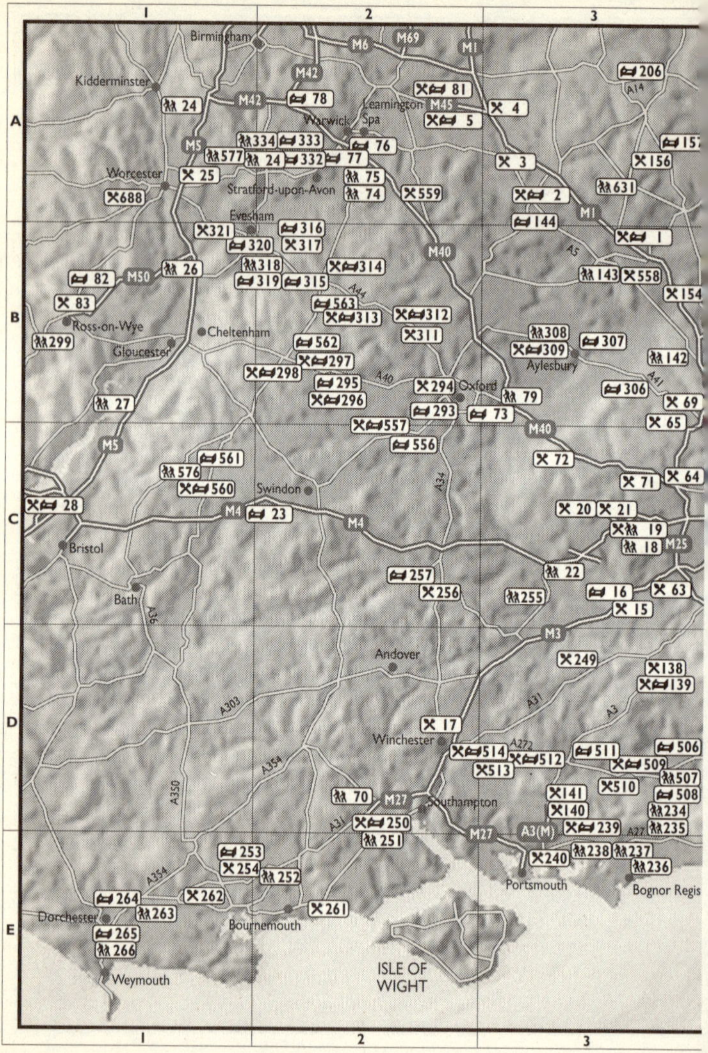

1
2
3
A
B
C
D
E
Birmingham
Kidderminster
Worcester
Warwick
Leamington Spa
Stratford-upon-Avon
Evesham
Ross-on-Wye
Cheltenham
Gloucester
Oxford
Aylesbury
Swindon
Bristol
Bath
Andover
Winchester
Southampton
Portsmouth
Bognor Regis
Dorchester
Weymouth
Bournemouth
ISLE OF WIGHT
M6
M69
M1
M42
M45
M5
M50
M40
M4
M25
M3
M27
A3(M)
A14
A5
A44
A40
A41
A34
A36
A303
A31
A3
A272
A354
A350
A27
206
81
78
24
4
5
76
334
333
577
24
332
77
157
156
25
75
3
688
74
559
631
2
144
1
321
316
320
317
82
26
318
314
143
558
319
315
154
83
563
313
312
311
308
299
562
309
307
297
142
298
295
294
306
27
296
79
69
293
73
557
65
556
72
561
576
71
64
560
28
23
20
21
19
18
257
22
16
63
256
255
15
249
138
139
17
514
511
506
512
509
513
507
510
141
508
70
234
140
250
239
235
251
240
238
237
253
236
254
252
264
262
263
261
265
266

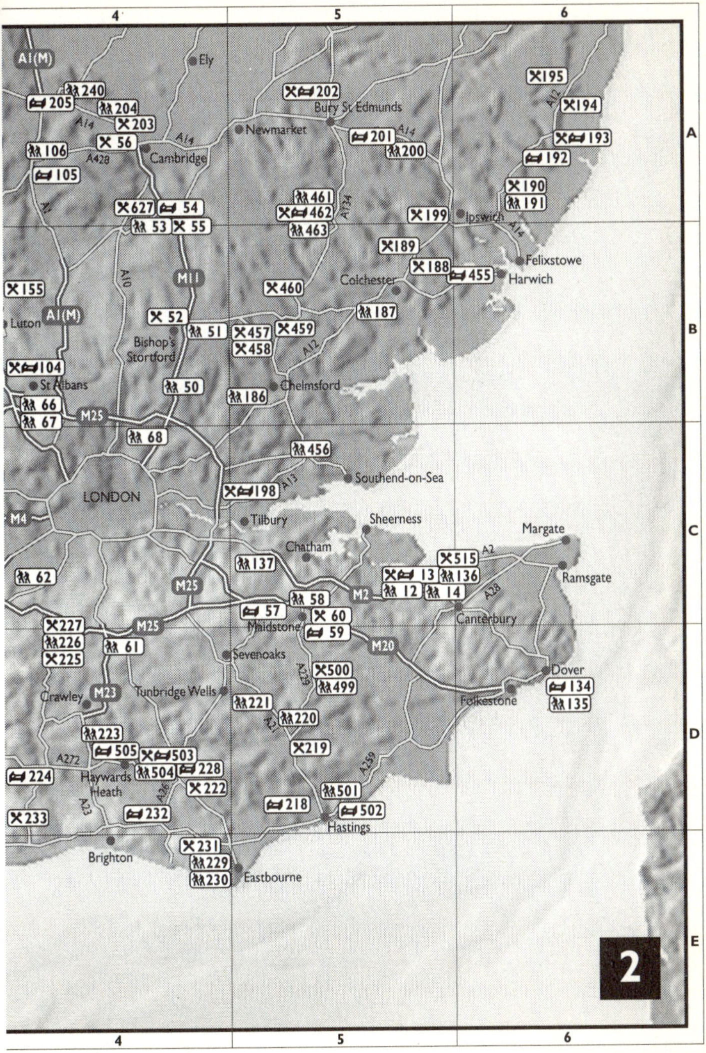

4
5
6
A
B
C
D
E
A1(M)
Ely
240
205
204
203
A14
56
A428
Cambridge
106
105
A1
627
54
53
55
Bury St Edmunds
202
Newmarket
201
200
A14
461
462
463
A134
195
194
A12
193
192
190
191
199
Ipswich
A14
189
188
455
Felixstowe
Harwich
Colchester
460
187
M11
A10
155
Luton
A1(M)
52
51
Bishop's Stortford
457
459
458
A12
104
St Albans
50
186
Chelmsford
66
67
M25
68
456
Southend-on-Sea
LONDON
198
A13
M4
Tilbury
Sheerness
Chatham
Margate
A2
515
136
137
13
12
14
Ramsgate
62
M25
58
M2
A28
57
60
Canterbury
Maidstone
59
227
226
225
M25
61
M20
Sevenoaks
500
499
A229
Dover
134
135
Folkestone
Crawley
M23
Tunbridge Wells
221
220
A21
223
219
505
503
A259
A272
224
Haywards Heath
504
228
222
501
A26
A23
233
232
218
502
Hastings
Brighton
231
229
230
Eastbourne
2
4
5
6

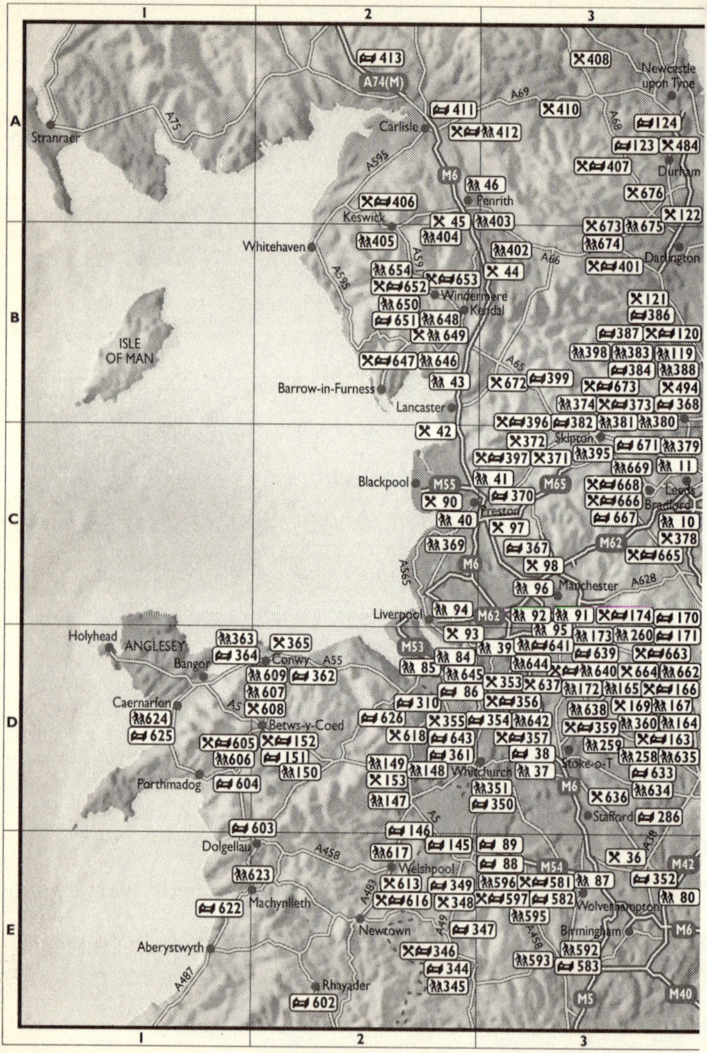

1
2
3
A
B
C
D
E
Stranraer
A75
A74(M)
Carlisle
A69
Newcastle upon Tyne
A68
Durham
A595
M6
Penrith
Keswick
Whitehaven
A591
A66
Darlington
Windermere
Kendal
ISLE OF MAN
A65
Barrow-in-Furness
Lancaster
Skipton
Blackpool
M55
M65
Leeds
Bradford
Preston
M62
A565
Manchester
A628
Liverpool
Holyhead
ANGLESEY
Bangor
Conwy
A55
M53
Caernarfon
A5
Betws-y-Coed
Whitchurch
Stoke-o-T
Porthmadog
Stafford
Dolgellau
A458
A38
Welshpool
M54
M42
Machynlleth
A483
Wolverhampton
A49
Newtown
Birmingham
Aberystwyth
A487
Rhayader
M5
M40

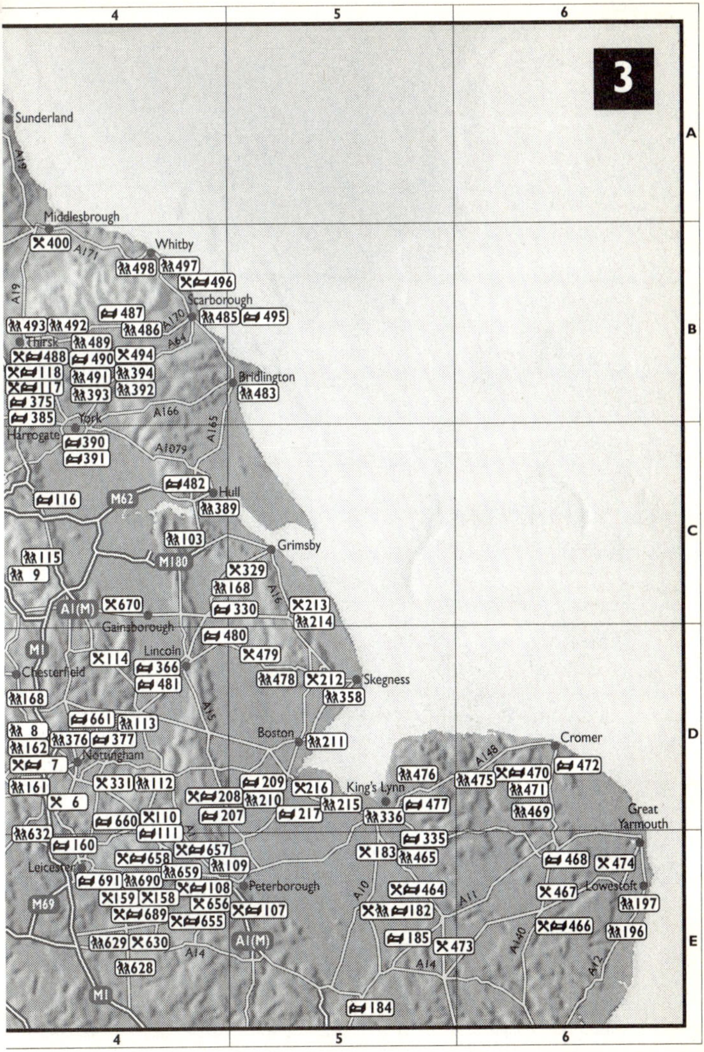

3
4
5
6
A
B
C
D
E
Sunderland
A19
Middlesbrough
400
A171
Whitby
498
497
496
A19
Scarborough
487
A170
485
495
493
492
486
Thirsk
489
A64
488
490
494
118
491
394
117
Bridlington
393
392
483
375
385
York
A166
A165
Harrogate
390
A1079
391
482
Hull
116
M62
389
103
115
Grimsby
M180
9
329
168
A16
213
A1(M)
670
330
214
Gainsborough
480
M1
Lincoln
114
366
479
Chesterfield
481
478
212
Skegness
168
358
A15
661
113
8
376
377
Boston
211
Cromer
162
Nottingham
A148
7
476
475
470
472
161
331
112
209
216
King's Lynn
471
6
208
210
215
477
207
217
336
469
Great Yarmouth
632
660
110
111
A1
335
160
657
183
465
658
109
468
474
Leicester
659
691
690
108
Peterborough
A10
464
467
Lowestoft
M69
159
158
656
A11
197
689
655
107
182
466
A140
196
629
630
A1(M)
185
473
A14
A14
A12
628
M1
184

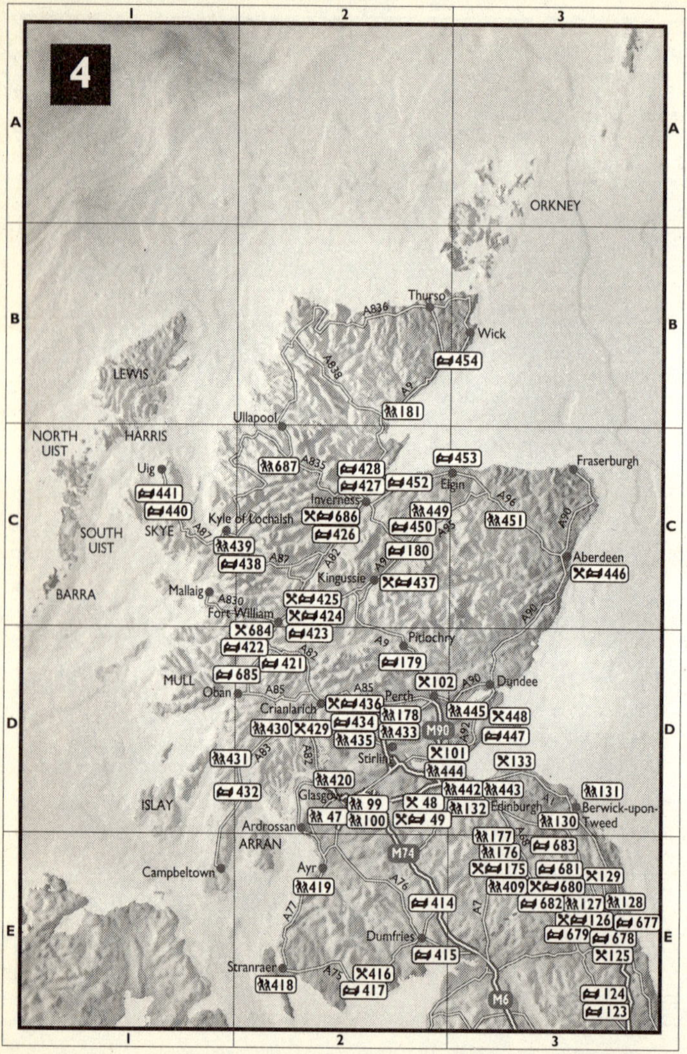
4
1
2
3
A
B
C
D
E
ORKNEY
Thurso
A836
Wick
A838
454
A9
181
LEWIS
Ullapool
NORTH UIST
HARRIS
687
A835
428
427
452
453
Elgin
Fraserburgh
Uig
441
440
Inverness
686
449
A96
451
Kyle of Lochalsh
426
450
A95
A90
SOUTH UIST
SKYE
A87
439
438
A82
180
Aberdeen
446
A9
Kingussie
437
Mallaig
A830
BARRA
425
424
Fort William
684
423
A90
Pitlochry
A9
422
A82
179
421
MULL
685
102
A90
Dundee
Oban
A85
A85
Perth
436
Crianlarich
178
445
448
434
430
429
433
M90
A92
447
435
A82
431
A83
Stirling
101
133
444
420
432
442
443
131
ISLAY
Glasgow
99
48
132
Edinburgh
A1
Berwick-upon-Tweed
47
100
49
130
Ardrossan
177
ARRAN
176
A68
683
M74
Campbeltown
175
681
Ayr
129
419
A76
409
680
A77
414
682
127
128
A7
126
677
Dumfries
679
678
415
125
Stranraer
416
A75
418
417
M6
124
123